The Suburbs

The Suburbs

J. JOHN PALEN

Virginia Commonwealth University

McGRAW-HILL, INC.

New York   St. Louis   San Francisco   Auckland   Bogotá   Caracas
Lisbon   London   Madrid   Mexico City   Milan   Montreal   New Delhi
San Juan   Singapore   Sydney   Tokyo   Toronto

THE SUBURBS

 This book is printed on recycled, acid-free paper containing 10% postconsumer waste.

1 2 3 4 5 6 7 8 9 0 DOC DOC 9 0 9 8 7 6 5 4

ISBN 0-07-048128-8

This book was set in Palatino by Ruttle, Shaw & Wetherill, Inc.
The editors were Jill S. Gordon and Caroline Izzo;
the production supervisor was Friederich W. Schulte.
The cover was designed by Initial Graphic Systems, Inc.
The photo editor was Inge King.
R. R. Donnelley & Sons Company was printer and binder

Cover Photo: Tom Hollyman/Photo Researchers

Photo Credits

Page 6: top, S. R. Pearson/Fairfax County Public Library Archive; *bottom,* Scott Boatright/Fairfax County Public Library Archive; *16: bottom left,* Peter Menzel/Stock, Boston; *top,* Barbara Alper/Stock, Boston; *bottom right,* Alexander Lowry/Photo Researchers; *26:* Bettmann Archive; *34:* Bostonian Society; *39:* Chicago Historical Society; *54:* Ralph E. Tower/Chicago Historical Society; *59:* Culver Pictures; *65:* Culver Pictures; *76:* Library of Congress; *107:* Jay Wiley/Monkmeyer Press; *109:* Mimi Forsyth/Monkmeyer; *110:* Paul Conklin/Monkmeyer; *133:* Rob Nelson/Black Star; *142:* Ovie Carter/Oak Park Housing Center; *151:* Tony Freeman/PhotoEdit; *155:* Bettman Archive; *165:* Wayne F. Miller/Magnum; *174:* Steve Takatsuno/Jeroboam; *191:* Courtesy of J. C. Nichols Company; *200:* AP/Wide World Photo; *213:* Dennis Brack/Black Star; *217:* Philip Langdon.

Library of Congress Cataloging-in-Publication Data
Palen, J. John.
    The suburbs / J. John Palen.
        p.   cm.
    Includes bibliographical references and index.
    ISBN 0-07-048128-8
    1. Suburbs—United States—History.   I. Title
HT352.U6P35   1995
307.74—dc20   94-7638

About the Author

J. JOHN PALEN is Professor of Sociology at Virginia Commonwealth University. His research interests include patterns of suburbanization and gentrification in the United States and urban change in Asia, especially Singapore and Taiwan. Palen is a Civil War buff and enjoys hiking through cities and Virginia's Blue Ridge Mountains.

Dr. Palen is the author of several books including *Urban America, City Scenes, Gentrification Displacement and Neighborhood Revitalization,* and *Social Problems.* His book, *The Urban World* is currently in its fourth edition with McGraw-Hill. He is the 1994 recipient of the Virginia Commonwealth University Humanities and Sciences Distinguished Scholar Award.

104061

For Karen
a city soul living in the suburbs

Contents

the Suburbs / Government Fragmentation / A Note on Political Representation

11. Outer Cities and the Malling of the Land   181

Older Patterns / Multinucleated Edge or Satellite Cities / The Rise of Private Cities / Shopping Malls / Early Centers / Strip Malls / Enclosed Malls / Regional Malls / Safety / Megamalls / A Suburban Downtown Alternative: Reston, Va.

12. Planned Utopias and Other Communities   203

Planned Suburbs / Llewellyn Park / Riverside / Railroad Suburbs / Designed Streetcar Suburbs / Visionary Communities / Planned Utopias / New Town Movement / Reston, Columbia, and Irving / Neotraditional Developments / Retirement Communities

13. Quo Vadis?   223

Current Status / Where We Are Going

Indexes

Preface

Suburbs are no longer *sub*. In terms of population, economics, and culture, America has been a suburban nation for a quarter of a century. Today more Americans live, work, go to schools and colleges, and do their shopping and recreation in suburbs than in cities. Yet we still continue to use models that view the city as dominant and the suburbs as peripheral. The assumption is that economically and socially, the downtown is still the center, while suburbs are outlying residential places that remain oriented toward the central city. For example, we still think of commuting as going into the city in the morning and returning to the suburbs at night. However, in reality most commuting is from suburb to suburb. Rather than being on the fringe or off center, today's suburbs are the metropolitan centers. Without fanfare, suburbs have become the new retail and employment "downtowns." More than three-quarters of the job growth during the 1980s in America's twenty largest metropolitan areas occurred in the suburbs. This suburban transformation is only now being recognized in literary or popular imagery. Still common is the old stereotypical image of suburbia as rows of look-alike homes interrupted by an occasional shopping mall. While most Americans no longer take for granted the employment, administrative, consumption, or even social dominance of the central city, we have yet to fully replace old concepts and models. This volume will examine the reality of contemporary suburbia.

The pages that follow will document the changes in suburbs from the early, affluent railroad suburbs of the nineteenth century to the streetcar suburbs of the early twentieth century to the rapid, mass suburbanization following World War II up to the more complex, diverse, and sophisticated contemporary suburbia. Over the past quarter of a century, the residential character of suburbia has undergone a dramatic transformation. Once overwhelmingly residential, suburbs now dominate the metropolitan business landscape. Suburban outer or edge cities now not only house the bulk of retail trade, they often have more office workers and office space than the traditional downtowns. Suburbia has become far more complex. Residential suburbs have become socially, economically, ethnically, and racially diverse to a degree unthought of even two decades ago. For example, throughout the 1960s the middle class suburbs surrounding cities such as Atlanta, Georgia and Washington, D.C. rigidly excluded minorities. Now the suburbs of these two metropolitan areas hold, between them, more than a million, overwhelmingly middle class, black suburbanites. This volume is among the first to both document and discuss this dramatic transformation from white to multicultural suburbs. Also discussed is the influx of Hispanics and Asians into suburbia. Additionally discussed are topics such as the evolving ideology of suburbia, the role of women in suburbs, the malling of America, the development of outer cities, visionary new suburbs, and even retirement suburbs.

The overall goal of this book is to sketch the scope and nature of contemporary suburbia and how we got to this point. Although I am an urban sociologist by training and an urban ecologist by inclination, I have consciously sought to include the research of a wide range of urban scholars regardless of their disciplinary or ideological affiliation. I, for instance, especially believe that urban historians have much to contribute to our understanding of contemporary suburban patterns, and thus I have included several chapters on the emergence and development of early suburbia. Understanding of how metropolitan patterns are evolving today is facilitated by some knowledge of how the patterns historically developed. Thus, while the major focus is on the contemporary suburban situation, the book begins with reviewing the past in order to help us better understand the present. I hope that this will aid in our understanding of how suburbs have socially, organizationally, and economically evolved to their present form.

I would like to acknowledge my debt to the urban scholars whose studies are cited in this work. Fortunately, while the subject of suburbs has not had widespread academic attention, the quality of the available work is generally high. I would also like to thank those who reviewed earlier versions of this work. Reviewers play an important role in strengthening a manuscript. I would like to thank Kenneth Eslinger, John Carroll University; Judith Friedman, Rutgers University; and Dale Spady, Northern Michigan University for their careful reading and critical suggestions. Jill Gordon, who worked on the project as sponsoring editor, saw the book through to publication. Especially deserving of thanks is Inge King, who, as photo editor, deserves credit for the fine photo program. Finally, I would like to thank Phil Butcher, executive editor at McGraw-Hill, whose enthusiasm encouraged me to develop the project.

J. John Palen

The Suburbs

CHAPTER 1

Suburban Ascendancy

INTRODUCTION

In a change virtually unheralded during the last quarter of a century, North America has gone from being a continent of city dwellers to a continent of suburbanites. Even more important, suburbs have gone from being fringe commuter areas to being the modal locations for American living and working. There has been a suburban revolution that has changed suburbs from being places on the periphery of the urban core to being the economic and commercial centers of a new metropolitan area form. Increasingly, it is the suburbs that are central with the cities being peripheral. Economically healthy and growing suburbs now find themselves sandwiched between older declining cities on one side and declining rural areas on the other. This transformation has been remarkably rapid. The suburbs are also becoming dominant socially, although this is not yet part of the public's store of general knowledge. However, whether the social dominance of suburbia is commonly recognized or not, and whether applauded or denounced, it has already largely occurred. At the end of World War II, the American city was the industrial, commercial, and cultural center of the world. Downtown was where the action was to be found. What wasn't recognized was that this was the peak; the following decades would witness a massive outflowing from the cities. Although it somewhat twists the language, suburbs are more and more frequently the center of the metropolitan area.

Daily, the inevitable transformation of America into a nation of suburbs becomes ever closer to demographic and economic reality. A quarter of a century ago, Herbert Gans opened an article on suburbs by opining that, "In this unpredictable world, nothing can be predicted quite so easily as the continued proliferation of suburbia" (Herbert J. Gans, "The White Exodus to Suburbia Steps Up," *New York Times Magazine*, January 7, 1968). In the intervening years nothing has changed, and everything has changed. Today we all know about suburbs; they are the place where most of us live. The 1990 census confirmed that within metropolitan areas, half again as many Americans now live in suburbs as in cities. Nationally, approaching half of all Americans are suburbanites. Thus, as we approach the new century it is appropriate that we examine both the substance of suburbs and the roles they play, for just as the twentieth century was the age of the American city, the twenty-first will be the age of the suburb.

In historical terms the growth of North American suburbs into a dominant demographic and social force has occurred with breathtaking rapidity. Suburbs housed only 15 percent of the nation's population in 1920, and by the end of World War II only 20 percent of the United States' population resided in suburbs. The central cities seemed destined to grow in population and influence. No one at that time saw suburbs as ever being anything but *sub* to the city. Certainly, no one saw suburbs as the dominant American location for shopping or employment. In 1950 a quarter of the United States' population lived in metropolitan-area suburbs. A decade later the figure had increased to a third of the nation's population, equalling that found in the central cities of metropolitan areas. Nonetheless, the city was still the prime focus of governmental and scholarly attention. The assumption was that the city was central, and thus programs such as urban action grants, model cities, and revenue sharing had an explicit urban focus.

Ironically, just at the time that President Lyndon Johnson gave his famous 1960s speech declaring America to be a nation of cities, that was ceasing to be the case. The president proclaimed the arrival of the era of the cities at almost the precise time that era was closing. The decades of the 1950s and the 1960s saw dramatic, more than doubling, growth, from 35 million to 84 million suburbanites, with the result that by the 1970 census, the suburban domains of metropolitan areas possessed larger populations than their central cities (U.S. Bureau of the Census, "Patterns of Metropolitan Area and County Growth, 1980 to 1987," *Current Population Reports*, P-25, No. 1039, 1987). Today suburbs are even more dominant. According to the 1990 census, some 115 million Americans lived in suburbs, while only 78 million lived in central cities and 56 million in nonmetropolitan places, that is, those places that are not cities of at least 50,000 persons, or the suburbs of such places. The census also revealed that there were fourteen states in which an absolute majority of the population were suburbanites. States where suburbanites already are more than half of the population include such populous states as California, Michigan, New Jersey, Ohio, and Pennsylvania. On a pragmatic note, over half of all voters now live in the suburbs—a matter of considerable political consequence as central-city mayors make increasingly frantic calls for additional state and national funding.

A Time Warp

Even today, when suburbs dominate metropolitan economic development, our imagery often remains locked into an earlier picture of suburbia as essentially an area of middle-class housing and culture. We seem to be caught in a time warp where we see suburbs not for what they are, but what they were. And even this picture is a warp of reality. In this 1950s- and 1960s-based version, suburbia is a place of neat identical homes set on green lawns, where "Ozzie and Harriet" or "the Beaver" can be found living next door. The suburbs of our mind are the dormitory suburbs of detached single-family homes in which the mother is a homemaker caring for young children and the father the breadwinner who commutes to his job in the city. This is the suburbia of the sitcoms in rerun. It never really reflected the diverse reality of the suburbs of the past; it certainly is misleading as a contemporary image.

The confusion, if not chaos, of contemporary suburban reality fits uneasily with this idealized image of suburbia as a never-never land of stable middle- and upper-middle-class white families living with their young children in ranch-style homes surrounded by wide yards of green. Today suburbs are this and much more. They also contain the elderly, single parents, blacks, Hispanics, high-rise buildings, most of the nation's household and personal trade, the bulk of the nation's manufacturing plants, and a growing share of the nation's offices. In the years since the 1960s, suburbia has become remarkably diverse, both in terms of residents and the variety of land uses. Reality, however, often leads perception. Suburbs, for example, are sometimes still discussed, even by scholars, as if they are still all but exclusively white. But reality has changed. When the media refer to metropolitan-area blacks, for instance, the image invariably is of a central-city urban neighborhood. Yet one out of every three metropolitan-area blacks is a suburbanite. According to the 1990 census, 32 percent of black Americans living in metropolitan areas resided in suburbs—a remarkable suburban increase of 6 percent over the figures from a decade earlier. As far back as the 1970s, African American suburban growth rates already exceeded those of whites.

Exemplifying the change is Prince George's County, Maryland, a suburban area of Washington, D.C.. In the 1972 presidential party primary, Prince George's County voted for George Wallace and white backlash. Today the majority of the Prince George's suburban residents are black, and most are comfortably affluent. Nonetheless, the old one-dimensional view of suburbs as solely residential locations of freestanding single-family homes inhabited by white middle-class families and their young children still persists, and such myths are remarkably resistant to modification. The actuality is that as we approach the twenty-first century, not only are Americans more likely to live in a suburb than in a city, town, or farm; they are also more likely to work in a suburb, shop in a suburb, and attend entertainment and sports events in a suburb.

Emerging Suburban Dominance

Mass suburbia is a post-World War II occurrence. The postwar years witnessed new suburban subdivisions sprouting from the potato fields or cornfields, that previously defined the boundaries of American cities. Wave after wave of suburban home building moved young families ever further from the old urban cores. Young couples, in what seemed like unending numbers, were marrying, having children, and moving to the suburbs. The cities' existing housing stock was unable to house the growing new families of the baby boom. The suburban single-family home became the American home and suburbia the American way of life. Most everyone was caught up in the desire for new single-family housing. Exceptions were some urban singles, childless couples, and a small but vocal group of urban professionals and intellectuals living in urban centers, especially New York City. The poor and urban minorities, of course, were left behind.

That, in time, became part of the attraction of suburbia. As central cities erupted in flames during the 1960s, the exodus to the suburbs meant more than the seeking of newer housing and more room. It also came to mean that the city, with its growing congestion, filth, problems, poor, and minorities could be escaped. Suburbia was thought to be safely white, middle-class, and residential. Cities, on the other hand, were dirty and dangerous.

In the decades immediately following World War II, there was a flurry of scholarly as well as popular interest in the life-styles, behaviors, and beliefs of the ex-GIs and their spouses moving into the new baby-boom suburbs. Often the concern was that suburbanites were trading individualism for conformity and "togetherness" (William H. Whyte, *The Organization Man*, Doubleday (Anchor), Garden City, N.Y.,

1956). However, this flash of attention was overwhelmed in the late 1960s by concern over the social upheavals and physical destruction occurring in the central cities. The urban revolts or riots of the 1960s were followed in short order by the central-city financial crises of the 1970s. Urban studies became virtually synonymous with the study or discussion of central-city and, particularly, inner-city problems. Meanwhile, suburbs, all but forgotten in the popular and professional literature, quietly became the modal place of residence for the American population.

The singular focus on inner cities, while understandable and perhaps even necessary, meant that the momentous changes occurring in the rest of metropolitan society went virtually unheralded. During this period North America went from being a continent of city dwellers to being a continent of suburbanites with remarkably little notice. For example, in the space of a little over a score of years, we have gone from shopping downtown to shopping at the suburban mall. Suburban shopping malls, as of 1987, accounted for 54 percent of all sales of personal and household items. Across North America there are now over thirty-five thousand malls, ranging from plain strip malls to Kmarts to regional malls to megamalls such as the Mall of America in Burlington, Minnesota, with its indoor amusement park and 400 stores. Regional malls such as Tysons Corner, Virginia, outside Washington, D.C.; Southcoast Plaza, in California's Orange County; and Galeria, in Houston, have become virtual tourist sites in their own right.

Employment as well as shopping also increasingly has a noncenter ZIP code. During the past quarter of a century, jobs as well as homes have suburbanized, with over twice as many jobs in manufacturing now being located in suburbs as in central cities. The industrial park has supplanted the central-city factory. Not only blue-collar but white-collar jobs are also rapidly suburbanizing. This now includes headquarters as well as back-office operations. Outer Dallas, for example, has three times the office space as does the central business district, while suburban Atlanta has twice the office space as the center city. Even in the New York metropolitan area, northern New Jersey has more offices than Manhattan. The movement of Sears is instructive. Two decades ago Sears topped the Chicago skyline, locating its operations to the world's highest building, the 110-story Sears Tower. In 1992 Sears moved its 5,000 Merchandise Group employees out from the Sears Tower to suburban Hoffman Estates, thirty-five miles to the northwest. Sears's new retailing headquarters, named Prairie Stone, is anything but a city skyscraper. Built on a former soybean field, Prairie Stone includes more than 200 acres of reconstructed prairie and wetlands. The highest building is six stories high.

Tysons Corner, Virginia, outside Washington, D.C., is typical of suburban outer cities insofar as it does not exist as a legal entity and thus cannot be found on state maps. This is in spite of having grown over the past twenty-five years from a crossroads to a major suburban shopping and office outer city containing more office space than the city of Tucson.

Economically as well as demographically, suburbs are no longer *sub*. Whether you call them outer cities, edge cities, technoburbs, suburban cities, or some other term, outer cities are coming to dominate the metropolitan landscape. Two-thirds of America's office space is now located in outer cities. Places unheard of a quarter of a century ago, such as King of Prussia, Pennsylvania; North Dallas, Texas; Dunwiddie, Georgia; and Costa Mesa, California, are now major economic and commercial centers. If current patterns continue, they will pass the economic power of their central cities of Philadelphia, Dallas, Atlanta, and Los Angeles. Older core-periphery models of urban growth with their assumption of a dominant central city hardly fit this new reality.

Overview

This volume seeks to provide a synoptic view of some of these demographic and social changes. The primary focus is on the process and consequences of American suburbanization. The book's original organization will be temporal and will move to more of a topic-based organization as we enter the contemporary era. We will begin by discussing how and why suburbs emerged and developed. We shall arbitrarily restrict our attention to the past 150 years of suburban development in the United States, with the heaviest attention given to the past 50 years of post-World War II suburban developments. We shan't ignore earlier twentieth- or nineteenth-century developments, though, because without an understanding of how suburban areas developed physically, politically, and socially, it is most difficult to understand current changes in suburbia. The goal is to provide an overview that will explore some of the historical background factors that brought us to the current state.

Next, we will give our attention to examining and summarizing our knowledge and understanding of the contemporary suburban scene. Here we look at the nature of the current economic, ethnic, racial, and social status of suburbs as well as their changing economic role. From this we hope to gain a better understanding of what suburbia looks like today. Finally, a few comments will be offered on the direction in which suburbs might be evolving as we approach the new century. If we are to plan for the future, or even hope to change our direction, it is essential to know what will occur if we do nothing. Knowledge of both past developments and the contemporary suburban scene gives us a base upon which to make decisions.

CHAPTER 2

Definitions and Paradigms

DEFINITIONAL CONFUSION

Everybody, it seems, knows what suburbs are. Over the years there has been a marvelous vague agreement in many volumes and professional articles written on suburbs that the term is so self-explanatory that no definition need be offered. Those who are comfortable with this approach might want to simply skim this chapter on defining the animal we are discussing. Since suburbs are something we all know something about, coming up with an agreed-upon operational definition has been fraught with surprising difficulty. H. Paul Douglas, perhaps the first scholar to focus attention specifically on suburbs as an aggregate, in the mid-1920s defined the suburbs as being "the belt of population which lives under distinctly roomier conditions than is the average lot of city people, but under distinctively more crowded conditions than those of the adjoining open country" (H. Paul Douglas, *The Suburban Trend*, Century, New York, 1925, p. 6). The criterion he used was basically housing density; the suburbs were the middle landscape. By definition, suburbs were residential. The definition also indirectly suggests that suburbs are more affluent by noting "roomier conditions" in suburbs.

A somewhat different dictionary definition of a suburb is that given by *Webster's New Collegiate Dictionary*, which states that a suburb is "a smaller community adjacent to or within commuting distance of a city" (*Webster's New Collegiate Dictionary*, G. & C. Merriam, Springfield, Mass., 1981, p. 1154). This definition has the advantage of simplicity but the weakness of assuming that suburbs are by definition smaller in population, and by implication space, than central cities. Today, with central-city populations often declining to the point that they are only one-third or less of their metropolitan-area population, it is becoming increasingly problematic that all suburbs are by definition "smaller communities." The definition also fails to distinguish between suburbs and satellite communities.

A more widely used definition of a suburb, and one traditionally used by academics, is that a suburb is a "community that lies apart from the city but is adjacent to and dependent upon it" (David Popenoe, "The Traditional American House and Environment: Social Effects," in Elizabeth Huttman and Willem van Vliet, eds., *Handbook of Housing and the Built Environment in the United States,* Greenwood Press, New York, 1988, p. 394). Historically, this definition fit rather well, and it is still commonly used. For instance, when discussing what he calls "middle-class suburbs of privilege," Robert Fishman states, ". . . I shall use the words 'suburb' and 'suburbia' to refer only to a residential community beyond the core of a large city. Though physically separate from the urban core, the suburb nevertheless depends on it economically for the jobs that support its residents. It is also culturally dependent on the core for the major institutions of urban life: professional offices, department stores and other specialized shops, hospitals, theaters, and the like" (Robert Fishman, *Bourgeois Utopias,* Basic Books, New York, 1987, p. 5). Such definitions emphasize the outer area's economic dependency on the central city and, additionally, suggest political separation from the central city. The definition gives the basic image of suburbs being areas of urban spillover across city boundaries. This image fits many of the suburbs we will be discussing, and virtually every American would recognize the picture. It certainly fits nineteenth- and early-twentieth-century suburbs.

Many North American suburbs today still are residential communities consisting of detached, owner-occupied, single-family, middle-class homes arranged in low-density and socially homogeneous communities located outside the central city but within commuting distance of the city core. However, as we move toward the new century, the assumption of suburban economic and social dependency on the central city becomes increasingly questionable. More and more suburbs are becoming the dominant metropolitan economic and social units. Definitions for contemporary suburbs that assume that suburbs are economically dependent and *sub* to their central cities are out of date.

Some urban scholars try to sidestep these difficulties by making more general definitions. Thus Mark Baldassare, in a 1992 review of suburban communities, states, "We offer the following broad definition of suburban communities. They are the municipalities and places in metropolitan areas outside the political boundaries of the large cen-

tral cities. Suburban communities differ from central cities in the presence of sprawling, low density land use, the absence of a central downtown district, and the existence of a politically fragmented local government" (Mark Baldassare, "Suburban Communities," *Annual Review
of Sociology*, Vol. 18, 1992, p. 476). Again, this is a picture of suburbia
that resonates with most readers. The definition has the advantage of
not assuming economic or social dependence on the central city.
However, the definition does assume that suburbs lack central retail,
commercial, and business districts such as are found "downtown."

Suburbs today, though, have grown to where deciding which business and retail districts are central and which are peripheral is no
longer simply a matter of geography. In many cases suburban shopping and business districts are now "central" to more people than are
the old traditional downtowns. All across America places such as
Tysons Corner or King of Prussia have become "downtowns" in their
own right. Tysons Corner, for instance, has more department stores
and commercial activity than does "downtown" Washington, D.C.
Other metropolitan areas show more extreme patterns. In the Detroit
area, for example, almost all major business offices, theaters, restaurants, and retail stores have long since moved to the outer city. Each
year fewer suburban or city residents even venture downtown. One
might ask, then, on what basis, other than history, does the old downtown of Detroit lay claim to being the central core district of the metropolitan area? Virtually all the economic and social activities we associated with "downtown" are found in the outer-edge cities surrounding
Detroit, not in the old central core. If the suburbs hold most of the business offices, shopping, and entertainment activities that defined the old
downtowns, can't suburban outer cites be said to be the new central
districts?

The existence of political fragmentation as a defined characteristic
of suburbs also can be a potential problem. It is true that suburbia is
often fragmented politically, but how significant is this fragmentation,
and is it characteristic of suburbia as a whole? As suburbs have become
spatially and demographically larger, and as industrial-era cities have
lost population, even the old assumption that the central city is, by definition, the largest demographic and spatial metropolitan unit may become uncertain. This author, for example, lives in a legally defined
suburban community that is both larger geographically and, as of the
1990 census, larger in terms of residents than the central city that it borders.

Complicating further our definition of a suburb is that the distinction between city and suburb is basically legal rather than sociological.
While local municipal boundaries may be significant in many ways, including financing, taxing, and the provision of public services such as

police and schools, they basically are arbitrary divisions. Sometimes the political and the social definitions don't match. The affluent Buckhead area of Atlanta, for instance, is often spoken of as being suburban. Clearly it is suburban in appearance and life-style, but it is legally part of the city of Atlanta. Another example of the affluent suburb-within-the-city is River Oaks, in Houston. Some writers, such as Fishman, sidestep the definitional difficulty by saying, "I should emphasize that the suburb, in my definition, is not necessarily a separate political unit" (Fishman, 1987, p. 5). Instead of legal boundaries of municipalities, suburbs could be defined using demographic definitions based on factors such as the population density of an area, the educational level of residents, or even the family status of those living in the area. Ecological definitions could also be used, such as the distance from the center of the city or the proportion of single-family housing. However, the traditional city-suburban legal division is overwhelmingly the most commonly used, and over time the city line has come to be viewed as also being an economic, social, and sometimes a racial boundary. A once permeable and movable boundary has developed an inevitably fixed character.

Interestingly, the Bureau of the Census doesn't officially use the term "suburb." The government definition most commonly used to approximate suburbia is the "MSA area outside the central city" (definition provided by the U.S. Government Office of Management and Budget) and is based on the definition of Metropolitan Statistical Areas (MSAs). A Metropolitan Statistical Area is a county or group of counties having a central city of 50,000 or more or twin cities of 50,000 or more. As of the 1990 census, there were some 284 areas designated as MSAs. The area in the county outside the central city and all of any adjacent counties that are judged by the Bureau of the Census to be metropolitan in character and socially and economically integrated with the central city is designated as the MSA "outside the central city." This metropolitan-oriented area outside the central city is what is commonly referred to as the suburbs. Census data on suburbs presented in the following pages reflect this government definition, which divides MSAs between central cities and county areas outside the central cities. (Prior to 1950 the Bureau of the Census defined metropolitan areas on an ad hoc basis for each census. The result was decade-by-decade change in suburban boundaries, making historical comparisons difficult. Additionally, central cities often annexed built-up suburban areas between census periods. This resulted in historically overestimating city growth and underestimating suburban growth. Suburban growth rates for earlier eras thus are best viewed as estimates—estimates that understate suburban rates of growth.)

The United States government's collection of data based on the territorial boundaries of counties rather than on population does have certain advantages. First, since county boundaries rarely change from decade to decade, it is easy to aggregate data over a long period. Second, many other data are also collected on a county basis, and thus it is easier to make comparisons. Finally, counties, better than any other civil division, realistically contain the territory economically and socially integrated with the central city. Unfortunately, there are also some real disadvantages to the use of counties. The main difficulty is that the area outside the central city, the suburban area, is actually a residual category. By lumping all the "suburban" areas outside the central city together, the census definition reflects more of the suburban reality than does the use of individual suburban boundaries, but it does so at the price of including everything that is not central city. In some cases the use of counties results in including in the category of suburbs considerable land outside the central city that cannot realistically be considered anything but rural. Thus, the extent of metropolitan growth is overestimated. However, since the population living in these "urban" areas is of limited size, the inclusion of such rural suburbanites does not substantially distort suburban population data.

In some cases the problem is not counting ruralities as suburbanites but including those who are essentially city dwellers as suburbanites simply because they live in a smaller city that lies near an even larger central city. Areas outside the largest central cities of New York, Philadelphia, Chicago, and Los Angeles may include large, long-established communities that, if located in Kansas or Montana, would be considered cities in their own right. Most of us, for example, do not think of old industrial cities such as Camden, New Jersey, across the river from Philadelphia, or Egin, Illinois, west of Chicago, as being suburban. Further complicating the definitional problems is the decision made by the Bureau of the Census back in the 1970s to create a new type of suburban metropolitan area not having any central city. Examples of such "suburban" SMAs are Orange County, south of Los Angeles, and Nassau and Suffolk counties, on Long Island, outside New York. In practical terms, these hybrid all-suburban metropolitan areas make sense; but they do stretch the old distinction between city and suburb.

A Working Definition

As the above indicates, there is no ideal or universally agreed upon definition of what a suburb is. When we speak of suburbs in this book, we will be referring to incorporated or unincorporated spatial communities of moderate density that lie outside the central city but within the metropolitan area. The area's primary economic activities are nonagricultural, and government is usually through independent and sometimes uncoordinated local units. Suburban areas do not have to be primarily residential, but their densities are moderate, and both their population and their economic activities are spread throughout a wide area. Contemporary suburbs are not necessarily dependent economically on the central city they surround, but they are tied to the city (and to other suburbs) by a dependency on the automobile. This means that except when noted otherwise, I will be using the term "suburb" in a manner similar to the way it is implicitly understood by most North Americans and in a way that conforms to the way data are aggregated and released by the Bureau of the Census.

Finally, it is the contention of this work that the American suburb is essentially a North American development. While areas of peripheral residential development are found worldwide, the North American suburbs have evolved significantly even from their English prototypes. American suburbs have a lower density and much larger lots than those in England. Americans are also more likely to be homeowners rather than renters. This remains true even given the proliferation of higher-density rental garden apartments over recent decades in North America. Compared to Western European patterns of suburban high-rise housing, the American pattern is even more diverse. Part of this difference has been due to differing government policies. For example, research since the 1960s has demonstrated that the general North America pattern has been for suburbs, regardless of racial composition, to have higher socioeconomic status than their central cities (J. John Palen and Leo Schnore, "Color Composition and City-Suburban Status Differences," in J. Palen and K. Fleming eds., *Urban America: Conflict and Change,* Holt, Rinehart and Winston, New York, 1972, pp. 114–120). By comparison, the working-class, Communist suburbs northeast of Paris have long been known as "the red ring," and suburban new towns in Germany and Sweden house heavy lower-status immigrant "guest worker" populations. In America suburbs are more likely to house the affluent than the economically and socially marginal members of society.

PERSPECTIVES AND MODELS

Metropolitan growth sometimes seems haphazard, but the historical reality is that growth has patterns. Thus, if we wish to examine suburbanization in the last century, it helps to first make explicit some of our current beliefs regarding the pattern of growth of suburbs and suburbanization. This then provides a reference point that we can use in making comparisons with earlier eras and patterns.

Ecological Paradigm

The theoretical approach or paradigm that doubtlessly has had the greatest influence on the spatial organization of suburbs and cities is that of urban ecology. Classical urban ecology (also called human ecology) had its period of early flowering during the 1920s at the University of Chicago. Under the leadership of researchers such as Robert Park and Ernest Burgess, the so-called Chicago School produced a large number of empirical studies focusing on the social-spatial organization of the city. This represented the first systematic assembly of actual urban research done without the social reform agenda of earlier decades. Areas of poverty, crime, mental illness, and other social problems were studied and mapped not for their own sake but to discover how the sociological, psychological, and moral experiences of urban life were reflected in spatial relationships. Park believed that changes in physical and spatial structure directly affected social behavior. In his words, "most if not all cultural changes in society will be correlated with changes in territorial organization, and every change in the territorial and occupational distribution of the population will effect changes in the existing culture" (Robert Park, *Human Communities: The City and Human Ecology*, Free Press, New York, 1952, p. 14). This postulate of "an intimate congruity between the social and physical space, between social and physical distance, and between social equality and residential proximity is the crucial hypothetical framework supporting urban ecological theories" (Ralph Thomlinson, *Urban Structure: The Social and Spatial Character of Cities*, Random House, New York, 1969, p. 9). In practice this meant that urban ecology was concerned with questions such as persistence of ethnic neighborhoods, patterns of racial segregation, problems of social control, local political behavior, and community and neighboring.

Classical urban ecological theories of human community were related to, and borrowed much of their terminology from, evolutionary theories of plant and animal development. In all these, competition—the Darwinian struggle for survival—played a central role. In the metropolitan area, as a consequence of the economic competition for prime space, there emerged distinct spatial and social zones. Just as someone traveling from desert to mountains finds that different physical environments produce different species of plants and animals, so, by analogy, would traveling from a city business district to outlying residential areas show different zones of development. Thus, the spatial organization of the metropolitan area evolved, according to the ecologists, not through planning or government action, but through competition influenced by the ecological processes of invasion, succession, segregation of new groups (e.g., immigrants), and new land uses (e.g., commercial usage replacing residential). Change occurs through new populations or usages invading an area and pushing out old groups and usages. Thus, succession of group and land usages takes place.

Burgess Growth Model

The most famous ecological model of the spatial-organizational development of the city is the concentric zonal hypothesis developed by Ernest Burgess in 1924 (Ernest W. Burgess, "The Growth of the City: An Introduction to a Research Project," *Publications of the American Sociological Society,* Vol. 18, 1924, pp. 85–97). This model still sets our stereotypes of suburbs and their relationship to the central city. The Burgess hypothesis is one of the centerpieces of the so-called Chicago School. It grew out of efforts by scholars at the University of Chicago to explain how cities change from simpler, preindustrial to more complex, industrial forms. It was assumed that economic and social changes in the metropolis would be reflected in the changing spatial patterns of the city. The model thus shows how cities change over time from a preindustrial pattern, in which there is no clear segregation of land for specific purposes (e.g., a specific downtown central business district and specific manufacturing and residential areas) to the complex functional differentiation characterizing contemporary urban areas. Generations of Introductory Sociology students have been exposed to the Burgess hypothesis as a static picture of the pre-World War II industrial city, but this is a somewhat bastardized version of the original hypothesis, which defined the model not as an existing reality, but rather as a description of urban *growth* patterns. This growth took place through invasion and succession (Otis Dudley Duncan and Beverly Duncan, *The Negro Population of Chicago,* University of Chicago Press, Chicago, 1957). In other words, what Burgess was hypothesizing was a model for urban change.

The Burgess model emphasized that in industrial cities, businesses, homes, and retail establishments were not randomly dispersed throughout the urban area. Rather, there was a clear pattern based on economic competition for space and social sorting that resulted in similar populations and land uses in certain areas. In other words, competition for space meant that businesses, institutions, and homes were not distributed in a random fashion. That all of this seems obvious to us today is a reflection of our acceptance of the work of the Chicago

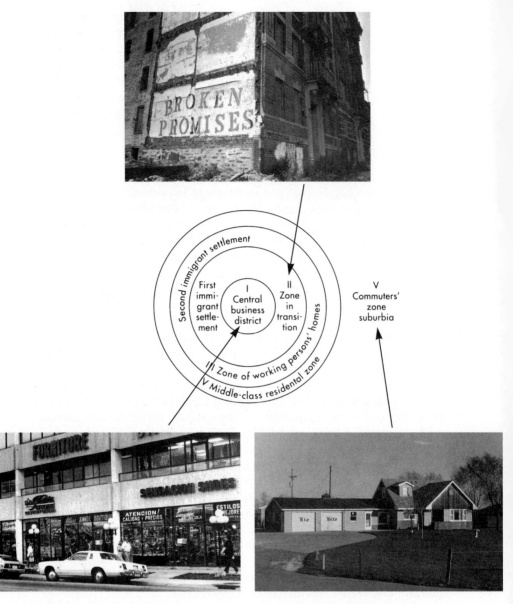

The Burgess Zonal Hypothesis provided the dominant model of how urban areas grew prior to the suburban changes over the last few decades.

school into our body of "commonsense" general knowledge. The Burgess growth hypothesis, with its emphasis on growth going from the center outward through a series of zones, also has had a profound effect on twentieth-century beliefs regarding real estate. Few realtors may be aware of it, but the filter-down housing model that has been implicitly used for decades to determine real estate values is based directly on the Burgess model of how cities grow and change. Although filtering down was not integral to the model, it suggested both that change came from outside the neighborhood, and that the pattern of invasion and succession was more or less inevitable. The implication was that once change began in a neighborhood, it was virtually impossible to reverse the pattern. This would suggest, for example, that once a neighborhood passed a certain tip point, racial succession was inevitable. This belief, widely held by realtors, would have a negative effect on housing practices for much of the twentieth century.

Crucial to Burgess' model was the belief that cities grow radially through a series of zones, with the most strategic and valuable land going to those users who were best able to afford the costs, both in terms of land costs and toleration of nuisances such as congestion and noise and air pollution. This meant that in the industrial city of Burgess's era, the most valuable land would be the central business district (CBD) located at the center of the transportation network. Intensive uses of space such as department stores, financial institutions, and business offices would thus tend to force out less intensive uses, such as housing. Land values would thus be highest in the center of the downtown and decrease in value as one moved further toward the periphery. Since outer suburban land was less valuable, lot sizes could increase, and single-family homes on large lots became economically more viable. This resulted in a pattern where the most valuable homes and the wealthiest residents lived on the urban fringe. Or, to state it another way, there was a tendency for an inverse relationship between the value of land and the economic status of those occupying it. The more affluent lived on the cheaper outer land.

This is the general picture of suburbs most of us carry around in our heads. That is, suburbs are thought of as peripherally located upper-income or middle-income communities of relatively low density on substantial lots holding free-standing single-family homes. However, this mental image of what a suburb is does not adequately reflect the contemporary scene and may deflect our attention from the different manner in which much of suburbia is evolving. It may make it more difficult for us to confront the more recent development of outer-city suburbs. Nor does this generally accepted view of suburbs being, in effect, a creation and extension of the central city always help us to understand the development of the first American suburbs.

Political Economy Perspective

For many decades the ecological model was "the" model of urban growth. However, during recent decades it has increasingly come under attack by scholars favoring neo-Marxian or political economy models. These models challenge the mainstream urban ecology perspective by emphasizing that urban patterns are not the result of "hidden hand" economic forces, but rather that urban patterns are deliberately shaped for private profit by elites in business and government. Thus, unlike ecological approaches, which explain suburbanization as occurring as a consequence of technological factors such as the streetcar or automobile, political economy, or neo-Marxian, views stress the role played by corporate and real estate interests in manipulating land usage and markets. Suburbia is not a consequence of individual homeowner choice, but a consequence of a deliberate decision by elites to disinvest in the cities. These elites are composed of "the industrial executives, developers, bankers, and their political allies (Joe Feagan and Robert Parker, *Building American Cities: The Real Estate Game,* Prentice-Hall, Englewood Cliffs, N.J. 1990).

This approach is sometimes also identified as the "new urban sociology." According to Smith and Timberlake, ". . . (T)he new urban sociology is usually based on assumptions of neo-Marxism and conflict theory" (David A. Smith and Michael F. Timberlake, "The New Urban Sociology," in J. John Palen, ed., *The Urban World,* McGraw-Hill, New York, 1992, p. 340). The term "new urban sociology" is a bit of a misnomer, since advocates of this approach or paradigm often are geographers, urban planners, or political scientists rather than sociologists. Although these perspectives differ in specifics, they all stress that urban development is a consequence of capitalist modes of production, capital accumulation, exploitation of the powerless, and conflictual class relations.

Gottdiener and Feagan argue that the basic concepts of the new approach are:

(1) Societies are specified according to their mode of production . . .
(2) In the United States and Western Europe as well as elsewhere societal development is dominated by the capital accumulation process . . .
(3) A central role in the process of accumulation is assigned to labor power—its use, management, and reproduction.
(4) Social spatial relationships, particularly the relationship between

capitalistic processes and space, are an intrinsic part of social development.

(5) Methodological individualism is overcome through specification of structure and its relationship to agency, although the articulation of this relationship varies among the new urbanists.

(6) Real-estate and its supporting infrastructure constitute a "second circuit" of capital (Mark Gottdiener and Joe Feagan, "The Paradigm Shift in Urban Sociology," Urban Affairs Quarterly, Vol. 24, December 1988, pp. 171–172).

Gottdiener and Feagan also suggest that "certain assumptions are common to the new critical urbanists." These are:

(1) Societal interaction is dominated by antagonistic social relationships. Consequently society is not a unified biotic community that experiences change from the outside, but a stratified and highly differentiated form of organization characterized by its own fissures, contradictions, and patterns of uneven development—features that flow from the (for example, the capitalistic) mode of production itself.

(2) Social development is unstable in societies with antagonistic owner relationships. Contradictions of development and inequalities of growth fuel antagonism and define the nature of political activities.

(3) Power inequality is a basic element in societal relationships and the exercise of power can be a factor in societal development.

(4) No society can be adequately analyzed without reference to either its long-term history or its global context (1984, p. 174).

The political economy, or new sociology, theoretical approaches were developed in the 1970s as a reaction against the mechanistic and ahistorical nature of much of the early urban ecological research. Manuel Castelles, in *The Urban Question: A Marxist Approach,* argued that urban sociology had become sterile, and he advocated a Marxist approach to cities, urban life, and urban questions (Manuel Castelles, *The Urban Question: A Marxist Approach,* MIT Press, Cambridge, Mass. 1977). Although he has since modified some of his earlier Marxist views, his critique of how urban sociology had become captive of its own comfortable assumptions resonated strongly with younger academics. Similarly influential was David Harvey's *Social Justice and the City,* which argued strongly that the social inequality, social conflict, and social problems of Baltimore were the predictable consequences of capitalist political economy determining real estate and land usage (David Harvey, *Social Justice and the City,* Edward Arnold, London, 1973). The Marxist argument about urban space, "begins from the idea that urban space (as well as space at other scales) is the specific effect of the kind of society in which this urban space is developed . . . and the capitalist city . . . is developed according to a logic that is internal to capital itself" (Neil Smith and Michele LeFaivre, "A Class Analysis of Gentrification," in J. Palen and B. London, eds., *Gentrification, Displacement, and Neighborhood Revitalization,* State University of New York Press, Albany, 1984, p. 53).

A systematic statement of how a non-Marxian new sociology political economy approach can be used to study how property markets work as social phenomena can be found in Logan and Molotch's *Urban Fortunes: The Political Economy of Place* (John Logan and Harvey Molotch, *Urban Fortunes: The Political Economy of Place,* University of California Press, Berkley, 1987). They argue that place is valued in two ways: first, as an object of exchange to be bought and sold, and second, when it is used to do business in or live in. In the latter case place has a sentimental and symbolic value associated with jobs, neighborhood, hometown, and community. However, the urban growth machine of corporate political elites is interested in land strictly as an investment and commodity to be bought and sold. Their interest is in creating "a good business environment" so that investments and new residents will come to the area and increase market value of the land, and aggregate rent levels will increase. This governmental and corporate emphasis on growth is at the expense of the interest of local residents and their communities. The needs of the general public are captive to the "growth machine" whose principal interest is in the transfer of wealth to rentier groups. "Use values of the majority are sacrificed for the exchange values of a few (Logan and Molotch, 1987, p. 96). Thus, community groups that advocate slow growth or neighborhood preservation are fought by the business elites that profit from maintaining the "growth machine."

In the pages that follow, the reader will note that most "explanations" of suburban social and physical change are implicitly based upon these models regarding both ecological change and the political economic growth machine. Our use of the models will be pragmatic rather than ideological. Rather than trying to fit the data into a predetermined ideological pattern, the explanations used will be based on what appears to be the patterns in the data. Others may, of course, interpret the patterns differently. They are encouraged to do so.

CHAPTER 3

Rural-Urban Ideals and Early Suburbs

NASCENT SUBURBS

While one can trace the existence of suburbs back to classical times, we will restrict ourselves largely to the period from roughly 1850 to the present. But it is useful to know how American suburbs prior to the 1850s were organized. Before that time American suburban areas differed in many ways from our contemporary ideas about suburbia. Our concept of suburbs as the outer extremities and extensions of central cities presents an incomplete and, in some ways, inaccurate picture of the first American suburbs. The suburbs before roughly one hundred and fifty years ago were not upper-middle-class residential appendages of the central city. Rather, they were far more mixed economic and social entities. As such they interacted with both the city and with the outlying countryside. According to historical research, the first suburbs were not add-ons to the city, but "a zone of manufactures and commercial activity relating to the city but not requiring regular contact" (Henry C. Binford, *The First Suburbs: Residential Communities on the Boston Periphery 1815–1860,* University of Chicago Press, Chicago, 1985, p. 10). Poor-quality roads, and the time difficulty of commuting to the city, meant that the great bulk of suburban-edge residents both worked and lived in their peripheral villages. They were neither socially nor economically tied to the nearby city. In this respect the American suburbs of one hundred and fifty years ago were in many ways better precursors of the emerging self-sufficient suburbs of the end of the twentieth century than they were of the residential suburbs of the 1920s. In this respect, early-nineteenth-century suburbs also

21

had more similarity to the new self-sufficient suburban outer or edge cities of today than they did to the central city that oriented and dominated post-World War II residential tract suburbs of the 1950s and 1960s.

In his influential work *Crabgrass Frontier*, Kenneth Jackson titles his first chapter "Suburbs as Slums" (Kenneth T. Jackson, *Crabgrass Frontier*, Oxford University Press, New York, 1985, p. 12). He does this to emphasize that before the transportation revolutions of railroad and horse-pulled streetcar that occurred in the mid-nineteenth century, suburbs were not easily accessible. Thus, the outskirts housed those who were socially as well as physically on the outskirts of the society. This thesis stressing the evils of early suburbs contains an element of exaggeration for emphasis, but it is true that seldom did one find in the suburbs the more "genteel" segment of the population. To stress this point, Jackson reprints comments from the 1849 diary of George Foster who wrote, "Nine-tenths of those who rascalities have made Philadelphia so unjustly notorious live in the dens and shanties of the suburbs." (Jackson quoting George R. Taylor, ed., "Philadelphia in Slices: The Diary of George G. Foster," *The Philadelphia Magazine of History and Biography*, XCIII, January 1969, p. 34.)

Certainly, it was the case that in the preindustrial era, areas on the outer fringes of the city often housed those who economically and socially were on the margins of society. In this housing of marginal people in marginal areas, America followed the European pattern, where one found respectable people of substance living in town. The French *faubourg* and the German *vorstadt* referred to places outside the city walls, and to be outside the walls was to be outside civil society.

English suburbs were, similarly, not places where the better sort resided. The placement of Shakespeare's Globe Theater not in London proper, but across the Thames in the suburbs, reflects the marginal position of theaters and actors in Elizabethan England. During the same period, houses of prostitution also moved to the outer areas, so whores became known as "suburban sinners." It should come as no surprise that it was considered an insult to label someone a "suburbanite." Until the nineteenth century, no less an authority than the *Oxford English Dictionary* said a suburb was "a place of inferior, debased, and especially licentious habits of life" (Robert Fishman, *Bourgeois Utopias: The Rise and Fall of Suburbia*, Basic Books, New York, 1987, p. 6).

Early suburbs in North America were perhaps not as colorful, but neither were they commuter zones for the upper middle class. As late as 1857, when Frederick Law Olmstead began building Central Park on 843 acres at the northern edge of New York City, the suburban site was described in less than glowing terms. According to Olmstead, Central

Park, which was to become one of New York's jewels, was a swamp "seeped in the overflow and mush of pigsties, slaughterhouses, and boneboiling works, and the stench was sickening." Living in the squalid squatter shacks in the area were many impoverished Irish immigrants who survived marginally as ragpickers and garbage scavengers. This is hardly the contemporary image of suburbia.

Thus, before the middle of the nineteenth century, the advantages of the city and the difficulties of commutation insured that commuters were not a significant proportion of the population of most cities. The historian Henry Binford argues that early suburbs, rather than being appendages or outgrowths from the city, were freestanding, thinly settled, semirural communities (Binford, 1985, pp. 8–10). Such communities included manufacturing and commercial activity related to the city, but the limited mobility of persons and goods meant that contact with the city was sporadic rather than daily. Going into the city just took too much effort. Before the late 1840s travel required considerable energy, time, and expense. In their social life and political organization, early suburbs were more villages than smaller clones of the central city. Only when transportation improved would fringe areas be transformed into commuter suburbs. In the meantime fringe locations would be hybrid communities.

Binford makes the point that even before the era of mass transportation and the period when the suburbs would have regular contact with the city, the suburban fringe had already begun to change in significant ways (Binford, 1985, p. 47). First, the suburbs had become more diverse villages, with a mixture of newcomers, some of whom had links to the central city and some of whom had economic and other links to the country. Second, partially as a consequence of the increased population diversity, there was increased social complexity. As the populations of the suburban villages became more diverse, their social organization became more complex, with overlapping circles of interest and involvement. Boundaries became more varied and flexible. People's social, religious, business, and political networks were increasingly likely to vary from individual to individual. Finally, the villages were changing politically. Newer and younger men had a wider range of interests, and they were more open to the growth of local government and its evolution from village to suburban forms.

However, not all American suburban areas of a century and a half ago were impoverished, housing only the poor and outcast. Outer areas had open land, and America's Jeffersonian agrarian heritage contributed to an ideology that encouraged open space while viewing cities as sources of discord and social evils. Since virtue (and cheap land) increased as one approached rural life, the goal of some urbanites was to be in the city, but just barely. The suburban development of Brooklyn as an independent suburban community, across the harbor from Manhattan, indicated how the dilemma of continuing urban business without abandoning the city could be resolved using the technology of the ferryboat. Living in Brooklyn, across the harbor from Manhattan, provided the prototype compromise. Kenneth Jackson refers to Brooklyn as the "first commuter suburb" (Jackson, 1985, p. 25). With its frequent ferryboat connection to Manhattan, Brooklyn Heights had easy access to the city while at the same time retaining the suggestion of a bucolic community. By 1841 half of the householders who had bought land in Brooklyn Heights commuted to offices in Manhattan. By no stretch could these commuters be characterized as social outcasts or those on the margins of society. Hezekiah Beers Pierrepoint developed Brooklyn Heights as a community, noting "Gentlemen whose business or profession require daily attendance into the city cannot better, or with less expense, secure the health and comfort of their families." Here in his comments were the themes that would be used to promote and advertise suburban living for the next century and a half. Suburbia claimed to offer a superior life-style, was a more healthful place to live, and was less expensive in the bargain.

ANTEBELLUM WALKING CITIES

Cities of the pre-Civil War era were compact walking cities. The radius of even the largest cities did not extend over three miles. Even in New York a walk of an hour would bring the stroller from the central city to open countryside. If one were adventurous and could afford it, a three-quarters-of-an-hour ride from Wall Street on the new horse-drawn streetcars would bring one to the norther boundary of the city, where a swampy area of suburban shacks was being transformed into what would become Central Park.

Not that many people rode in private or even public transportation. While the streets evidenced many carriages, owning such was a privilege restricted to the upper and some of the upper middle classes. Maintaining a horse and carriage in the city—with keeping the coachman and stable hands that were part of such ownership—was an expense beyond the means of ordinary citizens. Most cities, by the 1850s, had public omnibuses for middle-class usage. Omnibuses were essentially overcrowded urban stagecoaches. The poor quality of urban streets, however, made the omnibuses uncomfortable as well as crowded, slow, and expensive. Thus, before the advent of horse-pulled streetcars in the 1850s, most middle-class urban dwellers got where they were going by walking. In good weather it was both faster and more comfortable than riding the omnibuses. The poor, regardless of weather or distance, always walked.

The decades prior to the Civil War (1861–1865) saw the rapid expansion of existing cities and the founding of many new ones (see J. John Palen, *The Urban World*, 4th ed., McGraw-Hill, New York, 1992, pp. 66–74). All were densely packed walking cities. In the two score of years prior to 1860, cities grew at a pace faster than they grew before or ever since (Charles N. Glaab, *The American City: A Documentary History*, Dorsey Press, Homewood, Ill. 1963, p. 65). Of the fifty largest cities today, only seven were incorporated before 1816; thirty-nine were incorporated between 1816 and 1876; and only four have been incorporated since 1876. The effect of environmental factors on the growth of pre-Civil War cities is evident from the fact that of the nine cities that had surpassed a population of 100,000 by 1860, eight were major ports. The one exception really wasn't an exception. It was Brooklyn, which was an independent city until 1898, when it was incorporated into New York. Brooklyn, of course, shared the best natural harbor on the east coast with New York.

New York was by far the most important American city on the eve of the Civil War. It had a population of over 1 million in 1860 (only London and Paris were larger); it was the financial center of the nation; and its docks handled a third of the country's exports and a full two-thirds of its imports. However, in spite of its tremendous growth, even New York retained many preindustrial-city characteristics. The urban economy was still in a commercial rather than industrial stage. Business people were primarily merchants, although they intermittently took on subsidiary functions such as manufacturing, speculating, and banking.

In spite of the ready availability of land, the eighteenth- and nineteenth-century American city was remarkably densely packed. An examination today of the old central area of cities such as Philadelphia, Boston, Baltimore, or Charleston reveals block after block of tightly packed town houses. Lots were commonly only twenty feet wide and occasionally even narrower, with houses built right on the lot line. Front yards were nonexistent, with houses even of the wealthy fronting on the sidewalk, which in turn was immediately adjacent to the street. This tight housing pattern was in part a carryover of the European pattern. European cities were tightly packed in part because of the existence of city walls. Cities in North America weren't constrained by external ramparts as were the cities in Europe. Where log-wall fortifications had once existed, such as Wall Street in New York or Fort Dearborn in Chicago, they were rapidly dismantled once the sur-

A hundred years ago affluent town houses abutting Fifth Avenue in New York City represented the ideal of urban life. Note the minimal levels of traffic in such upper-class neighborhoods, and compare this with the congestion of the central business district shown in the first photo in Chapter 4.

rounding Indian populations had been extinguished and the threat of Indian attack eliminated. The Canadian exceptions of the stone-walled cities of Montreal and Quebec reflected a French rather than English tradition. They were exceptions that proved the rule.

However, high density did not occur in United States cities as a result of crowding within the walls for defense purposes. Far more important was the maintenance of high-density neighborhoods because of custom and fashion. The new homes of the wealthy in Georgian London were built cheek to jowl, and the eastern seaboard cities of the United States followed the London fashion. The existence of nearby open land did not, at first, sway American cities from following the European pattern. Even small towns built housing side by side while surrounded by mile upon mile of vacant land.

Overall, the American city mixed commercial, residential, and even manufacturing activities, but each large city had a few blocks of homes of the wealthy residents crowded near the center of the city. Often these elite homes were only a block or two from far more humble housing. Traces of this preindustrial walking city pattern of centrally located elite areas can still be seen in Beacon Hill in Boston, Chestnut Street in Philadelphia, and Washington Square in New York (Sam Bass

Warner, *The Urban Wilderness: A History of the American City*, Harper & Row, New York, 1972, p. 88). Having a central location was a sign of social and economic achievement. It was fashionable to have a central core address. Thus small central-city lots were extremely valuable, while within walking distance there was unbuilt-upon open land.

Cities were also densely packed as a matter of practicality. Before the era of rapid and inexpensive mass transit, it was a major inconvenience to be outside of the central area. Thus, peripheral areas were given over largely to the poor and those on the fringes of society. In an era of slow, uncomfortable, and expensive transportation, the families of means took the center, and the poor were more likely to be relegated to the periphery (Sam Bass Warner, *The Private City Philadelphia in Three Periods of Its Growth*, University of Pennsylvania Press, Philadelphia, 1968, p. 13).

Within the city one walked to work in the morning, walked home for lunch, walked back to work, and then walked home again in the evening. This was not a major chore, since home and business were never far removed. They might, in fact, be in the same building: "The first floor was given over to commerce, the second and third reserved for the family and clerks, and the fourth perhaps for storage. People lived and worked in the same house or at least in the same neighborhood" (Christopher Tunnard and Henry Hope Reed, *American Skyline: The Growth and Form of Our Cities and Towns*, New American Library, New York, 1956, p. 59). The separation of workplace and residence that was to become a hallmark of the industrial city was limited in the preindustrial American city. Virtually everyone lived less than a mile from their place of work.

The result of all of the above was that the walking city had little spatial separation of economic activities and residential areas. Nor was there the sharp division and spatial separation of socioeconomic status that we associate with contemporary urban areas. The wealthy clearly lived far more comfortable lives and on better blocks than the urban poor, but they did not live in neighborhoods that were physically far removed from the poor. Spacial and social seperation of socioeconomic classes would be a product of the technologies of the post-Civil War industrial era.

THE AFFLUENT COMMUTING FROM SUBURBS

Although outlying suburban areas existed prior to the 1850s, places we would clearly recognize as suburbs began to appear in greater number at that time. What made possible the suburb as we know it was a revolution in mobility. The emergence of a reasonable, reliable, and safe public transport for the first time made city-suburban commuting feasible. The long-standing advantages of central-city residence were being challenged for the first time by the possibility of another reasonable and feasible alternative—commuting. Transportation advances were transforming the walking city into a riding city. The old pattern of limited travel by foot and horse over unimproved roads to peripheral locations was first supplanted by regularly scheduled omnibuses and later by railroads.

Omnibuses were large horse-drawn stagecoaches. Such coaches meant one could travel to the urban periphery without having to have one's own horse and carriage. However, omnibus travel still involved considerable time, expense, and discomfort. Omnibuses also were slow, traveling at roughly three to four miles per hour, which was no faster than a brisk walking pace. Omnibuses also were almost uniformly uncomfortable as they jolted along washboard roads filled with bone-jarring potholes. Thus, the omnibus option had severe limitations. It was a serious option only to those who were able and willing to spend money and hours bumping along marginal roads rather than resting at home in the comfortable town houses of Boston, Philadelphia, Baltimore, or New York. It is not surprising that most men of business and property preferred to remain in the city.

What really changed the urban-suburban equation was the transportation technology of the railroad. Ironically, when the railroads first extended their lines outward from the major east coast cities in the 1830s, they had little interest in suburban commuters. Railroad managers tended to view commuters more as a nuisance than as a source of revenue. The interest of the railroads was in bringing goods from the hinterland, not passengers from relatively nearby. The lack of interest in local travelers partially reflected preset ideas regarding the uses of rail transport. It also reflected the nature and economies of steam engines. Rail-mounted steam engines consume large amounts of power to initiate movement and then accelerate slowly. Once the engines are moving, the power required for propulsion drops radically. Once they are going, railroad trains are also difficult to rapidly stop. Thus, the greatest efficiency of the railroad was, and is, in long hauls with minimal stops. Therefore, there was little initial interest in short hauls for commuter passengers.

Nonetheless, by the mid-1840s it had become clear that in large east coast cities, there was strong passenger demand for local suburban rail travel. Railroad officials rethought their opposition to local stops and were soon building commuter stations and offering long-term commuter tickets at reduced tariffs. The result was a selective suburban migration of bankers, businessmen, and other affluent professionals who could afford the time and costs of commuting by rail. By 1850 half of Boston's 400 lawyers already were commuters. By the end of the decade, Philadelphia had some forty trains a day making the commuter shuttle between Philadelphia and its northwestern suburb of Germantown. What began serving a limited number of suburban passengers in the mid-1840s had become a suburban institution by the 1850s.

STREETCAR LINES

The introduction of the horse-drawn streetcar in the 1850s further stimulated suburban growth by providing a more frequent and convenient means of transportation. Building and operating a horse streetcar line on light rails was far less expensive than operating a railway on heavy rails. Moreover, from the commuters' viewpoint the streetcar had the added advantage of frequent schedules at a low fixed fare. Most horse streetcars charged 10 cents, while the omnibuses charged 15 cents. Moreover, the streetcars could hold thirty to forty people and transport them at a speed of 6 or 7 miles an hour. This was twice as fast as walking or taking the uncomfortable omnibus. The effects of the horse streetcar lines will be discussed in detail in the next chapter.

The rapid expansion of horse streetcar lines during the 1850s meant that now not only wealthy businessmen using the railroads could be regular commuters, but also shopkeepers and tradesmen. By the advent of the Civil War, horse streetcar lines provided regular and dependable service both within and to the extremities of all larger cities. New York alone had some 142 miles of track, which transported almost 100,000 passengers a day.

It is important, however, not to overstate the impact these transportation advances had on the degree of early suburbanization. The vast bulk of the horse streetcar lines operated within the city. The city was where most of the passengers lived and, consequently, where there was the greatest demand and profit. The 1850s saw no mass exodus from the city as would occur a century later. The great bulk of those affluent enough to commute daily were quite comfortable in their urban town houses, and they were not eager to forsake the comforts and culture of the city for the more bucolic charms of the urban periphery. Not until the Civil War and its industrial changes transformed the center of the cities from the preindustrial pattern emphasizing trade, commerce, and limited local manufacture to the industrial pattern emphasizing a workplace filled with factories and tenement slums packed with immigrants would suburbanism become a distinctive way of life.

CHAPTER 4

The Way We Were

TECHNOLOGY AND METROPOLITAN CHANGE

SUBURBAN CONSEQUENCES OF INDUSTRIALIZATION

Steam Power

The Civil War (1861–1865) provides a good dividing line between the compact commercial-based walking city of the antebellum period and the large, sprawling industrial-based cities that followed the war. During the Civil War the economy of northern cities shifted from a mercantile or trade focus to an industrial economy. Aided by new Republican party protective tariffs that kept out cheaper foreign competition, northern industrialists began producing the bulk of the nation's steel, military hardware, and woolen goods. Prior to the war, most of these goods had been imported. The huge war-stimulated demand for goods, and the war-inflated profits, were a boon to new industries. The war's closing of the Mississippi hurt water-based St. Louis and was disastrous for New Orleans, but it boomed Chicago and other railroad cities. The old pattern of north-to-south river transport was permanently altered to one of east-west transportation using the railroads. The great cities of the east and midwest built much of their physical plant following the Civil War, particularly in the era from 1880 to the Great Depression. This was also a period of growth for affluent and middle-class suburbs.

Technology, particularly the technology of the steam railroad, was overcoming the hardships and blockages of the physical environment. This was particularly true west of the Mississippi, where, as Richard

Wade aptly phrased it, "The towns were the spearheads of the frontier." In the west the railroads had reversed the pattern of settlements and towns coming first followed by the railroad. Josiah Strong, writing in 1885, stressed the role of technology:

> In the Middle States the farms were first taken, then the town sprang up to supply its wants, and at length the railway connected it with the world, but in the West the order is reversed—first the railroad, then the towns, then the farms. Settlement is, consequently, much more rapid, and the city stamps the country, instead of the country stamping the city. It is the cities and towns that will frame state constitutions, make laws, create public opinion, establish social usages, and fix standards of morals in the West (Josiah Strong, Our Country: Its Possible Future and Present Crisis, Baker and Taylor, New York, 1885, p. 206).

This was an exaggeration, but it wasn't much of one; the railroad played a crucial role in the development of the west. One could own the best wheat-growing land in Kansas, but it was of little value unless it was within a reasonable distance to a railroad line so that the crop could be moved to urban markets. Railroad mileage during the last half of the nineteenth century expanded from 9,000 to 193,000 miles. The railroads opened the west and drastically changed eastern cities. Technology was also changing the farms, where the majority of the population still worked and lived. Changes in technology such as mechanical reapers, steel plows, and threshing machines heralded the shift from self-sufficiency to commercial farming. Jefferson's yeoman farmer was being converted into a business entrepreneur raising cash crops for distant markets. The railroad played an essential role in bringing the crops to market.

Concentration

The coming of the steam-powered industrial city did not initially encourage dispersion of population and industry, but rather their concentration. Steam is most efficiently generated in large quantities and must be used close to where it is produced. Steam cannot be transported more than short distances. In this respect it differs significantly from electric power, which can be transferred efficiently from a source of origin to users residing over hundreds of miles. Steam power encouraged the proximity of factory and power supply and thus a compact city. Thus, the introduction of industrialization initially encouraged centripetal rather than centrifugal forces. Urban densities increased, and cities became more crowded.

Within the cities the new manufacturing plants and industrial factories concentrated in areas near but not in the central core. Since property at the very center of the city was too expensive for industrial usage, industry usually located in a ring surrounding the central core. This provided good access to local markets as well as to rail and often water transportation. Rail lines rarely went into the very heart of the larger cities. Rather, the terminals were on the outer edges of the downtown commercial area. This was both because the downtown land was too valuable for such a usage and because steam engines spewed out not only filthy smoke but also sparks that started fires. Thus, both land economies and municipal regulations eventually banned steam locomotives from the central core of most cities. However, for manufacturing industries, location near the center of a rail line was essential since the plants depended on the railways to bring them raw materials and the coal used to fire their steam turbines. The rail lines were also crucial for shipping goods to nonlocal markets. The result was that in city after city, the zone just outside the downtown was converted from residential to manufacturing and commercial activities. The housing that remained in the zone consisted of high-occupancy tenements for the poorly paid workers in the local factories.

The post-Civil War concentration of industries in the so-called zone of transition also led to the concentration of storage and wholesale distributing as well as manufacturing activities in the same general area. This, in turn, made the zone around the downtown even less desirable as a residential area for those owning property. However, the changes in the zone of transition meant sharp appreciation in land values and, thus, large profits for those owning land. As areas went from good residential housing to factories and tenements, fortunes were made. Speculators often would buy properties in anticipation of even further rises as land usages changed. Hopes of profits from land use change also discouraged investment in improving the existing buildings. Rather, the existing buildings were turned into slum housing.

Older residential properties near the factories were commonly divided into many small units in order to house the unskilled—often immigrant—workers who worked for minimal wages in the industrial plants. Often working twelve hours a day six days a week, the industrial workers could not afford to live anywhere but near the factories. The slow and expensive nature of public transportation also ruled out any separation of place of work and place of residence. The result was that surrounding the factories, landlords converted existing homes to multiunit, one-room flats. They also built jaw-to-jaw, cheaply constructed tenements to cover every open space. These tenements were then packed to unbelievable densities with immigrant workers—first Irish, then German, Jewish, Italian, Polish, Black, and Hispanic. These slums provided immigrant laborers with housing close to the factories in which they worked—but at a horrendous price in terms of health and decency of life. Population densities in tenement zones sometimes exceeded 100,000 persons per square mile. These remarkably high levels of crowding contrasted with the declining housing-density levels in the more middle-class neighborhoods developing on the cities' periphery.

The post-Civil War city thus saw the preindustrial pattern of downtowns having a mixed residential and business usage being supplanted by the industrial pattern of downtown land being devoted to commerce and business while the next zone was one of industry and tenements for minimally paid workers. The latter part of the nineteenth century saw the remaining central-core residences quickly give way to business offices and retail establishments. Especially found in the city core were firms that thrived on crowds and congestion such as the new large department stores. High central-city land values were an inevitable result of a free-market system and a high business demand for a central location. Centrality meant access, and access was crucial to exchanging business information and making contacts. Nineteenth-century businesses a century before the era of fax machines, and even before telephones were in widespread business use, had real difficulties quickly exchanging information. To exchange information it was necessary that offices be close to one another. This was commonly done by means of office boys who served as messengers. If your business was out of the range of the office boys, you were out of the loop.

Several inventions of the late quarter of the century, such as Otis's practical steam-powered elevator and William LeBaron Jenney's iron-girdered buildings, further increased both the value of central-city land and the number of working people that could be officed on that land. Buildings could now grow upward. The development of a practical steam, and by the late 1890s, electric, elevator meant that the height of buildings was no longer restricted to the maximum five or six floors that anyone in good health was expected to climb. The iron- or steel-girdered building, first developed in Chicago in 1889, was even more revolutionary. Since the emergence of cities, buildings had been constructed to be supported by their outer walls. In the case of office buildings, this meant massive outer walls at the base of the building, with the walls becoming progressively thinner as height increased. Since the walls were load bearing, windows had to be small. This was a major limitation in the era before widespread use of electric illumination. This method of building by using the walls for support meant that the maximum number of floors any building could have was ten or eleven. The development of steel-framed buildings changed all this. Steel-framed buildings were constructed by erecting a frame of steel girders and then basically hanging the building's walls on this frame. Since the outer walls weren't load bearing, windows could be made much larger, as in the "Chicago windows" of Louis Sullivan's Carson, Pirie, Scott & Co. department store in Chicago's Loop. Steel-framed building techniques meant that offices, businesses, and hotels could now be stacked vertically one floor upon another as high as economics and local ordinances would allow.

Horse Streetcars

All of the above provided a strong incentive for middle- and particularly upper-class outmovement. What was needed was an effective means of daily transport for the middle class. Horse streetcars, as previously noted, provided a reasonably comfortable ride at twice the speed of the omnibus. Putting a coach on light rails also opened up peripheral land along the rail line to real estate speculation. Fortunes were made by promoting for suburban development what was previously low-valued out-of-town property. Sam Warner, Jr.'s classic study

Washington and Sumner Streets in downtown Boston of 1901, with their office buildings, stores, streetcars, and early autos, indicate both the congestion and vitality of the central city at the turn of the century.

Streetcar Suburbs documents the crucial roles of the horsecar, and later the electric trolley, in extending Boston from a pedestrian city having a 2-mile radius in 1850 to a metropolitan area having a 10-mile radius in 1900 (Sam Bass Warner, *Streetcar Suburbs,* Harvard and MIT Press, Cambridge, Mass., 1962).

However, in spite of their obvious advantages, horse streetcars also had serious limitations. Most of these had to do with the horse itself. Pulling a car loaded with thirty people was a major effort, particularly in the heat of the summer or when there was an incline. Not infrequently, overworked animals were beaten by drivers and collapsed under the strain. Estimates for the number of horses dying in New York streets during the peak years of horse streetcar usage are roughly 15,000 animals dying a year. When an animal pulling a streetcar died or was injured and had to be destroyed, the carcass was not only left on the street, but the riders had to wait for a new horse to arrive and be hitched. Moreover, horses spent the majority of the day in the stable, and whether they were used or not they had to be fed. Horses also caused tremendous waste and pollution problems. Each mature horse produced approximately 26 pounds of manure and several gallons of urine each day. As a result, at the beginning of this century, New York City each day had to deal with 2.5 million pounds of horse manure and 60,000 gallons of urine. Horse streetcars, thus, contributed in a major fashion to urban sanitation and public health problems. Horse-drawn streetcars brought manure and flies.

Cable Cars

Cable cars initially seemed to provide an answer to the disadvantages of horse streetcars. Cable cars were first used in San Francisco in 1873 as a means of coping with the city's steep hills. By the 1880s, cable cars had spread east and come into wide usage nationwide. Cable cars, which ran by clamping the cable car onto a moving cable that ran in a tunnel between the streetcar tracks, were far cleaner (no horse smell, manure, or urine) than horse streetcars. Moreover, they could go faster, pull heavier weights, and even go up hills and safely down the other side. The ability to go down a hill at a fixed rate of speed was the real achievement. Poor brakes not infrequently led to wagons going down steep hills breaking loose and out of control. Without the cable cars' ability to grip onto a cable that was always moving the same constant speed, streetcars, with their minimum friction between steel wheels and steel rails, would slide down the hills like a sled, even if wheel brakes were applied. During the 1880s large cities from New York to San Francisco built cable car systems along heavily traveled routes.

Chicago alone had 86 miles of cable car track and 1,500 cable cars (Kenneth Jackson, *Crabgrass Frontier*, Oxford University Press, New York, 1985, p. 104).

The problem with cable cars was that, for all their strengths, they also had some serious liabilities. The cable cars were pulled along by a single strand of twisted wire cable winding miles out from and back to the steam generator that turned the cable. Unfortunately, the cable wore out, and a break anywhere in the miles of cable meant the entire system was down until the break was spliced. Also, there were sometimes problems of operators not being able to disengage their grips from the constantly moving cable. This meant a runaway car could only by stopped if it hit something or was closed down. If the cable car that was unable to disengage from the cable couldn't stop, those cars ahead also had to stay engaged to the cable to keep from being rammed. Thus, one runaway created a whole series of runaways. Cable car systems were also wasteful of energy since the cable kept running regardless of whether cars were engaged on it, loading passengers, or out of service.

Cable systems were also far more expensive to build than horse streetcar systems, and unlike horse streetcar systems, they couldn't be gradually expanded. With a cable system, you couldn't add an extra mile of track and a few more horses and cars. You had to make a heavy front-end investment in both the heavy steam engines to move the cable and the expensive cable. Moreover, you had to pay to dig up the streets and then install the cable in its tunnel. This cost a great deal before the system was even operational.

Today, only San Francisco retains its cable cars. They are a tremendous tourist attraction and are kept now largely for that reason.

ELECTRIC STREETCARS

It is difficult today to fully understand the tremendous importance of the electric streetcar to the development of American suburbs. The electric streetcar literally changed the physical shape of metropolitan areas. It also contributed mightily to the modern residential pattern where one's area of residence tells a great deal about one's socioeconomic status. Electric streetcars permitted the construction of economically and socially homogenous suburbs.

There had been numerous attempts to build an electric streetcar, but the first successful—that is, reliable—system was put into operation in Richmond, Virginia, in 1888. The system was designed by Frank Sprague, an inventor and electrical engineer who had earlier worked under Thomas Edison. Sprague's system was relatively straightforward. Electric current was transferred from an overhead line to the electric motor powering the wheels by means of a troller, or trolley, that was held against the overhead line by means of a spring. However, when Sprague signed the Richmond contract in 1887, much of the necessary equipment had yet to be designed, much less built and tested. Moreover, his contract specified that unless he could build a fully working system within a year that was acceptable to the Richmond officials, they would pay nothing. Sprague assumed the full cost of designing and building the entire system. To the delight of the city fathers, the system worked as specified. Sprague's design was clearly superior to any of the experimental systems that had been tested elsewhere and found unreliable. Sprague's system proved to be both safe and reliable. Within a year twenty other cities had bought Sprague's system, and he was both a famous and a rich man.

Sprague's new electric streetcars were adopted in city after city with remarkable speed. Horse-drawn car lines, which accounted for two-thirds of all streetcar lines in 1890, the remainder being mostly cable system, had virtually vanished a mere decade later. Seldom has any invention so completely replaced its predecessors in such a short period. Electric streetcars had clear advantages over the earlier cable and horse-drawn systems. Electric streetcars could average 15 miles per hour, which was at least double and sometimes triple the speed of its cable and horse-drawn competitors. Moreover, the trolleys had over three times the carrying capacity of the horse-drawn cars without any of the pollution. The electric systems also cost far less to build and operate than cable systems. By 1902 electric trolleys accounted for 97 percent of all streetcar milage, with 2 percent still operated by cable car lines and only 1 percent of horse cars (Charles Glaab and Theodore Brown, *A History of Urban America*, Macmillan, New York, 1967, p. 144).

Social Consequences: Dividing Home and Work

The electric streetcars, which provided comparatively high-speed transit for a modest 5-cent fare, changed the way urban-area dwellers lived. There no longer was any necessity for middle-class families to live within walking distance of their place of work. Industrialization was making residence near one's work less attractive, while the streetcar meant it was now possible for middle-class employees to live in suburbs as far as 10 or even 12 miles from the central business district and commute both rapidly and inexpensively. Within a short period, new middle-class residential suburbs were being constructed along the right-of-way of the streetcar lines.

The burgeoning streetcar suburbs made it possible for the middle class to live in new housing areas on the city's fringe while still being able to commute within thirty minutes to downtown offices and even shop at downtown department stores. From 1890 to 1920, the streetcar dominated metropolitan transport. The very shape of the metropolitan area changed. Previously, outer growth had occurred more or less everywhere on the periphery where growth was not constrained by geography. The electric streetcar, by contrast, restricted growth to narrow, fingerlike developments along the streetcar tracks. Real estate developers built homes paralleling the tracks, but only to a depth of a few blocks on either side. The interstitial areas remained undeveloped. The special configuration of the American city changed from that of a compact city to that of a star-shaped metropolitan area.

The streetcar lines, which opened up outlying sites for development, often also made the existing city homes of the well to do and the upper-middle class living along major city thoroughfares less desirable. Living along an electric streetcar line was extremely noisy. Streetcars made a great deal of clamour with squealing wheels and clanging bells, and their constant passage created major noise pollution for those living in homes adjacent to the trolley line. On a hot summer's night, with all the windows open, the jarring sound of screeching metal on metal made sleep difficult. Once-quiet residential streets became noisy streetcar lines. As a consequence, those who could afford to moved to quieter and more sedate surroundings—usually further out. Because a location along the streetcar line was good for business, retail stores frequently opened stores in what were previously residences. A common pattern was for a storefront extension to be built out to the sidewalk on what was originally the front yard of a home. This pattern consisting of a shop in front with the original house behind can still be seen in many older cities today.

Street Car Suburbs

Middle-class residents of turn-of-the-century streetcar suburbs also found that their new homes had practical advantages beyond that of fast transportation to the city. Sewer lines, water lines, and gas lines tended to be installed along the street right-of-way, while electric and telephone poles paralleled the tracks. This was comparatively inexpensive for the utilities (usually private companies) to do, since it did not involve ripping up already-paved streets. Suburbanites, being well-off, were also ideal customers from the business standpoint. Thus, outlying streetcar suburbs often received the services of the new utilities well before they came to working-class areas of the city. Outer areas built at

This 1882 advertisement for homes in
Englewood, then a southwest suburb of
Chicago, emphasizes the availability of Lake
(city) water and sewage, and a 5-cent railroad
fare to downtown Chicago. The assumption
was that residents of Englewood would be
suburban commuters.

the turn of the century had from their time of construction "modern"
advantages such as toilets and electricity. By contrast, some poor city
neighborhoods still had to use outhouses and light their homes with
kerosene. At the time of World War I, three-quarters of American
homes still did not have electric service.

Even more important than the physical and quality-of-life differences between the city and the suburbs were the emerging social differences. Simply put, the suburban trolley lines allowed the upper-
middle and middle class to move out. The technology of the steam
railroad had allowed the well-to-do of earlier decades to separate their

place of work from their place of residence. Now the technology of the streetcar allowed the middle class to do the same. The new suburban areas were almost exclusively middle class. The poor were excluded from the new subdivisions. Homogeneous economic and social communities replaced the more mixed pattern of the earlier walking city. Segregation of population as well as of land uses was becoming the norm.

By providing the means for the middle class to move out of the city, the trolley provided a physical inheritance of housing type and distribution that we can still see throughout North America. Newer and more affluent homes on larger lots were built in outlying areas. As one would ride the streetcar from center to suburb, there would be a clear upgrading in the size and quality of residences. Even a century later, the pattern can still be clearly seen when traveling the old streetcar routes through the cities of the east coast and middle west. Today many of what were new middle-class neighborhoods at the turn of the century are residences of the metropolis' working class and poor, but the pattern of an inverse relationship between the centrality of residence and the socioeconomic status of those occupying the property persists. While the electric streetcar lines certainly did not invent social and economic exclusivity, the trolleys did facilitate the separation of the city into homogeneous socioeconomic, ethnic, and racial enclaves.

The suburbs, in addition to being heavily middle class, also differed in ethnic composition from the central city. The turn of the century was the high tide of southern and eastern European immigration to the United States. Ellis Island received over a million immigrants a year during the first decade of the twentieth century. The industrial cities of the east and midwest were the principal destinations of these Italian, Polish, Slavic, and Jewish immigrants. As of 1900, over three-quarters of the population of cities such as New York, Boston, Cleveland, and Chicago were listed by the Bureau of the Census as being of foreign stock. That is, the census listed them as being foreign born or having parents who were foreign born. Suburbs, by contrast, were overwhelmingly WASP (White, Anglo-Saxon, Protestant). The new suburbs allowed those who feared the menace of "rum, Romanism, and rebellion" to escape to segregated neighborhoods. Those who were uncomfortable living in a city teeming with foreign immigrants now had a convenient and comfortable alternative. Additionally, the suburbs offered middle-class WASPs the opportunity to remove themselves and their families from both the taxes and immigrant-dominated political machines of the city. Suburban enclaves were essentially homogeneous in social, economic, and ethnic composition. By the time of World War I, the pattern of a segregated urban area had become the norm. The poor and ethnic working class lived in the central city, while the affluent and middle-class nonethnics increasingly commuted from outer-city and suburban areas.

Streetcars and the Suburban Growth Machine

Speculators were quick to see the financial opportunities in building commuter suburbs. Many of those who invested in streetcar lines were primarily interested in real estate profits rather than managing transit companies. Real estate speculators realized that having a streetcar line running to their properties did wonders for sales. The trolley was a subdivider's dream, since previously marginal land that had been purchased at low cost could now be subdivided and sold at tremendous profit. Thus, for example, in Boston, the West End Line was originally established from Boston to Brookline by Henry Whitney to attract customers to his land (Warner, 1962, p. 60). Nor was land speculation restricted to the largest cities. In Richmond, Virginia, where the electric streetcar had been invented, William Ginter built a streetcar line at his own expense in order to boom his north side upper-class commuter suburb of Ginter Park. The streetcar line lost money, but the development more than made up for it in sold lots.

The most extensive system created primarily to sell real estate was developed by Henry E. Huntington in the Los Angeles area. His Pacific Electric Railway Company operated an extensive system of "Big Red" interurbans (heavier built streetcars for longer runs). Interurbans radiated out from Los Angeles throughout the Los Angeles basin area. Huntington consciously operated interurban streetcar lines to new areas at a loss in order to spur sales of his real estate holdings. Decades before the automobile was a potent force, Huntington's interurbans had invented urban sprawl. Tying together spatially separate new communities of homeowners, the streetcars created the multicentered Los Angeles of today. Automobiles are often blamed for the sprawl of the Los Angeles area; but the automobile didn't create the sprawl—it simply allowed the orange groves between communities to be filled in.

None of this is to suggest that trolley lines were not economic money-makers in their own right. Electrification of existing horsecar lines and consolidation of smaller companies into traction franchises made huge fortunes for company owners. The handful of owners of New York's Metropolitan Street Railway Company made $100 million in the decade between 1893 and 1902 (Jackson, 1985, p. 109). In Chicago, Charles Yerkes, by astute business sense and a willingness to use bribery and unethical practices, had consolidated most of that city's streetcars under his control. In so doing, he also became one of the most hated men in the city. His arrogant demand that he be given the sole franchise for the city for fifty years only failed to pass a bribed Chicago City Council because of the outrage of an armed mob of city residents who stormed City Hall. (Unrepentant, Yerkes moved to England and bought the London Underground.) Only after World War I did the streetcar companies, with their fixed nickel fares, increasing operating and maintenance costs, and aging equipment, become money-loosing operations. By this time, earlier excesses of the traction companies had made fare increases virtually impossible. In city after city transit systems went bankrupt and either went out of business or were bought by the municipality.

Electric streetcar usage reached its peak in the early 1920s, but even at the period of peak usage the future of public transit was clouded. Private transit companies were being sandwiched between rising costs and fixed revenues. Particularly during World War I, there were sharp increases in the wages paid transit operators, and older, heavily used equipment needed replacement. Most transit systems, however, were tied to a 5-cent fare, and any attempt to raise fares led to massive public outcries. Given the fortunes made by earlier transit owner "robber barons," there was little public sympathy for transit companies. Nor was there any support for public subsidies or tax relief for what were seen as private companies. The use of public monies for the building and maintenance of roads for automobile usage was, on the other hand, viewed as necessary. Streetcar companies thus cut back on service and equipment, which in turn caused them to lose more riders to the faster and more flexible autos. Nor could bus lines ever win back automobile users.

In spite of the riches initially going to the owners and investors, the electric street railways were a bargain for passengers. The standard fare was 5 cents, which was half the cost of the horsecars. Moreover, the consolidated trolley lines would take one anywhere in the system, and transfers were free. At the turn of the century, the trolleys were transporting customers to the extent of 2 billion trips a year. The streetcar had become an American way of life. From this point on, American city dwellers, and more important, suburbanites, would take easy and rapid mobility for granted as a basic right.

AGE OF THE AUTOMOBILE

While the electric streetcar made middle-class suburbanization possible, the automobile was to make suburbanization the dominant residential pattern. As the twentieth century opened, the automobile was strictly a novelty—a rich man's plaything. In all of North America, there were only 8,000 horseless carriages, and most of these were both expensive and highly unreliable vehicles. What changed North America into a continent of automobiles was Henry Ford's Model T. The Model T was first introduced in 1908 and remained in production until 1927. The use of assembly line techniques and few variations (e.g., Model T's came in one color—black) meant that the price of the "flivver" kept dropping during the two decades of its production. By the mid 1920s, a new basic Model T, which, when introduced, had cost $950, could be bought for under $300, while used models sold for as little as $50. (This promoted a social revolution as well, for it meant that young people with autos could easily escape the chaperonage of adults.)

Ford's assembly lines revolutionized auto manufacture by turning out a thousand completed cars every working day. The Model T looked ungainly, but although modestly powered, it was remarkably durable and dependable. Its high ground clearance meant it could navigate even rutted country roads, and it was so simple to repair that any farm boy could fix it. Moreover, the "Tin Lizzie" was cheap enough for the average middle-class urban or farm family to own. By the time Ford finally brought out his new Model A in 1927, some 16 million Model T's had been built, and every second vehicle on the road was a Ford.

The rise in automobile registrations indicated how Ford's assembly lines were bringing a revolution that was changing the face of America. Registrations jumped from 2.5 million in 1915 to 9 million in 1920. This was in spite of automobiles being defined as nonessential for production during the 1917–1918 period, when the United States was in World War I. By 1930 auto registrations had skyrocketed to 26.5 million, and in spite of the Great Depression, another 4.5 million cars were added during the 1930s. (Today the United States has almost four cars for every five persons.)

Automobile Commuting

The widespread usage of automobiles by the 1920s meant that cars were being increasingly viewed as necessities rather than as simply recreational vehicles. The Sunday afternoon ride in the car might still take place, but for those suburbanites not located near a rail or streetcar track, the auto was a commuting necessity. The automobile made possible the development of previously inaccessible land not served by mass transit. The consequence was a suburban middle-class housing boom during the 1920s. The wide interstitial areas between the transit lines could now be profitably developed. Land speculators, home builders, and those middle-class families owning an automobile no longer were tied to narrow corridors of development. By 1941 the Bureau of Public Roads reported that over 2,100 communities ranging in size up to 50,000 population were without any form of public transportation (Jackson, 1985, p. 195). Those commuters who could afford the cost of an auto could now drive to work and live where they pleased within a reasonable commuting distance.

Automobile suburbs were built at lower densities than earlier suburbs that were tied to fixed transit lines. Both newer and more established suburbs also began using the newly developed planning tool of zoning in order to exclude not only commercial activities but also inexpensive homes on small lots. Zoning laws came into widespread usage following the pioneering New York City Zoning Resolution of 1916 and subsequent court cases that ruled that zoning was a legal use of the police power of a municipality (see the section on zoning). Suburbs, whether upper or middle class, also sought to exclude not only less expensive homes, but also residents who did not match the racial, ethnic, and even religious makeup of existing residents.

This was done in two ways. The simplest and most effective was through pressure on realtors not to show or sell homes to unwanted groups. Thus, if it were an all-Protestant suburb, Catholics or Jews would be "steered" to other areas. The second method used was that of establishing for an area exclusive "restrictive convenants." Restrictive covenants placed legal restrictions on property deeds, which prevented the resale of the property to specific groups. Almost universally, restrictive convenants prohibited sale to blacks, and the exclusion of Jews and southern and eastern ethnic groups was also common. For example, Turks were almost always excluded, although most suburbanites had never seen a Turk and wouldn't know how to identify one if they did. As of 1950 over a third of the homes in Los Angeles had restrictive convenants. By means of restrictive covenants and informal real estate practices, pre-World War II suburbs were stratified tightly according to race, ethnicity, and socioeconomic status. Only in 1948 did the Supreme Court say such restrictions were unenforceable, and not until the 1968 Fair Housing Act were restrictive convenants declared illegal.

During the 1920s middle-class, auto-based suburbs sprang up surrounding every major city. The pattern of auto-based suburbs continued, although at a far reduced pace, throughout the Depression years of the 1930s. By the eve of World War II, the auto had become the prime means of suburbanites, and even many city dwellers, commuting to work. This was true even in the older suburbs having public transit. In fact, by the beginning of the 1930s, over half of the commuters in all but the largest cities already were driving to work. Commuters in New York and Chicago still relied primarily on mass transit lines, but most of those in Washington, Cincinnati, St. Louis, Milwaukee, Kansas City, and Los Angeles drove. New York, and to a lesser extent Chicago, retained reliance on public transport in the center of the city both because they had excellent public rapid transit subway systems and because there were few places for commuters to park their autos. Even today one finds New Yorkers who don't and can't drive. However, in smaller cities, even before the mass suburbanization following World War II, the American suburbanite was committed to automobile commuting.

Commuter suburbs built before the second World War largely were bedroom suburbs. They remained dependent on the central city for employment, entertainment, major shopping, and most services. However, they were fiercely politically and legally independent. The result was that the city, which had earlier lost its ability to annex suburbs along the railroad and streetcar corridors, now was virtually surrounded by suburban entities. The city had been encircled and banded by a ring of municipalities so that annexation was virtually impossible. (See the section in Chapter 10 on annexation.) All of the consequences of this inability to expand were not perceived in the 1920s and 1930s. During the 1920s, the cities were economically strong, and during the Depression the focus was on reintrenchment. There was little concern about the problem of suburbs limiting city growth. Only during the housing boom following World War II did all of the consequences of banding the city with a ring of independent suburbs become evident.

Government and the Building of Roads

The idea that government is somehow responsible for providing good roads is not a long-standing historical American belief. Prior to the Civil War, state governments and even localities sometimes became engaged in the building of turnpikes. However, this was most often done not so much as a statement of public policy but as a means of making money. Public corporations offered stock to investors on the assumption that the roads would turn a handsome profit. In practice this hope was rarely realized. Even within the city itself the improvement of a street commonly would be done by the city, but at private expense. Property owners facing the street generally paid special tax assessments for street improvements. The assumption was that the owners would benefit from the paving both in convenience and increased property values, and thus they should be assessed for the improvement.

Only in the latter-nineteenth century did business leaders and middle-class city residents become increasingly vocal over the need for municipalities to assume the responsibility for the paving and maintenance of streets in the city. However, what finally tipped the scales in favor of paving in many communities was not the coming of the automobiles, but rather the widespread bicycle craze of the 1890s. Bicycles needed evenly paved streets, and considerable lobbying from bicycle clubs and enthusiasts provided the extra pressure for well-paved municipal roads. By the turn of the century, most large municipalities were well along in replacing gravel, cobblestone, and brick streets with asphalt. Heavily traveled streets and new roads were often constructed with concrete.

Beyond the city lines was another matter. Auto travel outside of the city was a major adventure. Roads varied from improved gravel to unimproved cowpath. No national road system existed, and prior to World War I, coast-to-coast auto trips received national newspaper coverage. Completion of such difficult coast-to-coast ordeals, which commonly took months, were used by automobile manufactures to advertise the reliability of their products. Following the first World War, the U.S. Army even sent a convoy of trucks coast to coast across the United States to highlight the need for a national road. One of the officers leading the convoy was the then-Captain Dwight Eisenhower, who viewed the publicity stunt as a chance to see the country. The 1919 trip from Washington, D.C., to San Francisco took the army convoy sixty-two days. In the 1950s, President Eisenhower would sign into law the bill creating our present interstate highway system.

In the 1920s, responding to increasing pressure from the motoring public and an effective political lobby of auto dealers, road builders, tire manufactures, and the like, the federal government gradually accepted major responsibility for maintaining roads between major cities. In 1916 the Federal Road Act had provided funds for states to organize highway departments. The 1921 Federal Road Act got the federal government directly into the highway-building business. A Bureau of Public Roads was established to plan highways to all cities of 50,000 or more, and the federal government agreed to pay half the cost of highways designated as "primary roads." This was the effective beginning of the national highway system.

Some states, particularly the more prosperous ones outside the south, also established major road-building programs of their own. The best-known and most enduring of these state plans was that of New York. The regional planner Robert Moses built a series of landscaped, limited-access parkways radiating from New York City north to Westchester County and Connecticut and east into Long Island. The first of these parkways, designed to allow New Yorkers a pleasant means to escape the city, was the Bronx River Parkway. The parkways were designed for pleasure driving rather than business, so trucks and busses were banned. To prevent anyone from later changing this purpose, Moses deliberately designed the parkways to have many overpasses too low for trucks to pass under. Although today the various parkways carry several times the traffic for which they were designed, these 1920s parkways are still the most attractive routes into or out of New York City.

The period between World Wars also witnessed the construction of many new bridges and tunnels. For example, virtually all of Chicago's current bridges linking its Loop and downtown with the north and west of the city were constructed during the 1920s. New York City dramatically improved its automobile access when the Holland Tunnel opened in 1927 and the George Washington Bridge opened four years later (Peter Mueller, *Contemporary Suburban America,* Prentice-Hall, Englewood Cliffs, N.J., 1981, p. 42). Philadelphia's Ben Franklin Bridge, opened in 1926, greatly simplified access to that city, while on the west coast a decade later the San Francisco Bay Bridge and the Golden Gate Bridge assured San Francisco's continued development. The Golden Gate Bridge is today an internationally recognized symbol for San Francisco. The importance of the Bay Bridge to the economic activity of the city was dramatically emphasized in 1990 when the bridge had to be closed for months because of earthquake damage.

Truck Transport

It is easy to forget just how dependent contemporary life is upon truck transport. Trucks in many ways did for goods what the automobile did for people. Unlike railroads, trucks were free of fixed routes and fixed schedules. Their use eliminated the necessity of being on a railway right-of-way. Trucks were far more flexible; they could make door-to-door pickups and deliveries. Motor truck deliveries were also much faster than rail for short hauls. Moreover, motor trucks had no need of elaborate terminal facilities on valuable inner-city land (J. John Palen, *The Urban World,* McGraw-Hill, New York, 1992, p. 120). Truck registrations more than tripled during the 1920s, from one to three and a half million. Although it was not recognized at the time, the breakaway from reliance on central-city rail-accessible factories had begun. As truck transport grew, a central-city plant location next to the railroad line became less of a necessity. Increasingly, the more important factor was easy access to an interstate highway.

During the nineteenth and early-twentieth century period of industrialization, factories had located in an inner-city industrial belt surrounding the central business district. This had occurred largely out of necessity since raw materials and goods could not be transported without rail access. Steam-driven industrial plants also relied on the trains to bring the coal that powered the factories. The cost of inner-city land and congestion of an inner-city location were seen as inevitable prices of doing business. However, while moving goods by horse-drawn wagon was difficult and expensive in the city, it was impossible for intercity cartage. Prior to the 1920s, there was no alternative to the railroad. The technology of the truck changed this. Trucks could easily haul five to six times the weight a wagon could, and they could do it at ten times the speed. This meant an inner-city factory or warehouse location might no longer be a necessity. The widespread use of electric motors to replace steam generators also meant that the factory no longer needed to be dependent on coal delivered by rail for its power. Electric power lines could cleanly and efficiently accomplish what previously required large coal-fed steam generators.

The 1920s and 1930s, however, did not see trucks replace rail as the major form of interurban transport. That would occur after the building of the publicly funded interstate highway system following World War II. The truck's initial advantage was in the short haul. The 1937 report of the National Resources Committee showed that motor trucks had a lower cost per mile within the first 250 miles of the city (National Resources Committee, *Technological Trends and National Policy*, Government Printing Office, Washington, D.C., 1937). Lower equipment and maintenance costs indicated that motor cartage was superior in cost and speed for the short haul. Rail transport, however, retained a major advantage in both cost and efficiency for longer-distance travel. The longer the trip, the lower the cost per mile for rail transport. Also, the motor trucks of the interwar years were not able to carry the largest or heaviest loads. Nor were the highways suitable for carrying large loads at high speeds. Finally, the railroads continued to benefit from the fact that existing industrial plants were located along rail lines and from the history of shipping goods by rail. The continuation of old patterns was not seriously challenged during the Depression of the 1930s, since few new plants were built either in the cities' industrial zones or on more peripheral locations. Only the second World War, with its demand for huge war plants that could only be located on open suburban land, would demonstrate the feasibility of locating new commercial plants in peripheral locations.

CHAPTER 5

The Exodus

TWENTIETH-CENTURY SUBURBANIZATION

PREWAR SUBURBS

"Modern" Suburbia

The period of the twentieth century prior to the second World War was one of momentous changes in the volume of suburbanization. This was the era in which the city reached its zenith and suburbs fully came into their own. Cities were booming. The year 1920 was a watershed insofar as it marked the first time the nation was more than half (51.7 percent) urban. The Roaring Twenties exemplified the urban adolescence of a country that was now explicitly being shaped by urban goals and values. As stated during the Depression of the 1930s by the Report of the Urbanization Committee to the National Resources Committee:

> The faults of our cities are not those of decadence and impending decline, but of exuberant vitality crowding its way forward under tremendous pressure—the flood rather than the drought. The city is both the great playground and the great battleground of the Nation ... An unprecedented mobility arising from the harnessing of steam, electricity, and internal-combustion engine to men and materials is responsible for this phenomenal urban development. Swifter forms of urban and interurban transportation have further led to suburban migration and caused the emergence of metropolitan districts instead of individual cities as the actual areas of urban life. (Report of the Urbanism Committee to the National Resources Committee, *Our Cities: Their Role in the National Economy,* Government Printing Office, Washington, D.C., 1937, pp. vi–viii).

Thus, in the period before the second World War, the cities appeared robust and growing in economic and social dominance, not in decline and decay. Suburbs were part of the growth of the urban area, no longer simply a footnote. With some 17 million residents in 1930, suburbs were becoming a major component of metropolitan population. Suburban population already was 45 percent as large as the central-city population.

Comfortable Suburbs

Suburbs built between the first and second World Wars (1918–1942) represented the first steps toward mass suburbanization. Elite suburbs of the nineteenth-century model—that is, large architecturally designed homes—continued to be built. However, such suburbs, as, for example, Shaker Heights, east of Cleveland, were now more oriented to streetcar lines than railroads. Moreover, the growing upper-middle-class use of automobiles for commuting now put a premium on living in a quality suburb not too distant from downtown offices. Thus, across the country, upper-status inner-ring suburbs on the "good side" of the city saw fine homes constructed during the 1920s.

These pre-World War II suburbs were built to have the best of both worlds. They could appeal to the long standing antiurbanism of many Americans. They also appealed to those seeking to remove themselves from the heavy concentration of new immigrant populations in the central cities. The suburbs could also boast that with their greenery they were closer to nature and thus better places to raise children. All this could be enjoyed while residents remained within a short commute of the city and kept all the urban advantages. This meant not only the city's cultural life and nightlife, but more importantly, the advantages of the city's gas, electric, and telephone utilities. Inner-ring suburbs might have their own government, run their own schools, and collect their own lower taxes, but they were connected to city gas mains, electric lines, water and sewer systems, and telephones. Affluent suburban residents thus obtained all the practical advantages of living in the city while escaping the costs and problems. No wonder the popular middle-class women's magazines such as *Ladies' Home Journal, Redbook,* and *Good Housekeeping* extolled the benefits of suburban living. You could have the mythical house with the roses surrounded by the white picket fence while surrendering none of the urban comforts and advantages.

Housing styles in affluent between-war suburbs reflected the privileged positions of their owners. Depending on one's preference, the homeowner could build an ideal home in a Colonial New England style while next door was an English half-timbered Tutor and next to that a center-entrance Georgian and at the corner a Spanish-Moorish-style villa. The last style reflected the importance of the expanding Southern California movie industry. Films such as *The Sheik* created a fad for all things thought to be Moorish Arab, which, when combined with the Spanish influence in Southern California, produced an ersatz Spanish-Moorish style found in places as far from the ocean and sun as Milwaukee, Wisconsin. An excellent example of the ersatz style then called Spanish is expensive Palos Verdes, Estates outside of Los Angeles. The style has come to be known as Californian style; that is, low hacienda-style stucco-sided and red-tile-roofed homes with terraces and verandas. Overall, Palos Verdes produced a very pleasant and harmonious, if not exciting, physical perspective.

Architectural styles during the 1920s and early 1930s were often mixed in occasionally bizarre and eclectic fashions. For example, for a number of years this author lived in the suburb of Shorewood, just north of Milwaukee, in a marvelous 1930 Dutch Colonial home that had a living room done in Spanish-Moorish style complete with rounded arches and rough Spanish plaster. The builders of such homes created for themselves far more than housing; they created the romantic idealization of earlier eras. "A man's home was his castle," where he could live if not as a lord, at least as a latter-day country gentleman. And all this could be had while benefiting from twentieth-century urban technology of indoor plumbing, central heating, and electricity. In the words of President Herbert Hoover, "To own one's home is a physical expression of individualism, of enterprise, of independence, and of the freedom of spirit" (Speech quoted in *American Home*, February 1932, p. 253).

It should be remembered that most of the communities in which these "expressions of individualism" were located were deliberately racially, religiously, ethnically, and economically restricted. In Palos Verdes, for example, cost restrictions mandated minimum lot sizes, setback requirements, and minimum construction costs. Residential covenants attached to the deeds excluded blacks, Asians, and even Mexican-Americans who could not demonstrate pure Spanish ancestry. An exception was made for live-in servants. (Jews weren't excluded, since they weren't yet a significantly sized population.) The irony of excluding those of Mexican heritage from a community designed to copy Mexican-style hacienda architecture apparently never occurred to the developers or residents.

Bungalow Suburbs

Housing styles reflect the social values of particular eras. The planned suburbs of the nineteenth century had been designed for the affluent railroad commuter (see section on romantic suburbs in Chapters 6 and 12). However, by the turn of the century, the elaborate Victorian social customs and housing styles had gone out of fashion. By World War I, the once popular Victorian- and Queen-Anne-style homes were being attacked as "architectural atrocities" and "hideous landmarks of forty years ago" (Clifford E. Clark, Jr., *The American Family Home, 1800–1960*, University of North Carolina Press, Chapel Hill, 1986, p. 132). The ornateness and flourishes of the late-nineteenth century were supplanted by simpler and more efficient architectural designs. The prototype of this cleaner form would be the suburban bungalow design. The informality and more relaxed nature of this design could be seen immediately upon entering the front door. The elaborate entrance halls and parlors of the Victorian era were replaced by a simple doorway opening immediately into a less-formal general-purpose living room. Bungalows were built not for the affluent, but for the comfortable middle-class family.

Early in the twentieth century, many new suburbs sprang up filled with utilitarian bungalow and other frame models. Rather than being individually designed, these homes were often mass-produced from simple sets of plans. Homes would be individualized by small variations in ornamentation or materials. Thus, first the streetcar and then the automobile opened up suburbia as a place of residence for the comfortable middle class. Such simple, moderate-priced, and informal-style homes were needed to house this growing suburban population. Most common among these simpler designs were the foursquare and the bungalow. The foursquare, as its name suggests, was a basic four-sided model sometimes known as the box, the cube, or the classic box (Alan Gowans, *The Comfortable House*, MIT Press, Cambridge, Mass., 1986, p. 84). It was an efficient model set on a raised basement with a porch across the front reached by raised steps. The foursquare had its two stories capped by a low pyramidal roof containing generally a front, and sometimes a side, dormer. Inside, the rooms were generally of equal size, with the stairwell on the side wall near the front door. The foursquare was a solid and stable, if unexciting, style.

The bungalow-style home, by contrast, looked more "suburban" and was more versatile, permitting greater variation in the arrangement of interior space. External ornamentation could give the bungalow a colonial, shingle, Tudor, or even Spanish appearance. Often, essentially identical homes on the same street were given different external styles. The bungalow house was relatively little known in 1900, but by World War I it had become common in the outer reaches of the cities and the developing middle-class suburbs. The bungalow was very much an American creation, combining practicality, economy, and comfort. Bungalows, as noted, also suggested a more informal life-style than the earlier Victorian housing. Over time the term "bungalow" became virtually a generic name for any smaller, cozy, and comfortable home.

While Victorian homes had parlors, libraries, and sitting rooms, the bungalows were more modest and utilitarian. Large entrance halls and vestibules were replaced with front doors that entered directly into the living space. In the bungalow, "a pleasant living room with a cozy fireplace, bookcases, and an cupboard or two would serve the combined functions of library, parlor, and sitting room" (Clark, 1986, pp. 144–145). The bungalow cottage, most often simply called a bungalow, characteristically had a porch, living room, dining room, and kitchen downstairs and three bedrooms and a bath upstairs. The front upstairs windows typically were in a dormer extending out from the front roof. The style had limited space but used it very effectively. There were numerous regional variations of the standard bungalow. California bungalows often had only one floor, and in Los Angeles the term "bungalow" came to be used for any low suburban house. In the midwest the "Chicago bungalows" that covered much of that city's outlying northwest side and northwest suburbs were uniformly single storied (with a room that could be finished upstairs), and all were brick faced.

Bungalow homes were well suited for starter homes insofar as they were reasonably priced, and they seemed to exude a mood of solid middle-class comfort. For many new families, they suggested upward mobility. Suburban bungalows were efficiently laid out and could easily be managed by a middle-class housewife without the servants that had been part of large Victorian houses. Bungalows, many of which are still occupied today, substituted technology for hand power. Bungalows had all the modern conveniences of central heating, water heaters, indoor plumbing, and gas ovens and stoves. Bungalows also invariably had residential electric service. This made them very up-to-date residences. Electricity, for example, was by no means universally found in homes at the time of World War I. As of 1917 only one-quarter (24.3 percent) of all homes in the United States were electrified. Even many city homes were still lit by gas or, if the family was poor, by kerosene. Following the war electric service quickly became the norm. By 1920 the proportion of homes having electric service had jumped to almost half (47.7 percent), and by 1930 it was 85 percent (Ruth Schwartz Cowan, "The Industrial Revolution in the Home: Household Technology and Social Change in the Twentieth Century," In Thomas Schlereth, ed., *Material Culture Studies in America*, American Assn. for State and Local History, Nashville, 1982, pp. 222–397).

Suburban bungalows were smaller than earlier Victorian homes,

The northwest side of Chicago still has miles and miles of virtually identical well-maintained "Chicago bungalows" built in the 1920s. The Chicago bungalows had an unfinished second floor which was reached by entering from the kitchen. Over the years many owners converted the second floors into children's bedrooms.

partially because of smaller families and no live-in servants. However, most important in reducing floor space were the rising construction costs of building "modern" homes with built-in central heating, indoor plumbing, and electric sockets for plugging in lamps and modern labor-saving devices such as electric Hoover vacuum cleaners. In the east and midwest, bungalows commonly had concrete-floored basements with washtubs having running hot and cold water. This was a major advance. Earlier houses hadn't had semifinished basements entered from the house, but dirt-floored cellars entered by external lift-up cellar doors. Also, these basements differed from those of earlier years in that they were designed not as much for storage as to be electrically lighted and centrally heated places where the new electric washing machine with ringer could be kept, where the washed clothes could be hung to dry in winter, and where the husband could have a workroom. Following World War II, it became the fad for homeowners to enclose a "family room" in the basement. Often the new television set would be kept in this family room. Among the "modern" features in some bungalows were faux fireplaces with gas-fired logs. These went out of fashion in the 1940s, and many of the gas systems were disconnected for safety reasons. Ironically, as of the 1990s gas-fired logs are again in style among affluent and aging baby boomers who want a fireplace but don't want the bother of real wood.

The post-World War housing boom is usually blamed for identical housing styles, but the suburban bungalow had perfected the art of mass-producing suburban homes far before the postwar look-alike subdivisions. Even complete homes with all building materials included could by purchased from catalogs. The most long-lived of the mail-order builders was the Aladdin Company, but Sears, Roebuck and Montgomery Ward also were major sellers of prefabricated bungalows. Between 1908 and 1937, Sears sold roughly 100,000 mail-order houses, primarily in the midwest and the east. Sears, in their catalog, offered several prefabricated homes and all the precut parts. Everything from plans to lumber to doors to fixtures was dropped off at the nearest railway station. Both Sears, Roebuck and Montgomery Ward also pushed appliances and furniture to those purchasing homes, figuring that those who were buying a new house were excellent customers for purchasing household goods. The retailer thus not only sold the home but everything that went into it. Sears did not leave the mail-order housing business until 1937, when the Depression forced them out. Sears had made the mistake of not only selling the homes, but also financing them. Sears made too many installment loans to buyers who lost their jobs and thus could not pay their mortgages.

Changing Housing Styles

By the 1930s bungalows were out of fashion as the preferred small-home style. The term "bungalow" had become a pejorative usage among some housing writers in the same way the term "Levittown" did in the 1960s and 1970s. President Woodrow Wilson, who was a cultural patrician, was one of the first to use the term in this way when he dismissed the plebeian Warren Harding as possessing only "a bungalow mind" (Gowans, 1986, p. 74). During the 1930s bungalow styles were replaced by small "Williamsburg Colonials," which owed their popularity to the publicity given to the Rockefeller's restoration of Colonial Williamsburg, Virginia. Following World War II, the small colonials were largely replaced as the most popular small-home design by Cape Cods. These, in turn, gave way to low-profile ranch homes and, in the 1960s, their successor, the split-levels.

Postwar one-story ranch houses were built more for economy and utility than style. Since economy of construction was a major factor and space was at a premium, rooms often had multiple functions, such as a living room with a dining room or a combined kitchen and dining area. If the house had a study, it almost certainly doubled as a guest bedroom. Ranch-style homes, with their open floor plans and "family rooms," were even more informal than the bungalows. The simple one-story design with low-pitched eaves and the picture window suggested a casual and comfortable life style. To make the house seem larger, a sliding glass door commonly opened onto a patio so that the outside seemed an extension of the house. Millions of such ranch-style homes and their variations were built in the postwar years, as even a cursory viewing of suburban housing demonstrates.

Currently, ranch styles are less popular on the east coast, where colonial styles are back in favor. However, modified ranch California styles remain popular on the west coast. Regardless of the preferred housing style, across the country a relaxed family-oriented life style with an emphasis on outdoor activities has become the norm. Today in contemporary homes the emphasis on multiple-use space has resulted in the family room and living room often being replaced by a "great room," while the dining room has gone the way of the parlor. In recent years master bedrooms and bathrooms have grown far larger, while sun rooms, Florida rooms, and decks have become more common. However, in terms of sheer size, the largest room is invariably the garage.

Thus, by the onset of World War II, the patterns for mass suburbanization had been set. Suburbs had already lost their exclusivity as being communities containing homes of only the well-to-do. Suburbs also housed those who were comfortably middle-class. However, in the prewar era, when most Americans were still renters rather than homeowners, and when a typical mortgage was for only half the value of the house and could only be obtained for a period of five years, living in the suburbs was still beyond the hope of the "average" American. Not until the coming of the liberal mortgage terms of postwar Veterans' Administration loans would mass suburbanization of average Americans become a practical reality.

POSTWAR MASS SUBURBANIZATION

The Flood, 1945–1970

The World War II ex-GIs and their brides who moved to the new suburban subdevelopments after the war represented the beginnings of the mass suburbanization of North America. This postwar era was a period of economic boom and intense optimism. After all, the Depression was over, and America's productivity had won the war. That productivity meant that by the mid-1950s America, with only 6 percent of the world's population, was producing half the world's goods. The postwar prosperity showed in the 1950 census, which indicated that the United States now had become a nation of homeowners, with 55 percent of American householders now owning rather than renting. At the end of World War II, the average American family was renting. New housing starts in 1949 went over a million a year—a pace that would be maintained for forty years.

The veterans moving to the new suburbs were not only great in number, they also differed from earlier suburbanites insofar as they represented a wide swath of American society. Not all of the veterans obtaining VA loans were middle-class, and many were not WASPs. Suburbia was not only being enlarged, it was also ethically, economically, and religiously being democratized. The newcomers were Catholics and Jews as well as mainline Protestants; they were Irish, Italian, and Polish as well as English or northwest European; they were white-collar and factory workers as well as professionals and managers. While advertisements still stressed that moving out was moving up, the fact was that suburbs were coming to mirror mainstream America. One boundary, however, remained—that of race. Racially, postwar suburbs kept their pale complexion. Virtually all the newcomers were white. Blacks were not welcome.

There is no question that new metropolitan-area housing, and lots of it, was needed by the late 1940s. During the Depression new building starts for the nation had dropped to as low as 92,000 in 1933. During the war millions of people had been encouraged to migrate into the cities to take jobs in the expanding war industries. However, except for a limited amount of "temporary" housing, little new housing was built for the war workers. This was due in good part to the lobbying of banking and real estate interests such as the National Association of Homebuilders, who strenuously fought the government building defense housing (Arnold R. Silverman, "Defense and Deconcentration: Defense Industrialization during World War II and the Development of Contemporary American Suburbs," Barbara M. Kelly, ed., *Suburbia Re-examined*, Greenwood Press, New York, 1989, pp. 158–172). Real estate builders and sellers felt such housing would be a glut on the market after the war ended. As a result, by 1946 there were hardly any homes for sale or, for that matter, apartments for rent. Some 6 million families, unable to get their own housing, were doubling up with relatives. Something had to happen.

What occurred was a government-subsidized mass exodus to new tract suburbs of standardized single-family homes. With city landlords raising rents and landlords not wanting to rent to couples with young children, it is not surprising that middle-class and even blue-collar families flooded out from the cities to the greener opportunities of the suburbs. During the 1950s and 1960s, the suburban population of the United States dramatically increased from 35 million to 84 million suburbanites (U.S. Bureau of the Census, "Patterns of Metropolitan Area and County Growth," *Current Population Reports*, P-25, No. 1039, 1987, p. 137). This was a growth rate of 144 percent. By 1970, 37 percent of Americans lived in the suburbs. The 1990 census figure increased to 48 percent. Currently, half the United States population lives in suburbs. As we will see, many of the new postwar suburbanites settled in the subdivision tract suburbs being erected on the periphery of urban areas. They moved there because that is where new housing was available. Only in the suburbs could the goal of every family having its own home (and mortgage) be realized.

Reasons for Postwar Suburbanization

In examining America's postwar transformation of rural farm tracts into instant suburbs we must keep in mind several factors.

First, without doubt, by far the most important factor in making possible the postwar suburban exodus was the liberalization of loan-lending policies by federal government agencies. As noted earlier, prior to the war, mortgages would commonly only be given for a five-year period with a balloon payment at the end. A borrower would have to hope he could get a new mortgage when the note became due. Moreover, the mortgage would cover only half to at most two-thirds the value of the property.

The new Veterans Administration loans radically changed all this. The new Veteran Administration (VA) loan guarantees made loans available to veterans at low interest rates, below conventional mortgages, with no money down and with a twenty-five- or thirty-year repayment schedule. The Federal Housing Authority (FHA) similarly liberalized its lending policies for nonveterans. The government, in effect, guaranteed the lending institutions profits by agreeing to make good any loans on which the borrower defaulted. This was a truly radical change. Banks suddenly wanted to make loans to millions of middle- and lower-middle-class families who they previously would have spurned. Families with a steady breadwinner could, for the first time, realistically expect to get mortgages to purchase their own homes. Moreover, it was easy to do. The whole process was streamlined by developers such as the Levitt brothers so that all the paperwork could be completed in a few hours. In an era when closing costs

Following World War II, developers rushed to build acres of new suburban subdivisions. The homes were small and inexpensive, especially designed to be marketed to ex-GIs and their new brides. These were financed by the new Veterans loans which offered no money down and long mortgages. The small suburban house in the ad could be bought for a total principal and interest payment of $636 a year, with a 4 percent mortgage for twenty-five years. Given such terms, veterans could hardly afford not to move to the suburbs.

run thousands of dollars, it is worth noting that the *total* closing cost as of 1954 at the second Levittown outside Philadelphia, in New Jersey, was $10.

Government lending policies—whether by design or accident— actively fostered purchasing suburban over city homes. Following World War II, VA and FHA government-guaranteed loans were readily available for new homes in the suburbs. Young veterans could and did purchase new—sometimes still-to-be-built—VA and FHA approved suburban subdivision homes with nothing down and mortgage rates below the conventional amount. The above-mentioned Levittown in New Jersey sold homes in the mid-1950s for $8,990. Veterans were required only to place a $100 good-faith deposit, which was returned at the time of closing. Nonveterans needed only $450 down. To purchase existing city homes required far larger down payment. The low housing prices, and particularly the availability of a long-term, no-money-down mortgage, was a crucial factor for new families just becoming economically established. By 1972 the FHA alone had made some 11 million new-home loans.

Also important was the fact that purchasing in the city took time. Existing older homes in the city would have to be inspected to see if they met FHA standards, and this took weeks or months. By contrast, once a developer's plans were approved, all the standardized models of that home he built automatically qualified. A family could drive out to a new subdivision, pick a lot, put down a $100 deposit, and do the majority of the paperwork in a Sunday afternoon. Conventional mortgages were also easier to obtain in suburban locations. Two wars later, this was still the case. The author, a Vietnam-era veteran with three young children and barely enough for a down payment, found mortgage funds readily available on suburban homes. For homes across the line in the city the funds were harder to obtain, and came with higher interest rates.

Second, the Federal government further subsidized out-movement from the cities by initiating, in the 1950s, the construction of a federally financed metropolitan freeway system. Secretary of Commerce Weeks described the building of the national freeway system as, "the greatest public works program in the history of the world" (Mark Reutter, "The Lost Promise of the American Railroad," *Wilson Quarterly*, Winter 1994, p. 28). Without the newly built freeways, many of the new suburban subdivisions would have been all but impossible to reach. Automobile commuting would have been out of the question. The freeways meant distance from the city was now measured in time rather than mileage. Developers often put up billboards advertising their tract development as being, "Only 25 minutes from here." Ironically, the very freeways that speed commuters from the city were originally pushed to be built by downtown business interests and city mayors. They mistakenly expected that the new roads would bring more shoppers and business downtown. They forgot that the roads could be used to go out rather than in.

Third, Following World War II, open land for buildings was almost by definition suburban land (J. John Palen, *The Urban World*, 4th ed., McGraw-Hill, New York, 1992, p. 189). By the 1950s cities had largely developed all the land within their legal boundaries. This was particularly true of the cities in the eastern and midwestern sections of the country. Without annexation, additional growth in urban areas would thus, by definition, have to be suburban growth. By the end of the war, there was an extreme need for new housing. As noted earlier, for over a decade and a half little had been built. The 1930s were the years of the Great Depression, and during the first half of the 1940s, there was World War II. Thus, by the 1950s there was a tremendous pent-up demand for housing, and this demand could only be met in the suburbs. It wasn't so much that families were fleeing the city;

rather, it was that most of the land available for development was, by definition, suburban.

Fourth, for the decades following World War II, young families bought homes in the suburbs not so much for "togetherness" or to escape the supposed ills of the city, but because houses in suburban subdevelopment were both more available and less expensive than houses in the city. In attempts to analyze the postwar move to the suburbs, this basic economic motivation is often given less weight than it deserves. Economics, more than social-psychological needs for togetherness, propelled young couples to the suburbs. In many cases it was cheaper to buy in the suburbs than to rent in the city. A family with a mortgage on a tract house in the suburbs found that the monthly principal and financing costs usually were lower than on available housing in the city. Moreover, taxes were almost always lower than in the central city. This was in part because developers rarely put in the "extras," such as city water, sewers, parks, sidewalks, curbs, street lighting, and, of course, schools that were taken as givens in the city. In time the demand for services and the assessments to pay for them increased in new suburbs. However, the initial front-end costs were low and in a rough fashion met the needs of those at the beginning of their work careers who expected their incomes to increase with time. The 1950s and 1960s constituted a period in which unionization had brought even blue-collar workers high wages and benefits.

Fifth, survey data consistently show that Americans have a strong preference for single-family homes on their own lots. This is the type of housing that was most commonly built in the suburbs in the decades following the war. The homes in the original Levittown in Long Island were simple Cape Cod boxes built on a slab, but people stood in line for days waiting to get one. Planners and architects decried these subdivisions of little boxes, "all made out of ticky-tack and all in a row," but they were a huge hit with the buying public. Lewis Mumford and other critics might rail about the problems of poor design and one-social-class communities, but people literally lined up to buy houses in the newly opened Levittown and other suburban developments.

Actually, there wasn't a choice even if buyers wanted one. Apartments weren't covered by GI loans, and town houses weren't being built. Still, even if people are given a choice between high-rise units, town houses, or single-family homes, suburban sprawl will win every time. This is true even for those without children. Research indicates that most families living in apartment buildings view their residency as a temporary location before moving to a single-family house (William Michelson, *Environmental Choice, Human Behavior, and Residential Satisfaction*, Oxford University Press, 1977, p. 191). If a suburban home is too expensive, a suburban town house, or even a garden apartment, may be temporarily substituted. Even those academics holding neo-Marxian views, which see suburban sprawl as a product of conscious decisions made by powerful economic interests, still acknowledge that people want single-family homes on separate lots (Joe Feagan and Robert Parker, *Building American Cities,* Prentice-Hall, Englewood Cliffs, N.J., 1990, p. 215). Suburban critics may feel that such housing is a blight on the landscape, but there is no question suburban sprawl is what the mass of the population wanted after the war and still wants at the close of the century.

Finally, postwar suburbia was "caused" by demographic changes. The return of both the veterans and of economic prosperity created a marriage boom that was followed in short order by the famous "baby boom." The latter lasted from 1947 to 1964. Existing housing in cities and towns was simply not adequate for absorbing the exploding number of new families. Some 10 million new households were created in the decade after the war. In the tight postwar market, they were not welcome as renters. The result was that young couples with children were more or less forced from the overcrowded cities toward the newly built standard-format suburbs. They needed space to grow families—a need that suburban developers were delighted to fill.

Popular Misconceptions Regarding Postwar Suburbanization

Missing from the above list are most of the popular-wisdom reasons cited today for suburban moves. For example, nowhere in the list is there any mention of the filth and crime of the city. Nor is there any mention of sharply rising urban taxes. Most noticeably by its absence is any mention of race, and the "white flight" that is commonly believed to be a major cause of suburbanization. For example, Kenneth Jackson, in *Crabgrass Frontier,* lists the two causes of American residential deconcentration as "racial prejudice and cheap housing" (Kenneth T. Jackson, *Crabgrass Frontier,* Oxford University Press, New York, 1985, p. 287). However, while race, taxes, crime, or all of these factors doubtlessly were important for individual families, researchers have known for decades that such "commonsense" explanations tend to be overrated as major contributors to postwar suburbanization. In reality, they had little impact on the massive suburbanization that occurred before the late 1960s, when these explanations first became fashionable. This is not to say that race, crime, poor schools, urban decay, and high taxes are not factors in white flight from the city today. However, it is a mistake to project today's situation back into the past.

The fact is that during the 1940s, 1950s, and much of the 1960s, cities were doing reasonably well in terms of crime and taxes. Today it is hard to imagine a New York City in which, including family and criminal violence, there were under fifty murders a year, but that was the case during the 1940s. In 1942, for example, there were only forty-four murders in all of New York City. Moreover, white flight to the suburbs was largely irrelevant, because virtually all housing in the United States, city and suburban, was *de facto* segregated. Urban whites, particularly those living in the large industrial cities of the north and midwest, already lived in segregated, all-white neighborhoods. Until the federal open-housing legislation of 1968, city housing was segregated by law in the south and by custom in the north. This meant blacks and whites were in separate housing pools. In northern as well as southern cities, African Americans could only find housing in segregated black neighborhoods. New housing units were added to the minority housing pool through expanding the racial ghetto by blockbusting. During the 1940s, 1950s, and 1960s, publicly sanctioned racial segregation kept blacks confined within specific ghetto neighborhoods. Established patterns of housing segregation meant that for the vast majority of middle-class whites, "white flight" would have been meaningless. Only during the last thirty years does white flight emerge as a major variable. Following World War II other factors were more important.

The mass suburbanization exodus of young couples during the decades immediately following World War II was not caused by flight from the city so much as by the baby boom and by government subsidies for new suburban housing. The available lower-cost new housing was largely in the suburbs. Research shows that suburbanization in the decades immediately following World War II represented a movement *toward* the values associated with suburban living, such as privacy, space, cleanliness, and other suburban amenities, rather than a fleeing *from* perceived urban ills (Amos H. Hawley and Basil Zimmer, *The Metropolitan Community: Its People and Government*, Sage Publications, Beverly Hills, 1970, pp. 31–33). The suburbs were where young families could find new, inexpensive, single-family housing subsidized by government loans. Not surprisingly, young white families suburbanized in massive numbers.

Levittown

The prototypical example of the tract suburb was Levittown. The Levitt brothers, Bill and Alfred, had a construction company that had built upper-middle-class housing on Long Island during the late 1930s.

Early in World War II, they had obtained a government contract to build 2,350 mass-produced homes for war workers in Norfolk, Virginia. In the process they had learned just how many things could go wrong, but they also learned how to cut constructions costs by standardizing the building process. Bill later served with the Seabees in the Pacific Theatre, where he learned how to invent new ways to put up airfields in minimal time. He came back with ideas about how to revolutionize the housing industry. Instead of building one house at a time, he proposed to mass-produce housing. He did to housing construction what Henry Ford had done for automobile manufacture. In 1946 the Levitts began building what was at that time the largest private-housing development in North America on 4,000 acres of potato farms they had purchased some twenty miles from New York City on Long Island. They named it Levittown.

The community made history in a number of ways. First, Levittown was not designed as an upper-middle-class housing development; rather, it was built expressly for young working and middle-class ex-GIs. This originally meant a single housing style having a 12-by-16 foot living room, a kitchen, two bedrooms, and a bath.

Second, the Levitts were the first developers to use mass-production techniques. They did not have an actual assembly line, but they came closer to this approach than any other large builder of the time. Setting Levittowns apart from other developments was that they were built on a scale not previously attempted. Most builders then (and now) would build only a handful of houses at a time and use the monies from the sale of one home to purchase materials to build another. The Levitts built hundreds of homes at a time and, in effect, had their own finance company. Whole areas went up at once. Teams working on specific tasks went from house to house completing each task in assembly line fashion. Construction was broken down into a number of simple steps so it could be done by semiskilled workers who would repeat the same process over and over. Homes were built on identical concrete slabs laid out on identical cookie-cutter 60-foot lots. All the cement foundations in a neighborhood would be laid at the same time; all the walls went up at the same time; and all the interiors would be finished simultaneously. Even tree planting was routinized. One crew would machine-dig a similar hole in each front lot; another crew would drop a tree off a truckbed near the hole; and a third crew would plant the tree in the hole. Levitt claimed they were able to complete a house ever fifteen minutes. To keep down costs and prevent being stopped by strikes, the Levitts even had their own subsidiary timber company in Oregon. They even owned their own lumber yards and nail works.

Levittown revolutionized the housing industry after World War II by using mass production techniques in the construction of thousands of houses on what had been potato fields. The Levitt brothers claimed their techniques enabled them to complete a house every fifteen minutes.

Finally, and very importantly, the Levitts did all this at a price well below that of comparable homes while making a profit well above that of competitors. They were able to do so because of standardization. Variety, as with the early Fords, was severely limited. In fact, originally, all houses were identical 800-square-foot four-room Cape Cods with an unfinished upper floor that could be finished and expanded into two bedrooms as the family grew. The price for all this was only $7,990, and a Bendix automatic washer was included. A more expensive rancher model was later added. A rancher at the new Levittown outside Philadelphia cost the new suburbanites $8,990 in 1954. For this home, a veteran would have to put down no down payment, and the monthly payment on a thirty-year VA loan would be only $59 a month. This was well below contemporary urban rental costs, much less other suburban subdevelopments. Total closing costs were only $10. Levittown was designed to be mass suburbia. The original Levittown was planned as an entire community housing over 80,000 people in almost 17,500 single-family homes.

Levittown from the first was praised by the popular press and magazines and severely criticized by architects and planners. New York's intellectual elite scorned its repetitive commonness, and the term "Levittown" entered the language as a derisive term meaning a mass-produced suburb of look-alike homes housing look-alike people.

Levittown, however, was an immediate and overwhelming success with the public. Levitt particularly designed his communities for the young veterans and growing families. Before its opening, young couples lined up for days to get one of the homes. On one single spring day in 1949, some 1,400 families signed purchase contracts for their own Levittown homes. Mass suburbanization based on subdivisions of detached single-family homes was underway, and suburbia would never be the same.

We now take the postwar era of building subdivisions for granted, but it was not inevitable that American mass suburbanization would take the form it did. In Great Britain the government sponsored new towns filled with row houses, while in Sweden the emphasis was on suburban high-rise housing. By contrast, in the United States, postwar federal government home loan policies and the response of builders like the Levitts virtually assured acre upon acre of identical free-standing homes. Without these government policies, suburbia today might look far different.

Conclusion and Future

Rapid and sustained economic growth following World War II led to rising affluence and optimism regarding the future. For the first time large numbers of Americans had enough money to purchase homes and could also obtain automobiles and household durables such as washing machines. Not until 1950 did half of all husband-wife families become homeowners. This era of consumer confidence lasted from the mid-1940s through the 1960s (Richard T. Curtin, "Consumers' Powerful Role," *Institute for Social Research Newsletter,* Vol. 17, No. 3, 1992, p. 7). The decade of the 1970s was one of uncertainty and discontent, but the ethos of prosperity still prevailed. People expected the boom and bust of the 1970s to be an aberration, with prosperity and continual economic expansion to continue. By the 1980s expectations had shrunk to where most consumers simply sought to stay where they were and not fall further behind. The 1990s continue the pattern of uncertainty. Postwar suburbanization was fed by economic growth, and median family income adjusted for inflation today is not appreciably higher than that of two decades ago.

The real difference is that maintaining that family income today requires two breadwinners. Even if interest rates are low, the cost of home ownership is going up. In the mid-1950s the average thirty-year-old worker could carry a mortgage on a then median-priced home for 14 percent of his gross earnings (Frank Levy, *Dollars and Dreams: The Changing American Distribution,* Russell Sage, New York, 1987). Three decades later, it took a full 44 percent of the average thirty-year-old worker's gross earning to purchase the median-priced home. This means that purchase of the average home now requires two incomes to accomplish what a single income could afford in the 1950s. It is now harder to buy that starter home in a nice suburb. In 1980, 62 percent of all married couples aged thirty to thirty-five had bought their first home. By 1990, the percent of such couples in their first home had gone down to 52 percent (U.S. Bureau of the Census, "Housing in America 1987/86," *Current Housing Reports*, series H-121, No. 19, 1989; and *New York Times*, "Real Estate Report—Residential Properties," September 10, 1989, pp. 4–5). For younger couples, aged twenty-five to twenty-nine, the decline in homeowning was from 43 to 36 percent. For many young couples the buying of the first home is far more difficult than it had been for their parents.

It is possible, though, that housing costs might decline somewhat during the decade of the 1990s. Declines early in the decade were recession-related, but later in the decade another factor comes increasingly into play. That is the much heralded aging of the baby boom generation. As boomers age, they are followed by the "baby bust" cohorts. The smaller size of this latter group should result in some weakening demand for housing, and thus some slackening of prices, particularly for first homes. This should be good news for young couples seeking their first home. It will be much less popular with those boomers who bought at peak prices in the late 1980s, particularly those who purchased their homes as investments rather than as places to live. During the 1980s housing prices rose considerably faster than incomes or inflation. This is less likely to be the pattern of the 1990s. Houses are likely to be purchased more as homes in which to live rather than largely as investment properties.

CHAPTER 6

Myths, Ideology, and Imagery

IDEALIZED SUBURBIA

The American suburb is more than a geographical location. Suburbs also are more than various collections of certain types of residences. Nor are suburbs simply the abodes of certain types of people. American suburbs are all the above and far more—for suburbia is not just a place, it is an idea. This suburban ideal is called, in one urban scholar's felicitous term, a "bourgeois utopia" (Robert Fishman, *Bourgeois Utopias: The Rise and Fall of Suburbs*, Basic Books, New York, 1987). The suburbs that best met this idealized goal were the nineteenth-century suburbs of privilege. These well-to-do suburbs represented not only a place, but also a romanticized and idealized image of nature and of the role of the family in such an idyllic setting. The suburb was the humane alternative to the dehumanizing aspects of the city. To popular writers of the time, the suburb represents an escape from the filth, noise, and debauchery of the nineteenth-century industrial city. Suburban life was portrayed in a highly idealized light that stressed numerous advantages, and all but ignored inconveniences and liabilities. Suburbs were to allow families to achieve the benefits of the Jeffersonian rural ideal without having to forgo the comforts and convenience of the city. The suburb was said to be the perfect merger of the energy of the city and the charm and openness of the country. Here proud parents could raise healthy children in the safety and openness of the country.

Early country small towns copied the compact pattern of the city. This meant crowding existing structures together and building right up to property and street lines. Such small towns saw themselves as nascent cities, and as such they copied city patterns. The goal of the designed romantic suburb we will presently discuss was quite different. Rather than ape the city, the suburb consciously sought to return its residents to nature. Winding roads and large lots with trees, foliage, and ample lawns all were designed to suggest the virtues of a comfortable home nestled in benign nature. The goal of the idealized romantic suburbs was an improved-upon naturalism. For housewives, living in such planned naturalism—the fresh air, wide vistas, and comfortable cottages—was to allow them to develop their spiritual, sentimental, and intellectual capacities. For the male, the home was to be a refuge from the crowded, dirty, noisy, and dense city. The romantic suburb was designed to counteract the unnatural aspects of urban confusion with the balm of peaceful nature.

Romantic Ideals

The American romantic suburb had both American and English roots. It can be seen as an artifact of both Jeffersonian ideals and nineteenth-century British romantic era sensibilities in arts and philosophy. The Englishman J. Hector St. John de Crevecoeur, writing in 1782, stated that the new American man lived in a village, "where far removed from the accursed neighborhood of Europeans, its inhabitants live with more ease, decency, and peace than you can imagine; where, though governed by no laws, yet find in uncontaminated simple manners all that laws can afford" (J. H. de Crevecoeur, *Letters from an American Farmer*, J. M. Dent, London, 1912, p. 211). The image of the self-sufficient American was pure Jeffersonian, and it was one of the more enduring symbols of the romantic era. To nineteenth-century writers such as Emerson and Hawthorne, the rural landscape was far preferable to that of the squalid city. Creations of nature were preferable to the artificial creations of men. In the view of Emerson, urbanization was a potential danger to the nation in that it was fostering false and artificial tastes. This superficiality was undermining the rural simplicity that was the bedrock of the national greatness. As expressed by Emerson, "We pave the earth for miles with stones and forbid the grass. We build street on street all round the horizon and shut out the sky and wind." If such calamities were to continue, not only the artistic sensibilities would suffer; there also would be a sharp undermining of the people's natural rural virtue.

Onto these essentially Jeffersonian beliefs, writers of the nineteenth century then grafted the artistic works of the poets, painters, and writers of the romantic era. Examining the poetry of Wordsworth and

Tennyson, or even that of Byron or Shelley, is to see a world of picturesque villages and cottages in a bucolic landscape. In American art of the time, the paintings of the Hudson Valley School similarly present a view of nature that is highly idealized and almost mystical. Nature is pure, it is virtuous, and it is basically benign. There is no suggestion that nature can be capricious, evil, violent, or dangerous. It is the nature of Rousseau rather than that of Hobbes.

The romantic garden suburb was a pragmatic American response, insofar as it was an attempt to practically prepackage the rural virtues of the affluent suburbanite. The romantic suburb was to provide the jaded urbanite a healthful, restorative return to nature. Thus, moving one's family from the crowded, sinful city to the pure and open country was not just a practical decision; it was a moral choice. Moving one's family to a suburban villa, or a large country "cottage," signified one's moral rectitude (Kenneth Jackson, *Crabgrass Frontier*, Oxford University Press, New York, 1985, p. 50). It was a sign that the homeowner was not only well-off, but stable and dependable. In simplest terms, he was a family man. He was putting down solid roots. He cared for his family. He might have to spend his days in the hellish city, but his wife and children would be spared. They would abide among flowers and greenery in rural-like domesticity. The line between the home itself and the idealization of the family was blurred. Having the right home became a moral as well as a practical choice.

Early Suburban Ideology

Even before the Civil War, the image of the large welcoming house with a front porch, a garden, and a spacious tree-shaded lawn was on its way to becoming an American icon. It is generally accepted that architectural and social-morality writers were particularly influential in spreading the gospel of the morality of the suburban villa set in a gracious tree-lined lawn. The most influential of the latter was Catherine Beecher, the sister of Harriet Beecher Stowe who wrote the immensely popular antislavery potboiler *Uncle Tom's Cabin*. Catherine Beecher was the combination Miss Manners, Dr. Spock, and Ann Landers of her day. Her *Treatise on Domestic Economy*, first published in 1841, became the authority on everything domestic. The book is still a marvel, including everything from how to exercise, to proper manners, to the proper way to eat healthfully, to methods of best caring for infants, to how to raise plants, to skills needed to decorate a parlor, to how to design a more efficient kitchen (Catherine Beecher, *Treatise on Domestic Economy*, Marsh, Capen, Lyon, and Webb, Boston, 1841). Over a quarter of a century later, in 1869, Catherine and her sister Harriet Beecher

Stowe wrote a new version of *Treatise on Domestic Economy* titled *The American Woman's Home,* which expanded on the idea that not only the home, but also the surrounding community, should provide a tranquil escape from the city (Catherine Beecher and Harriet Beecher Stowe, *The American Woman's Home,* reprinted Stowe-Day Foundation, Hartford, Conn. [1869], 1975). The sisters' canon of domesticity stressed that the home, run by the mother, was to serve as a shelter and a refuge from the turmoil outside. The home, under the nurturing guidance of the housewife, became a religious place—a sacred home promoting loyalty and family support (Kirk Jeffery, "The Family, a Utopian Retreat from the City: The Nineteenth Century Contribution," *Soundings,* Vol. 55, 1972, pp. 21–41). Also, as the sisters became increasingly doubtful as to whether the city could be reformed and redeemed, the location of the home gradually became as crucial as the home itself.

It is one of those interesting side notes of history that Catherine Beecher, the expert on everything domestic and the advocate of suburban homes, never married or had a home of her own in the suburbs or anywhere else. Nonetheless, for several decades her works publicized the moral as well as practical advantages of living in a suburban country environment outside the city. In her view, women were morally superior to men, and the proper feminine sphere was providing husband and children an elevated home environment. While she never directly advocated leaving the city, it was clear that suburbia, in her view, best provided an environment as free as possible from the corruption of the male-dominated city life. She also stressed the practical and healthful aspects of living a quiet, countrylike life. While relatively few families could afford the ideal suburban villas she championed, Catherine Beecher was very influential with women in setting the image of the suburban home as the physical and moral ideal. (See Chapter Nine, Women and Families in the Suburbs—Beyond Myths, for further elaboration of this point.)

The second writer of great influence was the landscape architect Andrew Jackson Downing. Downing had considerable popularity. He even designed the largely undeveloped Mall in Washington, D.C., into a parklike area having winding carriage drives and a naturalistic setting of trees. (Only at the turn of the century, under the general guidance of the architect Daniel Burnham, did the Mall adopt the classical architecture and proportions with which we now are all so familiar.) However, Downing and his disciples, such as Calvert Vaux, were primarily concerned with domestic architecture and were great popularizers of the picturesque suburban villa or cottage. Downing's popular book *Cottage Residences* provided models of Italianate, Gothic, rustic, and Victorian-style comfortable middle-class housing, as did his later

The Architecture of Country Houses and *Victorian Cottage Residences* (Andrew Jackson Downing, *Victorian Cottage Residences,* Dover Publications Reprint, New York, [1873], 1981). Downing saw domestic cottage architecture as providing a sense of balance and tranquility to counter the unsettling negative energy of the city.

Downing's work was immensely popular, and his *The Architecture of Country Houses* went through nine printings in the fifteen years following its publication in 1850 (Andrew Jackson Downing, *The Architecture of Country Houses,* G. T. Putnam, New York, 1850). As Robert Fishman documents, in design, ideology, and concept he "borrowed" heavily from English precedents (Robert Fishman, "American Suburbs/English Suburbs: A Transatlantic Comparison," *Journal of Urban History,* Vol. 13, No. 3, 1987, p. 242). However, although Downing borrowed heavily from the ideas of the English landscape architect John Claudius Loudon, he had innovative designs and used new building techniques (Clifford E. Clark, Jr., *The American Family Home, 1800–1960,* University of North Carolina Press, Chapel Hill, 1986, p. 16). For example, Downing used the new balloon frame made out of two-by-fours spaced 18 inches apart rather than the older, and more expensive, post-and-beam method of construction. Balloon-frame homes did not require skilled craftsmen and could rapidly be constructed by two or three men having basic carpentering skills.

Housing reformers such as Downing preferred to refer to the more elaborate homes as "villas," which suggests a Roman estate for one of the patrician class rather than the more humble designation of "cottage." The home, in Downing's view, was to be republican, but not egalitarian. Suburbia was to be a place for those of taste, not for the urban masses. Similarly to Catherine Beecher, Downing and Vaux stressed the moral value of the suburban home as a refuge from the hectic businesses and moral vices of the city. Suburban homes in their design, size, and furnishings were to express the moral superiority of their inhabitants. Domestic architecture was not only to reflect taste and beauty, but also the spiritual ideals and moral development of the inhabitants. As noted by Clark, the architectural reformers of the mid-nineteenth century believed, for example, that Gothic-revival style, with its emphasis on verticality, not only harmonized well with nature but also symbolized an eminently Christian type of dwelling (Clark, 1986, p. 19). Dwellings were not simply functional, they also possessed a moral element.

Thus, whether the American suburb was a unique American phenomenon, as Kenneth Jackson suggests, or a virtual clone of earlier English models, as Robert Fishman argues, American suburbs soon developed into something quite American. Compared to early English estates, the American suburban vision of the ideal home was considerably reduced in scale. The American suburban home also carried in its designer's eyes an explicit tie to the agrarian Jeffersonian republican ideal. In Downing's words, the home had to be, "built and loved upon the new world, and not old world, ideas and principles; a home in which humanity and republicanism are stronger than family pride and aristocratic feeling" (Downing, *Country Houses*, p. 270). The American suburban home was more than a place, it was an ideology. The homeowner would not only be a better citizen, he would be a better person because of the more "natural" character of suburban life.

INTELLECTUALS AND SUBURBIA

Early-Twentieth-Century Views

H. G. Wells, writing in 1901, predicted for his British readers the reasons why the nineteenth-century pattern of movement from countryside to city would be reversed in the twentieth century:

> The first of these is what is known as the passion for nature . . . and secondly, there is the allied charm of cultivation, and especially gardening, a charm that is partly also the love of dominion, perhaps, and partly a personal love for the beauty of trees and flowers and natural things. Through that we come to the third factor, that craving . . . for a little private imperium such as a house or cottage "in its own grounds" affords; and from this we pass on the intense desire many women feel . . . for a household, a separate sacred and distinctive household, built and ordered after their own hearts, such as in its fullness only the country permits. Add to these things the healthfulness of the country for young children, and the wholesome isolation that is possible from much that irritates, stimulates, prematurely, and corrupts in crowded centers, and the chief positive centrifugal inducements are stated . . . (H. G. Wells, *Anticipations*, Harper & Brothers, New York, 1901, pp. 55–56).

However, in spite of all this glorification of the suburbs, the dominant role of the central city was explicitly or implicitly acknowledged. Suburbs were clearly *sub*. It was automatically assumed that suburbs were appendages of cities, and it was assumed that the great bulk of the urban population would remain city dwellers. Suburbanization was for the affluent, not the average. Thus, suburbanization and suburban imagery prior to the contemporary post-World War II period did not imply any abandonment of the city in other respects. The city was still the core and the suburbs a residential property. Moving one's families to the suburbs meant a residential decision and no more.

Factories, offices, and retail establishments stayed in the city. Men of business routinely commuted into their offices in the central district without any thought that the offices should suburbanize. One might move one's family out of the city, but that in no way meant family members were exiling themselves outside the city walls. The same rail-roads that allowed businessmen to commute provided frequent service to allow women and children to shop in downtown department stores, eat at downtown restaurants, and attend downtown theater and con-certs. Unlike today, suburbanites of the 1890s, or of the 1940s, routinely went downtown for shopping or an evening out. Until into the 1960s, the best restaurants and the first-run movies still were located down-town and were routinely supported by commuting suburbanites. The railroad and the electric streetcar, by converging their tracks on the center of the city, emphasized rather than diminished the role of the downtown as the core of the metropolitan area. Until the mass subur-banization following World War II, the role and economic strength of the core was further increased rather than weakened by adding outly-ing residential suburbs.

To social reformers and progressives of the early century, the spread of suburbanization not only provided better housing for those who could afford it, it also helped alleviate the terrible crowding and human deprivation of central-city slums. Suburbia was to be the hope of the future. Suburbanization and its accompanying decentralization were seen as reducing central-city densities. Decreasing urban housing densities was seen as permitting urban children to be brought up in a more healthful environment. Basically, social reformers were express-ing what would become known half a century later as the theory of trickle-down housing. As the affluent left older neighborhoods for new housing on the outskirts, those city working class and poor who could not move out themselves could at least move into the better housing being left behind. When mentioned at all, suburbs were often por-trayed not as a social problem, but as a social solution.

Literary Treatment

Since suburbs during the first half of this century were seen as little more than outlying residential areas, it is perhaps understandable that they attracted minimal literary or scholarly attention. For example, George Babbitt sold real estate in the suburban Glen Oriole develop-ment, but he lived in the city of Zenith (Sinclair Lewis, *Babbitt*, Harcourt Brace, New York, 1922). Authors and writers in the early decades of the twentieth century largely ignored suburbs while stress-ing the evils of the city. Typical was Carl Sandburg's poem "Chicago," which praised the raw vitality of the city but also noted the city's wickedness and brutality (Carl Sandburg, *Chicago Poems*, Holt, New York, 1916). By comparison suburbs were nonplaces.

Overall, it is not an exaggeration to suggest that until the post-World War II era, major American writers generally ignored the suburbs. True, Ernest, Hemingway caustically referred to Oak Park, where he had grown up, as a community "of wide lawns and narrow minds," but he apparently didn't think it merited a novel. Sinclair Lewis's exposure to the meanness of small-midwestern-town life in *Main Street* (1920) is far more typical of cosmopolitan writers of the first half of the twentieth century. In *Babbitt* (1922) Lewis, with equal acid, detailed the life of George Babbit, a small-city real estate developer and subdivider. Lewis's fictional city of Zenith was a literary twin of the empirical study by Robert and Helen Lynd of *Middletown*, which was actually Muncie, Indiana (Robert S. and Helen M. Lynd, *Middletown*, Harcourt Brace, New York, 1929). Generally, writers of the era agreed in their viewing small-town and small-city values as fostering dull conformity and repression of creativity. Only in the large metropolitan areas could one be truly free. Not until the suburban housing boom following World War II were the charges that early-twentieth-century writers had leveled against the small towns and small cities redirected at suburbia and suburban life-styles. The evils of Sinclair Lewis' fictional Gopher Prairie became those of Levittown.

One major exception to ignoring suburbia as either a literary site or a literary metaphor is F. Scott Fitzgerald's 1925 classic, *The Great Gatsby*. Fitzgerald places the rootless Gatsby in West Egg, one of the newly developing wealthy suburbs of Long Island. These were places without a background for people who were also reinventing themselves. Although he did not further expand the theme in later works, Fitzgerald is the first to hint at suburbia as a conscious and artificial creation especially designed to accommodate those possessing shallow roots. Whether it is Gatsby's wealthy new suburb or the post-World War II mass suburbia of Levittown, suburbia began to be portrayed not as a place of stability, but as a temporary residence for transients.

Popular-culture images of suburbia prior to the suburban exodus of the 1950s and 1960s was generally more charitable. Images of suburbia tended toward the comfortable and mildly comic, such as Norman Rockwell's *Saturday Evening Post* cover showing suburban wives, still in their bathrobes, driving their husbands in the family station wagon to the suburban commuter train station. Movie versions of suburbia were also benign and inclined toward the small-town nostalgia of Andy Hardy-type communities. The comic dimension of the upper-middle-class city dweller seeking a semirural retreat was reflected in the success of stories turned into movies such as *Mr. Blandings Builds*

The suburban backyard barbecue became an
American cliché during the 1950s. It symbolized the close national association of suburban
life with family values. This picture originally
appeared on the September 13, 1958, cover of
The Saturday Evening Post.

His Dream House and *Please Don't Eat the Daisies.* Interestingly, the former began as a cautionary article in *Fortune* on the perils of suburban
living (Eric Hodgins, "Mr. Blandings Builds His Castle," *Fortune
Magazine,* April 1946, pp. 138–189). On the other hand, Jean Kerr's
Please Don't Eat the Daisies was a satiric and ironic look at women's life
in the 1950s suburbs (Jean Kerr, *Please Don't Eat the Daisies,* Doubleday,
Garden City, N.Y., 1957).

It also has to be said that prior to the 1960s, urban-area scholars
were not particularly astute or insightful in examining the phenomenon of suburbanization. Social science's treatment of suburbs can be
described in few words: suburbs essentially were ignored. They were
the focus of neither theorizing nor research. Even textbooks in the
rapidly developing field of urban sociology went little beyond Ernest
Burgess's 1924 description of suburbia as an outer-commuter's zone.

No one seemed to think the area, or the process, merited further elaboration. The major scholar of suburbia, Harlan Paul Douglass, in his 1934 article on "Suburbs" in the *Encyclopedia of the Social Sciences,* portrayed suburbs as limited to the well-to-do. Living in the suburbs, in his words, was, "virtually limited to the most highly paid types of labor and to the upper middle classes" (Harlan Paul Douglass, "Suburbs," *Encyclopedia of the Social Sciences,* Vol. XIV, New York, 1934, p. 434). Even as late as the 1950s, Queen and Carpenter, in the urban sociology text *The American City,* (McGraw-Hill, 1953), gave only 4 of its 383 pages to even a mention of suburbs.

Postwar Critics

Then suddenly in the 1950s, urban-based intellectuals discovered the suburbs. And what they discovered, to their horror, was an aesthetic and social wasteland filled with tract housing, station wagons, and organization men. Attention was riveted almost exclusively on the supposed negative consequences of suburbanism as a way of life. The overwhelming consensus of city-oriented intellectuals, particularly those living in New York City, was that the postwar suburbs were an unmitigated aesthetic and social disaster. Suburbia was equated with the emergence of a popular mass culture dominated by the mass media. The blandness of popular tastes was blamed on the suburbs. They became a scapegoat for all that the cosmopolitan critics disliked about modern life. Often, this was accompanied with glorification of the past. In *The City in History* Lewis Mumford bemoaned the growth of middle-class suburbs:

> While the suburb served only a favored minority, it neither spoiled the countryside nor threatened the city. But now that the drift to the outer ring has become a mass movement, it tends to destroy both environments without producing anything but a dreary substitute, devoid of form and even more devoid of the original suburban values (Lewis Mumford, The City in History, Harcourt, Brace and World, New York, 1961, p. 506).

Further this mass exodus to suburbia was resulting in:

> . . . a multitude of uniform, unidentifiable houses, lined up inflexibly, in uniform distances, on uniform roads, in a treeless communal waste inhabited by people of the same class, the same income, the same age group, witnessing the same television performances, eating the same tasteless prefabricated food, from the same freezers, conforming in every outward and inward respect to a common mold manufactured in the central metropolis (Mumford, 1961, p. 486).

Mumford, like other cosmopolitan critics, seemed particularly offended that suburbia was developing not as planned communities for those of taste, but as mass suburbanization for the common man. Often, as in the above quotation, the characteristics of the housing and the characteristics of the suburban residents were directly linked. And both were clearly found wanting. The critics embraced an extreme form of environmental determinism in which the characteristics of the area determined the character of the inhabitants. According to a 1964 *New York Times Magazine* article by elitist Ada Louise Huxtable, the long-time *New York Times* architecture critic, "It is a shocking fact that more than 90 percent of builders' homes are not designed by architects . . . and the consequent damage "is social, cultural, psychological, and emotional, as well as aesthetic" (Ada Louise Huxtable, "Clusters Instead of Slurbs," *New York Times Magazine*, February 9, 1964, pp. 37–44).

Suburbia was a dismal place where mediocrity ruled and about which no intellectual could say anything favorable—even if they lived in one. The same criticism of popular tastes and cultural uniformity was delivered with far more humor in Malvina Reynolds's folksong "Little Boxes." Sung for decades by Pete Seeger to the point where it has become an American classic, the opening lines go:

> Little Boxes on the hillside,
> Little Boxes made of ticky tacky
> Little Boxes on the hillside,
> Little Boxes all the same.
> There's a green one and pink one
> And a blue one and a yellow one
> And they're all made out of ticky tacky
> And they all look just the same.

This point that the little boxes and the people who live in them are all the same was a core belief of the city-based intellectual critics of suburbs. It was a given that suburbs bred conformity. Ironically, the children born in the little boxes would spawn the cultural revolution of the late 1960s and early 1970s. It was the children of the suburbs who celebrated at Woodstock.

Finally, it should be noted that this pattern of urban cities detailing the ills of suburbia is not a phenomenon common only to earlier decades. Even in 1993, in *The New York Times*, one could find a feature article bemoaning the isolation and lack of intellectual and cultural activities in suburbia. As stated in the article, "escapees from Manhattan have found that along with the gains have come unexpected nuisances, even deep feelings of loss. And what is more, the unpleasant surprises are often the flip side of precisely the attractions that drew them to the suburbs in the first place. The emigres discover they can walk virtually anywhere at night without fear. But where to walk? So few places worth walking are open after dark. . . . Some discover that at times their snug home on its separate lot, without a doorman downstairs or neighbors above and below, makes them feel lonely and more vulnerable, not more secure. And when pipes leak and the heat shuts off, they learn that the joys of the suburbs do not include supers" (Joseph Berger, "Emigres in Suburbs Find Life's Flip Side," *New York Times*, January 24, 1993, Metro p. 30).

However, there are significant differences between contemporary articles, such as that quoted above, and the typical piece written during earlier decades. While both might decry the absence of all-night Chinese take-out, current articles acknowledge that in addition to opera, the city also has serious problems, such as the menace of muggers and aggressive panhandlers. Contemporary laments are also less likely to be angry diatribes and more likely to be done tongue-in-cheek, with humor. Finally, the authors of contemporary suburban criticisms are more likely to be themselves suburbanites. They miss the city, but they, like most American having the choice, have chosen to live elsewhere. The writer of the *New York Times* piece, for example, had moved to Westchester from the West Side of Manhattan some twenty months earlier.

SCHOLARS AND SUBURBS: POSTWAR DECADES

While the studies done about suburbs and suburbanization do not always fall into neat categories, it is possible, with a bit of shoving, to see suburbs and suburbanization since World War II as falling into four social and chronological eras. Each of these eras or phases has had a somewhat different emphasis.

1950s—The Myth of Suburbia

The first phase of study of suburbs was simply the discovery of suburbia as an area and a topic worthy of scholarly and popular attention. By the early 1950s suburbia had been discovered by the popular press and magazines, but there was a dearth of actual research. Magazines such as *The Saturday Evening Post* began to focus on the homogeneity of suburbs' physical appearance and how this was reflected in the social similarity of new suburbanites. While popular portrayals of the ranch houses, neat lawns, station wagons, and car pools had an element of humor, many of the novels, such as *The Man in the Grey Flannel Suit, The Crack in the Picture Window, Bullet Park,* and *No Down Payment,* painted a darker picture. While outwardly benign, suburbia's underside was portrayed as one of alcholicism, adultery, and quiet despair. (By contrast, the new medium of television painted a far brighter, if blander, picture. Shows such as "Ozzie and Harriet" in the 1950s, "Leave It to Beaver" in the 1960s, "Happy Days" in the 1970s, and "The Wonder Years" in the late 1980s and early 1990s presented an essentially warm and benign image of suburban life.)

During the late 1940s and the 1950s, scholars also discovered the suburbs, and what they found was that living in the suburbs produced a unique way of life. This came to be called "the myth of suburbia." Starting the process, although the book really wasn't about suburbs per se, was David Riesman's 1950 book, *The Lonely Crowd,* which, with its emphasis on the "other directed" personality type, emphasizing social conformity, set the stage for what was to follow (David Riesman, *The Lonely Crowd,* Yale University Press, New Haven, Conn., 1950). As portrayed by Riesman, postwar suburban housing developments were conformist and coercive. The indictment was that such areas produced look-alike, other-directed personality types who were governed by group norms rather than an inner moral compass.

Commonly acknowledged as the best sociological analysis of the new suburbs was William H. Whyte's best-selling book, *The Organization Man* (William H. Whyte, *The Organization Man,* Doubleday Anchor, Garden City, N.Y., 1956). Whyte, not a sociologist but the editor of *Fortune,* was impressed by the demographic composition of the postwar suburbs burgeoning on the urban periphery. Not only was the housing relentlessly similar, but the young corporate businessmen and their wives living in these suburbs seemed to be developing a way of life or "social ethic" strongly emphasizing group interaction. To test these ideas, Whyte studied a "typical" suburb, Park Forest, Illinois, some thirty miles south of Chicago on the train line. Park Forest was not just a subdivision, but a fully planned community having its own shopping center and community facilities.

Whyte suggested that in Park Forest, and other like suburbs, the corporate ethic, with its emphasis on teamwork and on the downplaying of the solo individualist, was creating a new social way of life. The new suburbs, with their interchangeable houses and families having shallow community roots, were simply reflections of the corporation ethic. Both corporations and suburbs were being populated by bland managers stressing the importance of getting along. In the suburbs, belongingness and frenetic socialization took the place of the individuality of an earlier age. Group conformity and not rocking the boat were supposedly the suburban goals.

Whyte's *The Organization Man*, in its portrayal of the burgeoning post-World War II suburbs as centers of conformity and "togetherness," set the suburban stereotype. Supposedly, the ethic of the organization, with its emphasis on mass-produced uniformity, produced newly constructed suburbs of considerable compulsive socialibilty and group activity but little originality. For example, in this era before most middle-class women worked, the wives living in Park Forest were expected to leave doors open to neighbors and engage in daily coffee klatching while their husbands were at work. Those who did not participate were ostracized; belongingness was a way of life.

Moving to the suburbs also was portrayed as more or less automatically producing a number of personality and behavioral changes. These ranged from turning city introverts into suburban joiners to the converting of urban Democrats into suburban Republicans. According to a 1957 *Newsweek* article, "When a city dweller packs up and moves his family to the suburbs, he usually acquires a mortgage, a power lawn mower, and a backyard grill. Often although a lifelong Democrat, he also starts voting Republican" (*Newsweek*, April 1, 1957, p. 42). The stereotype was that new suburbanites who previously were Democrats automatically abandoned their long-standing voting patterns to become instant Republicans. The suburban Eisenhower landslides of 1952 and 1956 were interpreted as being a sign of a permanent voter shift. Such analysis often downplayed the degree to which the vote was for the immensely popular Eisenhower rather than for the party. Such statements as that in *Newsweek* also did not give sufficient attention to the fact that similar Eisenhower landslides also occurred in many supposedly Democratic city wards.

The real voting pattern was more complex. In 1960 the old, established WASP suburbs voted solidly for Richard Nixon, while newer suburbs, particularly those with substantial Catholic populations, voted for John Kennedy. There also are rare cases of suburbs voting overwhelmingly Democratic. Barry Goldwater's 1964 campaign witnessed Goldwater losing every single suburban county in the northeast from Baltimore to Boston, illustrating that the suburbs were far from being bastions of Republicanism. (Kevin P. Phillips, *The Emerging Republican Majority*, Arlington House, New Rochelle, N.Y., 1969). However, the political myth persists, and it is commonly believed that Democrats cannot win in middle-class suburbs. As the myth was expressed in a 1992 *Atlantic* article, "Presidential politics these days is a race between Democratic cities and Republican suburbs to see who can produce bigger margins. The suburbs are winning (William Schneider, "The Suburban Century Begins," *Atlantic*, July 1992, p. 35).

It is true that Republicans seeking a middle-class constituency are generally more comfortable in suburbs than those Democrats still trying to revive the inner-city, ethnic-racial-economic coalition of the New Deal. It is also true that politically suburbia tends to be more conservative than the central cities. Between 1960 and 1988 city voters became more Democratic and suburban voters more Republican. The suburban proportion of the electorate grew from 33 percent in 1960 to 48 percent in 1988, while the urban proportion shrank from 33 to 29 percent (Schneider, p. 35). However, the suburban vote is not monolithic. Bill Clinton ran well in the suburbs in 1992. Congressional Democratic party candidates ran even better.

Ideologically, most suburbanites generally see themselves as being in the center rather than to the right or left. The supposed right-wing proclivities of Orange County, south of Los Angeles, may be fascinating to journalists, but such right-wing voting is not typical of suburbia nationally. Nonetheless, the myth that the growth of suburbs sounds the death knell of the Democratic party is a half-century-old myth that keeps being revived every national election.

Environmental Determinism

Implicit in the developing myth regarding suburbanites and their lifestyles was a naive determinism that assumed that the characteristics of the built environment changed how people believed and acted. Thus, moving from city to suburb could and would change patterns of socialization to say nothing of modifying political, religious, and child-rearing practices. In brief, suburban residence changed social behavior. Whyte, if willing to make broad-stroke statements about life in Park Forest, was more careful in his generalizing to other types of suburbs and suburbanites. Other writers showed no such restraint. Even some scholars such as David Riesman got carried away, charging that the suburban family was surrendering all individuality and creativity (Riesman, "The Suburban Sadness," in Wm. Dobriner, ed., *The Suburban Community*, G. P. Putnam Sons, New York, 1958, pp. 375–408). Implied was the view that all suburbs were similar and all produced conformity and a long list of social maladies. As portrayed in the postwar caricatures, suburbia was a producer of conformity, compulsive socializing, adultery, alcoholism, divorce, and boredom. Psychiatrists argued that the stress of suburban living additionally led to psychosomatic illnesses, suicide, and mental illness in general (R. E.

Gordon, K. K. Gordon, and M. Gunther, *The Split-Level Trap*, Dell, New York, 1962).

Typical of the stereotypic statements was that of the late Margaret Mead, who stated that, "Settled in their new homes and finding themselves with nothing to do at home, suburbanites are caught in the boredom characteristic of the American family when its members are imprisoned with one another." Suburban life had, in her view, degenerated into "a living room or a recreation room which often resembles a giant playpen into which the parents have somewhat reluctantly climbed" (Margaret Mead, "Freedom to Choose," in Charles M. Haar, ed., *The End of Innocence: A Suburban Reader*, Scott, Foresman, Glenview, Ill., 1972, pp.20–21). Particularly influential was an article by David Riesman, "The Suburban Dislocation" (later reprinted as "The Suburban Sadness"), which further popularized the stereotype of suburbs as a monocultural destroyer of urban diversity. Suburbs were, in his view, antithetical to developing a true urban culture, which could only be found in the density and diversity of large urban centers. Moreover, when men (and Riesman's focus in this earlier era, when there were few female suburban commuters, was on males) moved from the city to the suburbs, they were accused of removing their attention and abilities from important urban concerns and problems. They were portrayed as wasting their talents on parochial suburban activities such as Little League. They had become obsessed with family concerns to the detriment of their civic responsibilities. Such portrayals of suburban life were widely accepted as factual. Interestingly, the criticisms of husbands being overinvolved with family matters was the reverse of the criticism of progressive writers at the turn of the century. Then, the concern was that middle-class husbands did not become sufficiently involved in, nor spend enough time with, their families. According to the wisdom of the 1950s, suburban husbands and fathers were too family focused. Currently, the pendulum has swung again, and fathers are again portrayed in popular magazines as needing to be more involved in day-to-day family life.

A much-quoted social-psychological study of an affluent suburb, *Crestwood Heights* (actually not a suburb, but an outer-city neighborhood of Toronto), carried out by John Seeley and his colleagues, seemed to provide empirical support for the belief that suburban lifestyles were bad for one's mental health (John R. Seeley, R. Alexander Sim, and E. W. Loosley, *Crestwood Heights*, Basic Books, New York, 1956). *Crestwood Heights* was in many respects a fine ethnology of a suburb, but its analysis was prone to psychological overanalysis. Also, there is the technicality of Crestwood Heights not being a suburb, but an outer area of Toronto. In Crestwood Heights there supposedly was little individuality. Children were carefully socialized to conform to their parents' culture of status consciousness and using their homes more for status display than for living. Suburbia, thus, was seen as encouraging pathological family and child-rearing behaviors.

In all of the above works, women played a distinctly subsidiary role. Their place was seen as restricted largely to child rearing, consumerism, and coffee klatching. The postwar studies took it for granted that suburban women did not work outside the home. The studies also assumed that all suburban women were married.

The studies, with the exception of *Crestwood Heights*, also said relatively little about the effect of suburbs on children, although suburbia was criticized for having a particularly pernicious impact on child-rearing practices (Urie Bronfenbrenner, "The Split Society: Children vs Adults," in Charles Haar, pp. 23–28). It is amazing, in retrospect, that article after article would purport to show parents suffering from suburban-induced conformity, alcoholism, or sexual promiscuity, but little of this seemed to rub off on the children. Suburbia might be deadly for adults, but there was little suggestion that suburbia ruined children or was in any way bad for them, as it was for their parents. The studies gave no indication that for the suburban adolescents growing up in this simpler age, there were any serious family or community problems with delinquency, drugs, or dropping out. These topics were noticeable for their absence. Reading works of the 1950s, one gets the impression that the most serious problem facing teenage males was "momism," brought on by overprotective and overpossessive mothering. According to one of the most quoted books of the time, an excess of female-dominated domesticity was raising a generation of sons lacking independence from the domination of their mothers (Philip Wylie, *A Generation of Vipers*, Ferrar and Rinehart, New York, 1942). Other problems rarely surfaced. Only in the occasional controversial movie such as *Rebel Without a Cause* was there any suggestion that there could be a dark side to growing up in the suburbs. And even in the movie, James Dean's problems were clearly blamed on his parents' drinking and neglect. Not surprisingly, adults criticized the "negativism" of the film, while teenagers in that simpler era "rebelled" by seeing the movie over and over.

Evaluation of the "Myth"

The myth of suburbia, like all myths, contained elements of fact. That the new suburbs were architecturally similar was beyond dispute. However, the claim commonly made that this conformity also included all cultural tastes, child-rearing practices, levels of social activity, and patterns of neighboring carried the argument to caricature. While the image of compulsive conformity and socialization was a caricature, it is true that people in the suburbs were more socially homogeneous and more likely to engage in social interaction. (Sylvia Fleis Fava, "Suburbanism as a Way of Life," *American Sociological Review*, Vol. 21, 1956, pp. 34–37). There was general agreement that there were some differences, but their consequences were minimal. Nor was there any consensus on why, in suburbs, there was greater involvement with neighbors (Claude S. Fischer and Robert M. Jackson, "Suburbs, Networks, and Attitudes," in Berry Schwartz, ed., *The Changing Face of the Suburbs*, University of Chicago Press, Chicago, 1976, pp. 279–307). Part of the difference, doubtlessly, can be explained by the presence of young children and higher family incomes, but even with these variables taken into account, differences remain. The more localized nature of suburban friendship networks might simply reflect the relative isolation of the suburb and the greater difficulty of maintaining ties with those more distant (Claude S. Fischer, *The Urban Experience*, Harcourt Brace Jovanovich, San Diego, 1984, p. 256).

It also was suggested that suburbanites self-select for personality traits favoring sociability. In this view those who opt for the suburbs have chosen a life-style that emphasizes "familism" over alternatives such as "careerism" and "consumership" (Wendell Bell, "The City, the Suburb, and a Theory of Social Choice," in Scott Greer, Dennis L. McElrath, David Milnar, and Peter Orleans, eds., *The New Urbanization*, St. Martin's Press, New York, 1968, pp. 132–168). However, the data do not appear to support this explanation (Fischer, 1984, pp. 255–256). Research does suggest that the suburban neighborhood does foster somewhat greater political participation (Scott Greer, *The Urbane View*, Oxford University Press, New York, 1972, p. 97). Suburbanites as a group tend to be somewhat better off than city dwellers and desire a more familistic life-style (David Popenoe, "The Suburban House and Environment," in Elizabeth Huttman and William van Vliet, eds., *Handbook of Housing and the Built Environment in the United States*, Greenwood Press, New York, 1988, p. 397).

It appears that those living in suburbs have some minor differences in tastes from city dwellers, for example, preferring gardening and rating cultural affairs lower (Joseph Zelan, "Does Suburbia Make a Difference?" in Silvia Fava, ed., *Urbanism in World Perspective*, Oxford University Press, New York, 1968, pp. 401–408). However, there is no evidence that suburban living changes tastes. Rather, those who value nature tend to gravitate toward suburbs, just as those who prefer easy access to a full cultural life tend to prefer the city. There is no evidence that suburbanites make less use of museums, concerts, and art galleries than do otherwise equivalent city dwellers. Expressways allow suburbanites to get to many events as fast as those living in outer-city neighborhoods. In recent years popular culture, such as first-run movies or sports events, have occurred outside the central city. For example, the Detroit Pistons' basketball stadium is outside Detroit, and the New York Giants play their football in New Jersey.

Needless to say, postwar suburbanites did not view themselves as living lives devoid of culture or as being excessively conforming, hyperactive joiners. They already knew what researchers such as Bennett Berger and Herbert Gans would confirm (Bennett M. Berger, *Working Class Suburbs*, University of California Press, Berkeley, 1960; Herbert J. Gans, *The Levittowners*, Random House, New York, 1967). That is, the new suburbanites had not given up their individuality, political affiliation, ethnic identity, or religious heritage as they moved houses.

For good or ill, studies from the era of the 1950s achieved widespread popular as well as professional attention. *The Organization Man* was a widely read and discussed best-seller. It and its ilk helped set out contemporary view of suburbia—a view that later critics would call "the myth of suburbia." However, in spite of their popular appeal, the early studies of suburbia suffered from some serious limitations. One of the most obvious problems was rooted in the authors having preset expectations. Additionally, questions can be asked about how and why the various study sites were chosen. Rather than being "typical" suburbs, it is clear today that the sites were chosen precisely because they were "interesting." That is, they were selected because they were in some respects atypical, not because they were just like everyplace else. This approach to selection of a community may lead to more interesting reading, but it by definition limits generalization. The suburbs written about, for example, were almost invariably new, large-scale developments sprouting at the urban periphery. Little or no attention was paid to other types of suburbs, such as industrial suburbs, working-class suburbs, or even old established WASP suburbs. The focus of the studies was on the new middle-class subdivisions built to house young ex-GIs, their wives, and their children. Although it was not scientifically, or even logically, valid to generalize from these new suburbs to all suburbs, this was commonly done.

Additionally, many of the studies fell into the so-called ecological fallacy of trying to generalize from the characteristics of an area to the characteristics of all individuals who live in that area. Finally, their observations of supposedly typical suburban lifestyles were based on a single look at a new suburb immediately following the first wave of settlement. We now know that a mature community viewed ten or twenty years later shows a different pattern. For example, the supposed social-ability of postwar suburbia can be attributed in good part to the fact that because of the limited housing types in each subdevelopment, most of the new inmovers were approximately the same age, had the same aged children, and had the common experience of all moving into similar new houses at the same time. Most of the men also shared the common experience of military service. Under such circumstances, it would be unusual if there was not a high degree of social interaction.

1960s—The Era of Revision

While the first generation of post-World War suburban studies discovered alleged widespread suburban conformity, the 1960s research saw the effects of suburbanization as being far more problematical. Sociologists such as Bennett M. Berger, William Dobriner, and Herbert Gans began examining how much of the popularly accepted view of suburbia was reality and how much was myth. The empirical question being asked was whether the commonly accepted "facts" regarding suburbia were indeed facts or simply widely accepted beliefs. In simple terms, did moving from city to suburb change social behavior? A major attempt to answer this question was Bennett M. Berger's *Working Class Suburbs*. Berger carried out an empirical study of the actual effects of suburbanization on new working-class suburbanites. Berger was able to carry out a natural experiment by studying a group of northern California autoworkers who were forced to suburbanize from industrial Richmond, California, in order to keep their jobs at a Ford Motor Car assembly line that was being relocated to a suburban location at Milpitas, California. The possible effects of social class were all controlled, since all the workers were working class and from the same plant. Berger thus was able to examine the effect of the change of location on the workers' behaviors, attitudes, and values. He was particularly interested in the effects of the move on political behavior, religion, leisure activities, and social mobility.

What Berger, somewhat surprisingly, discovered was that two years after the move, the workers' values and social behaviors were virtually unaffected by the suburban move. They did not join neighborhood groups, change their religious affiliation or practice, or switch from the Democratic party. Nor did they have expectations of social mobility; they knew they were going to remain at their current level. He thus labeled the widely held belief that suburbanization affected beliefs and behaviors "the myth of suburbia." As stated by Berger:

> The studies that have given rise to the myth of suburbia have been studies of *middle-class suburbs*, that is suburbs of very large cities pop-

ulated primarily by people in the occupational groups often thought of as making up the "new middle-class—the engineers, teachers, and organization men (Berger, p. 11).

William Dobriner further reinforced this view that there wasn't one suburban life-style but rather that there were a number of life-styles. He focused on differences between middle-class and working-class suburbs by showing how the original Levittown on Long Island was becoming more heterogeneous as more blue-collar and Catholic families moved into the suburb (William M. Dobriner, *Class in Suburbia*, Prentice-Hall, Englewood Cliff, N.J., 1963). Social class rather than suburban residence was the important variable. Suburban newcomers, for instance, were voting on the bases of socioeconomic and ethnic factors rather than the location of their homes. Dobriner also pointed to the age of the community as a second defining variable.

Reinforcing the above was Herbert Gans's now classic participant observation study, *The Levittowners* (Gans, 1967). This was a detailed look at a new Levitt and Sons suburban development being constructed 17 miles east of Philadelphia in New Jersey. (The community later changed its name to Willingboro to escape the Levittown stereotype.) A new Levittown of 12,000 homes was being constructed, and Gans and his wife became two of the new homeowners. He wanted to discover how living in such an instant suburb would affect social behavior. After two years of residence and a study of two sets of Levittown newcomers, Gans found there were few differences that occurred in life-style that could be attributed to city-suburban differences. There were some differences, such as more sociability among neighborhood couples over back fences while doing lawnwork. Gans, however, suggested that the sociability that occurred within Levittown was not a result of suburban residence, but rather a direct consequence of the homogeneity of residents' backgrounds, particularly in age and income.

He also discovered that there was more diversity in terms of ethnicity, regional background, and religious beliefs than critics of suburbs had allowed. Active sociability only occurred when neighboring residents shared common values and tastes and had similar child-rearing practices. Gans also discovered that Levittown more than met the social and limited cultural needs of most of its residents while providing good housing for the price. There was no evidence of the suburb creating mental illness or social pathologies. He suggested that any differences from city dwellers that occurred were because of suburbs attracting people with different needs and interests rather than because of the suburban environment per se. In other words, suburbs and cities were home to different sorts of people. Rather than the suburbs forcing people to conform, the move allowed the new suburbanites to have the greater interaction with neighbors they had always wanted. The effect of the environment itself was seen as negligible. Residence was seen as having little if any effect on behavior—a view we have had to modify as being as extreme as the earlier view that residence determined behavior.

It also deserves noting that the limitations of suburban life stressed by critics have not been echoed by suburban residents. National surveys going back several decades indicate that suburban residents have a higher degree of satisfaction with their communities than do city residents (Angus Campbell et al., *The Quality of American Life*, Russell Sage, New York, 1976; Mark Baldassare, *The Growth Dilemma*, University of California Press, Berkeley, 1981). Suburbanites also are more likely to rate the cultural opportunities and activities in their areas slightly higher than do city dwellers. Suburbanites, additionally, are much more satisfied with a whole range of community facilities and services including schools, police protection, parks and community services. Suburbanites are also more likely to know their neighbors and have friends among neighbors. (For a fuller discussion of neighboring see "Ideology and Imagery," p. 92.) Residents of new fast-growing suburbs tend to express somewhat lower satisfaction than longer-term residents of more established areas (Baldassare, 1981). However, even residents in fast-growing suburbs are more satisfied with their communities than are city residents.

It is likely that differences in evaluation of suburbs and central cities reflects some self-selection, with those desiring a more familistic and neighboring orientation gravitating toward suburbs (William Michelson, *Environmental Choice, Human Behavior, and Residential Satisfaction*, Oxford University Press, New York, 1977). For those seeking home ownership and yard space, the suburb clearly is the preferred choice. Also listed as influencing satisfaction with suburbs have been the general economic advantage of the suburbs and the greater predominance of traditional family patterns (Brian J. Berry and John D. Kasarda, *Contemporary Urban Ecology*, Macmillan, New York, 1977; Amos Hawley, *Urban Society*, Ronald Press, New York, 1971). Greater length of residence in the community has also been found to encourage neighboring (John D. Kasarda and Morris Janowitz, "Community Attachment in Mass Society," *American Sociological Review*, Vol. 39, June 1974, pp. 328–339). The end result, whatever the causes, is that suburbanites clearly and consistently indicate a preference for suburban living. If decades of suburbanites have been living the shallow lives of quiet desperation portrayed by some novelists and critics, it has been kept secret from most of them.

1970s—The Lost Decade

The early 1970s appeared to be the dawn of increasing scholarly focus on suburbs. While popular attacks on suburban "rootlessness," such as Vance Packard's *A Nation of Strangers*, occasionally still surfaced, serious scholars had left the cliches behind (Vance Packard, *A Nation of Strangers*, David McKay, New York, 1972). Early in the decade a number of good collections of articles were published. Titles of suburban readers such as *The End of Innocence* (Charles M. Haar, ed., Scott, Foresman, Glenview, Ill., 1972), *North American Suburbs: Politics, Diversity, and Change* (John Kramer, ed., Glendessary Press, Berkeley, Calif., 1972), and *Suburbia in Transition* (L. N. Masotti and J. K. Hadden, eds., Franklin Watts, New York, 1974) emphasized the maturation of suburban studies and the realization that suburbs were no longer peripheral to American society. Urban problems were now also part of the suburban agenda. Crime, racial conflict, and drugs had all come to the suburbs.

This focus on suburban change was short-lived. Events on the national and international scene soon shifted attention elsewhere. The outbreak of urban riots in central cities, the focus on the War on Poverty, and growing protests regarding the continuing war in Vietnam all contributed to attention sharply shifting away from suburbs. The focus of researchers, politicians, and citizens now was on the inner city. The pressing needs of the city eclipsed other urban activities. The emphasis was on "relevancy," and suburban patterns and concerns were not judged to meet the test. With all the inner-city problems, why "waste" attention on suburbs? By the late 1970s the terms "urban research" and "urban studies" had all but become synonymous with the study of central-city problems such as poverty, racial conflict, crime, and drugs. Suburbs continued to rapidly expand, but there was only minimal interest by researchers and funding agencies in carrying out new suburban-based research. As a result, new suburban-oriented research came to a virtual halt.

There were a few exceptions to the general fixation on inner cities. One of the most promising was the emergence of urban history as a distinct and viable area of historical research. During the 1970s several good analyses were published, including Howard Chudacoff's *The Evolution of American Urban Society* (Prentice-Hall, Englewood Cliffs, N.J., 1975) and David Goldfield and Blaine Brownell's *Urban America: From Downtown to No Town* (Houghton Mifflin, Boston, 1979). However, relatively little of the new interest in urban history was concerned with the history of suburbs. That would not occur until the next decade. Another addition to our knowledge was a major study by

Michelson of housing choice preferences (William Michelson, *Environmental Choice, Human Behavior, and Residential Satisfaction,* Oxford University Press, New York, 1977). Done in Toronto, the study showed that the preferences of city dwellers and suburbanites were somewhat different. City residents emphasized the importance of location, while suburbanites ranked the quality of house and the characteristics of neighbors ahead of location.

Another sign of our growing understanding of suburbs was the comparative examination of suburbanization in different settings. David Popenoe's *The Suburban Environment,* which studied the different approaches to suburbanization in the United States and Sweden, broke new ground by comparing a Levittown in the United States with the planned new town of Vallingby in Sweden (David Popenoe, *The Suburban Environment: Sweden and the United States,* University of Chicago Press, 1977). The higher-density garden apartment and high-rise suburbs in Sweden were built both to be self-contained and to have easy access to the city by public transportation. By contrast, the dispersed American pattern of detached single-family homes provides less social support and access to the larger area for groups such as women and children.

1980s—The Consequences of Growth and Historical Studies

The 1980s saw the study of suburbanization experience a mild revival. Suburbia was losing its solely residential character. Looking toward the future of multicentered metropolises, Peter Muller's *Contemporary Suburban America,* published in 1981 (Prentice-Hall, Englewood Cliffs, N.J.) was prophetic in its description of the newly emerging outer cities. Studies such as Mark Baldassare's *Trouble in Paradise,* (Columbia University Press, New York, 1986) looked at Orange County, California, to further examine the consequences of continued suburban growth. Baldassare was particularly concerned with how rapid residential growth was viewed by residents as exacerbating problems of transportation and environmental degradation.

The 1980s also saw scholars extend our view of suburbs into the past, with the publication of historical studies documenting the emergence of nineteenth-century suburbs. After Kenneth Jackson's *Crabgrass Frontier* (Oxford, New York, 1985), it was no longer possible to view contemporary residential suburbs simply as a consequence of the availability of automobiles and post-World War II housing needs. Sam Bass Warner's earlier *Streetcar Suburbs* (Harvard and MIT Presses, Cambridge, Mass., 1962), which examined the streetcar's effect on suburban growth in nineteenth-century Boston, now was augmented by additional volumes, such as Robert Fishman's *Bourgeois Utopias*, (Basic Books, New York, 1987) which allowed nineteenth-century residential suburbanization to be examined in a wider context.

1990s—New Outer Cities

The 1990s may be the decade in which suburban research fully comes into its own. Currently, there appears to be a Janus-like emphasis of both looking back to a fuller historical understanding of early suburbanization, and looking toward the future by examining the impact of the relocation of business offices as well as commerce from the central core to the emerging edge metropolises. It is increasingly being recognized that the outer cities are not an aberration from, or extension of, the old core-periphery model. Rather, outer cities represent a new organizational model. The increasing role of minorities in suburbs also is beginning to receive major attention. It is now apparent that for North America, the twenty-first century will be suburban dominated. This represents a major departure from how we have for centuries viewed our urban places.

IDEOLOGY AND IMAGERY

Overlapping but somewhat separate from the question of suburban life-styles is that of a unique suburban ideology. By ideology we mean the set of beliefs that provides a symbolic rendering of social reality. Community ideologies not only provide shared views of the world as it is perceived to be, they also provide a community moral landscape of what is identified as the "good life." In the case of suburbs, the mass postwar migration was for many the pursuit of the "American Dream." This was the belief that there was something about living in lower-density, single-family homes outside the city that produced new forms of community. This is what was discussed earlier as the "myth of suburbia."

Here, when we discuss ideology, as was the case with life-styles, the focus is on the ideology of upper-middle and middle-class residential suburbs. We definitely are not speaking of older industrial suburbs such as Cudahy, Wisconsin; Calumet City, Illinois; or Hamtramck, Michigan. In fact, our image of what a suburb looks like, who lives there, and how they view themselves doesn't at all fit these old, working-class, industrial communities.

Urban Ambivalence

Americans continue to have an ideology that is largely ambivalent about, if not antagonistic to, great cities. There is nothing particularly recent about this ambivalence. Throughout the nineteenth and most of the twentieth century, Americans have been pouring into the cities while idealizing the country. The writings of Thomas Jefferson are typically American in equating the city with the evils and corruption of the old order while having the yeoman farmer typify wholesome virtue. As expressed by Jefferson in a letter to his friend and neighbor James Madison:

> I think our governments will remain virtuous for many centuries as long as they are chiefly agricultural; and this will be as long as there shall be vacant land in any part of America. When they get piled upon one another in large cities, as in Europe, they will become corrupt as in Europe (quoted in Charles N. Glabb and A. Theodore Brown, *A History of Urban America*, Macmillan, New York, 1967, p. 55).

The image of the Jeffersonian self-sufficient yeoman working the earth as the real genuine American as opposed to someone associated with the pomp, artifice, and degeneracy of the city still resonates today. The anti-Washington ideology of recent political campaigns certainly is, in some respects, a lineal descendant of Jefferson's views as to the corrupting effects of urban life. American ideology for two hundred years has viewed individualism and self-reliance as more compatible with rural than urban habitats. The frontiersman clearing the wilderness or the cowboy riding the range have been glorified into American myths. Immigrant factory workers or poor women garment workers slaving in sweatshops are somehow less laudable. In practice, we behave as if we consider the history of our urban ancestors as somewhat discreditable and, thus, best forgotten. Henry David Thoreau, sitting in rural solitude at eventide at Walden Pond, is ideologically acceptable. Thoreau sitting on his front stoop in Boston during the evening rush hour creates a less acceptable image.

Surveys clearly demonstrate the abiding strength of antiurban images and ideologies in American life. According to polls some 43 percent of Boston residents, 48 percent of those living in Los Angeles, and a full 60 percent of those living in New York City say they would leave the city if they could (Schneider, 1992, p. 33). The extent of suburban disconnection from central cities was brought home by a *New York Times* poll done back in 1978 that showed that among New York's suburbanites over half (53 percent) visited the city for nonbusiness purposes fewer than five times a year; a quarter of the suburbanites totally avoided the city, and three-quarters felt their lives unaffected by what occurred in the city. However, most disconcerting to those believing the Big Apple is the essential center of the universe was that over half (54 percent) the New York suburbanites felt they didn't even belong to the New York area. They did not want to be thought of as New Yorkers. Ideologically, they had disassociated themselves from the city.

At the same time we denigrate urban living, we idealize rural life. The mental construct of "rural" living continues to enjoy an existence that is antithetical to reality. This can be clearly seen when Americans are polled on the basic question of where they *desire* to live. The *reality* is that America counts over half its population living in metropolitan areas of a million or more, while less than two percent of the population still reside on farms. Americans, nonetheless, show a considerable gap between where they say they want to live and where they actually live. Put in simplest terms, Americans live in cities and metropolitan suburbs, but they *say* they prefer farms and small towns. Three-quarters (77 percent) of Americans live in metropolitan areas of over 100,000 persons, but slightly less than a quarter (23 percent) say they want to live in metropolitan areas that large. Polls over the years have continued to demonstrate the lure of rural and smaller places. Today only 2 percent of the population still live on farms, but 17 percent of the population express the wish to live on a farm, and an additional 8 percent would like to live in a rural area but not on a farm (Gallup Poll, *Los Angeles Times*, March 24, 1985). Practice goes one way, ideology the other.

Rural images and supposed rural values continue to hold popular appeal (often while simultaneously being judged to be dull and confining). It seems to make no difference that our ideas of what constitutes rural life and the nature of rural values come to us largely from the urban-based mass media. For most of us, our image of small-town life comes to us from television productions written in New York or Los Angeles and produced in Hollywood. Commercials also play to our yearning for open spaces and honest relationships. Advertisements for everything from cereal to cars rely heavily on a Norman Rockwell nostalgia filled with friendly "down-home" folks. The manipulative use of old cars, farmhouses, and porch swings fills out the essentially bogus images of rural life.

How much of this glorification of rural and small-town life is nostalgia for a world that is now gone, and that most Americans alive today never knew, is difficult to say. There is also considerable expressed support for small-town living. Nonetheless, it is clear that among those saying they want to move out to rural areas, there is no real desire to isolate themselves from urban advantages. Research continues to indicate that the bulk of those seeking to live in smaller places still wish to live within 30 miles of a big city (Glen V. Fuguitt and David L. Brown, "Residential Preferences and Population Redistribution: 1972–1988," *Demography*, Vol. 27, Nov. 1990, pp. 589–600).

Suburban Middle Ground

The suburban ideology fits somewhat uncomfortably into the urban-rural dichotomy. Suburbs are neither one nor the other. Proponents of suburban living historically have resolved this by emphasizing how suburbs ideally combine the best features of urban and rural living. Opponents stress that they contain the worst of both worlds. The argument that suburbs have the best of both is not new. An 1873 promotional tract pushing development of the North Shore of Chicago proclaims, "The controversy which is sometimes brought, as to which offers the greater advantage, the country or the city, finds a happy answer in the suburban ideal which says both—the combination of the two—the city brought to the country. This is a practical and valuable reply. The city has its advantages and conveniences, the country its charm and health; the union of the two (a modern result of the railway), gives to man all he could ask in this respect" (*North Chicago: Its Advantages, Resources, and Probably Future*, Chicago, 1873, p. 8). As the earlier section on romantic suburbs indicates, the suburb was to allow the nineteenth-century city man of business to have it both ways. He would make his fortune during the day in the dynamic and vital industrial city and then retire by commuter railroad to the health and domestic tranquility of the picturesque suburb.

Although homes in turn-of-the-century streetcar suburbs were far less grand and often occupied minimal size lots, the imagery of suburbs being at least surrounded by country persisted. Sometimes the open spaces lasted only until all the planned housing was constructed. Automobile suburbs built prior to the second World War, if anything, accentuated and sharpened the image of suburbs as being distinct from the city. Real estate developers and realtors found it was good for business to foster the image of both spatial and social distance from the central city.

The mass suburbanization during the postwar years may have changed the reality, not the ideology, of suburban exclusivity. Builders and developers continued to advertise based upon the image of suburbia as an exclusive enclave where one's fellow suburbanites would all be upwardly mobile and community-involved.

Advertisements spoke less about square footage than about "moving up" and the "quality of life." Nonetheless, the reality was that suburbia was now open to virtually all. Exclusivity had come down to the basics of being employed and being white.

Some of the postwar criticisms by cultural elites of the new suburbs were, in fact, a recognition of this change. Literary and cultural criticisms of standardized subdivision housing as an aesthetic wasteland, and the attacks on the middle-brow values of those inhabiting such housing, were in part an elitist response to rapid social change. This "there goes the neighborhood" response, combined with a glorification of the past, was clearly evident in the comments of influential intellectuals such as Lewis Mumford. One can feel the disdain when he describes postwar suburbia as "a multitude of uniform, unidentifiable houses, lined up inflexibly, at uniform distances, on uniform roads, in a treeless communal waste inhabited by people of the same class, the same income, the same age group . . . conforming in every outward and inward respect to a common mold. . . " (Mumford, 1961, p. 486). To many of the urban critics of the 1950s and 1960s, the major crime of the new suburbs was that they were common. Unlike the affluent and exclusive suburbs of earlier decades, the new suburbs, and suburbanites, were seen as lacking the true urbanite's sense of good taste. Underlying the criticisms is the assumption that the new suburbanites went to the wrong schools, read the wrong books, and even bought the wrong furniture. It was as if former workers and service help had aspired to rise above their true station in life.

Differences

Overall, both city dwellers and suburbanites tend to overemphasize the differences between them. Actually, when one controls for income and other social-status variables, there is little difference between the city and country cousins. There is little that makes suburbanites stand out from other similar-status persons. As stated by Herbert Gans in his classic study of Levittown:

> When one looks at similar populations in city and suburb, their ways of life are remarkably alike . . . The crucial difference between cities and suburbs, then, is that they are often home for different kinds of people. If one is to understand their behavior, these differences are much more important than whether they reside inside or outside the city limits . . . If populations and residential areas were described by age and class characteristics, and by racial, ethnic, and religious ones, our understanding of human settlements would be much improved (Gans, 1967, pp. 288–289).

The truth is that those living in the suburbs are not all that different from city dwellers with similar backgrounds. In many respects suburbs have been maligned by being portrayed as a monochromatic landscape of little boxes holding look-alike middle-class families. Suburbs now house half the American population, and this population is remarkably complex in terms of age, family status, income, ethnicity, and race. Individual suburbs, as is true with urban neighborhoods, are often homogeneous, but suburbia as a whole is diverse. There is a mosaic of suburbs: upper-income, lower-working class, industrial, Hispanic, Black, Jewish, Republican, and mixed. In discussing suburbs and suburbanites, it is important to remember their complexity as well as their commonalities.

Not everyone would agree with the portrait of suburbs presented in the above paragraphs. A more negative view of suburban life, and especially suburban family life, is presented by Baumgartner in her *The Moral Order of a Suburb* (M. P. Baumgartner, *The Moral Order of a Suburb*, Oxford University Press, New York, 1988). In a social-anthropological examination of an upper-middle-class commuter suburb of 16,000 outside New York, she describes a community that appears to fit Riesman's, and others', 1950s criticisms of suburbia. Baumgartner argues that the pattern she found in the community can be generalized to suburbia elsewhere (or at least upper-middle-class suburbia). She describes suburbia as a place of a "culture of weak ties" and "moral minimalism." The surface tranquility of suburban life covers an unwillingness to address real conflicts and tensions. Weak bonding to family and neighbors leads not to discussing and resolving conflicts, but to conflict avoidance and suppression as major characteristics of suburbia. As put by Guest in his review of the work, "Since ties are weak and unimportant, suburbanites have allegedly little reason to resolve differences. Thus, almost paradoxically, the apparent harmony of suburbia stems from a lack of communal feeling (Avery M. Guest, review of *The Moral Order of a Suburb*, *Contemporary Sociology*, Vol. 18, No. 5, 1989, p. 739).

To summarize, suburbia at the end of the twentieth century is too diverse to be simply and uniformly categorized. In general, one can say that suburbs have characteristics that tend to fall between those of cities and those of small towns. When one compares suburbs with small towns, suburbs have less neighboring, less community participation, and less localism (Popenoe in Huttman and van Vliet, 1988, p. 398). Suburbs also are more private and anonymous, possibly because they are not "whole" communities but only the residential piece. They lack the overlapping social networks found in small towns where people work and shop as well as live together. In most suburbs residents must commute outside the proximate community for work or shopping. Suburbs, while having more neighboring than cities, have less than small towns. Suburbs similarly lack the strong informal social-control mechanisms of small towns, which leads to suburbs having greater freedom, more anonymity, and more delinquency and crime than small towns. Socially as well as physically, suburbs are a middle landscape.

Imagery

City and country dwellers usually have sharp images of their environments, but suburbanites express some difficulty when asked to describe the communities in which they live. They tend to paint an image of suburbia as a middle landscape. Suburbanites delight in not being part of the city, but they know they are not country or small town either. David Hummon, in his study of the extent of community ideology and identity, says there are three sets of imagery salient to the suburban ideology that are frequently volunteered by suburbanites (David M. Hummon, *Commonplaces: Community Ideology and Identity in American Society*, SUNY Press, Albany, N.Y., 1990, p. 100). First, suburbanites describe suburbs as "clean, quiet, and natural places." Residents view suburbs as small and quieter places with an easygoing ambience. They lack the frenetic pace, and perhaps also the excitement, of the city. On the other side, the suburbs may not be country, but they have openness and provide access to natural things such as birds and trees.

Second, the suburbs are seen as a place of "domesticity." Suburbanites view themselves as interested in home, family life, and children. Suburbs are seen in the suburban ideology as "the best of both worlds." This is particularly true when the focus is on raising children. Children are believed to receive a good education in an environment where they have both freedom and security. Third, suburbs are viewed as being much different from cities insofar as suburbs are "safe." The safety of the suburb, in turn, is seen as making other values, such as sociability, family, and good rearing of children, possible. To the extent that crime has moved to the suburbs, it is seen as endangering other values.

The suburban ideology of the middle landscape as described above is somewhat vague and hazy. It lacks the sharpness with which central-city or country residents define their areas. Perhaps this hazy image is because suburbs are often defined by being contrasted with the clearer vision of the city or country. Hummon suggests there is an additional reason for the lack of a compelling image. Based on his interviewing in

Northern California, he states that only one of three suburban residents even designates his or her area as a suburb (Hummon, 1990, p. 100). In addition to those suburbanists who express a suburban ideology, Hummon suggests there also are "suburban villagers" and "suburban urbanists" (Hummon, 1990, p. 112). The first are those residents who think of their community as being a small town rather than a suburb. They identify suburbs, and supposed suburban problems, exclusively with suburban tract-housing developments. Subdivisions, thus, are suburbs, but older and more diverse housing areas are thought of as small-townish. By contrast, the suburban urbanists, including those who have previously lived in the city, are in some respects reluctant suburbanites. They explain their suburban residence in terms of the suburbs being more distant from cultural and other activities, but being a more attractive place to raise children. They believe the suburbs are a good place to live, but their enthusiasm is somewhat muted.

Hummon suggests there is one image of suburban life that is missing from suburban dwellers' own descriptions of the suburban landscape. The missing element is any discussion of race or housing segregation. There are several possible reasons for this absence. It might be because suburbanites do not consider housing segregation as uniquely suburban. They might think more in terms of specific neighborhoods rather than entire communities. For some others the urban versus suburban differences in racial composition may not be important. However, for others the avoidance of the topic may simply reflect that it is not considered socially acceptable to speak favorably of housing segregation. In this view the suburban ideology of clean, peaceful places of good housing and domesticity provides an acceptable vocabulary of motives to explain moving to the suburbs (Hummon, 1990, pp. 107–108). Finally, race may not be spoken of because it simply is not an issue in racially homogeneous communities. Whatever the reason, race is rarely mentioned.

Contemporary Changes

The "myth of suburbia," which saw the suburban future as one of togetherness and homogeneity, is now a relic of history. It has now been supplanted by a new popular myth, which sees suburbia not as a place of compulsive group conformity, but rather as one of competitive self-advancement and self-fulfillment. Supposedly, the community counts for less and status and success for more. According to an examination of Naperville, Illinois, as the "new suburbia," "the suburbs and, by extension, middle-class Americans have gone from glorifying group bonding to glorifying individual happiness and achievement"

(Nicholas Lemann, "Stressed Out in the Suburbs," *The Atlantic*, November 1989, p. 46). "Self-actualization," "self-fulfillment," and "self-expression" have become the bywords of contemporary suburbia. The argument goes that while suburbanites have become more prosperous, they have also become more anxious about their standard of living. This greater affluence is largely due to women working. While the suburban women of the 1950s were overwhelmingly homemakers, women today also work full time outside the home. In fact, the younger the couple, the greater the likelihood of the wife working. The result is that the couple has more money but also more stress. There is simply not enough free time. Because people are busier, there is less time for the socializing that was so often seen as characterizing the suburbs of the 1950s. There is now less social cohesion and sense of common community, but also less conformity—that is, if one accepts that living a life-style where everyone is concerned about self-advancement isn't conformity.

An interesting point about the above picture of suburbia as the home of self-oriented and self-concerned status seekers is that it is largely identical to the stereotype of the 1980s self-centered thirty-something baby boomers. Yuppie baby boomers were characterized as focusing on self and success rather than on family and community. Popular wisdom has it that the decade of the 1990s is reflecting a return to more traditional and communal values. This may, in part, reflect tougher economic times as well as simply the aging of the baby boomers. It will be interesting to see if a new generation of examinations of suburbia will again report residents heavily involved in community and socialization. Or has the general movement of women into the work force, as opposed to the 1950s, changed the equation? Do women who are still responsible for much of home and family work have the time for social activities such as preparing dinner parties? Does the time for casual coffee klatching still exist?

CHAPTER 7

Contemporary Suburban Variation

TYPES OF SUBURBS

We all at times fall into the habit of speaking of suburbia as if it is a relatively homogeneous area. That is, a place of free-standing single family homes with lawns where everyone is white, middle-class, and has children. We of course know better; we are aware that there are rich suburbs and poor suburbs, estate suburbs and garden apartment suburbs, residential suburbs and industrial park suburbs. Still we keep the standard image as a convenient shorthand and tend to forget that some suburbs vary widely from the norm. There is a remarkable range of types of suburbs. In terms of income, suburbs range from the very rich, such as Kenilworth, Illinois, outside Chicago, where the 1990 per capita income (not family income, but per person income) was $62,000, and Bloomfield, Michigan, outside Detroit, where it was $60,000, to the poorest of suburbs, such as Ford Heights, Illinois, outside Chicago, where the per capita income was $4,900, or Cudahy, California, outside Los Angeles, where it was $5,200.

In addition to the above income category, we can differentiate suburbs in a number of fashions. Suburbs can, in addition to socioeconomic status of income, education, and occupation, be differentiated by age, ethnicity, race, and function. In categorizing suburbs we can contrast older versus newer, growing versus stagnant, ethnic versus WASP, and incorporated versus unincorporated. The fact is, suburban settlements are so diverse that no single typology adequately encompasses all suburban types. One of the most used postwar typologies is between those suburbs that essentially serve as bedroom communities (residential suburbs) and those that have primarily a manufacturing, trade, or business function (employment suburbs). Mixed-usage suburbs, combining the characteristics of the other two, can also be delineated. In Leo Schnore's path-breaking research during the 1960s, he demonstrated that there were clear differences among these three categories of suburbs in terms of age of residents, ethnic composition, fertility rates, population growth, socioeconomic status, and housing characteristics (Leo F. Schnore, "The Social and Economic Characteristics of American Suburbs," *Sociological Quarterly*, Vol. 4, 1963, pp. 122–134). Using a sample of some seventy-four suburbs surrounding New York and a second sample of three hundred suburbs found within the nation's largest urbanized areas, he empirically demonstrated systematic differences in social and economic characteristics. Employment suburbs contained higher proportions of both foreign-born and nonwhite inhabitants than did residential suburbs, with mixed suburbs in the middle. Socioeconomic status, as measured by percentage having completed high school, percentage in white-collar occupations, and median income level, was highest in the residential suburbs. The mixed suburb was in the middle, and the employment suburbs were lowest. Residential suburbs as a group also had faster growth rates than employment suburbs.

Other systems of categories have also been developed. Within the general category of residential suburbs, the pollster Louis Harris a number of years ago classified suburbs in four categories on the basis of income level and the rate of growth (Louis Harris, *Time*, March 15, 1971, p. 15). The categories were:

First, *affluent bedroom:* Affluent bedroom communities would include places such as New Canaan, Connecticut; Leawood, Kansas; and Irving, California. They come closest to the traditional stereotype of a suburb. Such places rank at the top in terms of resident income levels, degree of home ownership, and proportion of residents employed as professionals and managers.

Second, *affluent settled:* Affluent settled communities such as Oak Park, Illinois; Cherry Hill, New Jersey; and Fairfield, Connecticut are past their period of growth and may even be losing population. Since their land is developed, they are beyond the building-boom stage, and some may have considerable older housing. The housing stock is in good repair, and the neighborhoods are comfortable. Affluent settled communities tend to have a wider range of economic activities and to be more self-sufficient and less purely residential than affluent bedroom suburbs.

Third, *low-income growing:* Low-income, growing suburbs are often the home of upwardly mobile white-collar and blue-collar workers. These communities, such as El Monte, California; Sylvania, Ohio; and Millerica, Massachusetts are much less likely to fit the stereotype of suburbia.

Fourth, *low-income stagnant:* Low-income stagnant suburbs are places that are suburbs by definition but do not at all fit the suburban stereotype. Places such as East Orange, New Jersey; McKeesport, Pennsylvania; and Joliet, Illinois are essentially satellite cities rather than suburbs, and they have the full range of economic activities associated with a city. They also have the full range of problems, such as crime and drugs, associated with central cities.

Today we would probably make some additions to the above list, such as the mixed, nonresidential and residential outer-city suburbs that combine office parks, shopping malls, and residential neighborhoods. But whatever typology or categories are used, the important thing to note is that there are predictable patterns of variations. Suburban growth is not as random or chaotic as it is often portrayed. Persistent and systematic differences exist. Suburban growth, in spite of its bad press, is not haphazard.

Suburban Status Persistence and Change

We take it for granted that city neighborhoods will change in socioeconomic status over time. One-time prosperous neighborhoods are expected to decline and possibly be rebuilt or gentrified. For example, a neighborhood may have been built as upper-middle class at the turn of the century, drifted down to middle class by the 1930s, become a rooming-house area by the 1950s, and been gentrified in the 1980s. This model of local community status change is basically a life-cycle model and is consistent with the earlier Burgess concentric zonal theory, which posited neighborhood change due to competition for land and the outgoing movement of affluent populations (Ernest Burgess, "The Growth of the City," in Robert Park, Ernest Burgess, and Roderick McKenzie, eds., *The City*, University of Chicago Press, Chicago, 1925, pp. 47–62).

However, when our focus shifts to suburbs, the assumption of status change is supplanted by the assumption of status consistency. Suburbs are seen as changing less than cities. There is a greater tendency to view suburban areas as locked in time. It is as if suburbs are not subject to the same laws of aging and change. For example, Chevy Chase, outside of Washington, and Berwyn, west of Chicago, remain, respectively, upper-middle-class and ethnic-working-class just as they were seventy-five years ago. This status-persistence model suggests that early in a suburb's history, its socioeconomic status tends to fix its position in the metropolitan area's ecological structure.

Initial research done on suburban status persistence suggests that this assumption of less economic and social change over time in suburbs has a base in reality. Research done by Reynolds Farley and replicated by Avery Guest suggests that there is suburban persistence, with suburbs holding their position over time (Reynolds Farley, "Suburban Persistence," *American Sociological Review,* Vol. 29, 1964, pp. 38–47; and Avery M. Guest, "Suburban Social Status: Persistence or Evolution," *American Sociological Review,* Vol. 43, 1978, pp. 251–264). Farley examined 137 suburbs of twenty-four cities and found that at least for the older established suburbs there was considerable consistency. In fact, one could accurately predict the educational level of a suburb by looking at the school attendance records of the high-school-age population forty years earlier. Guest further found that in the postwar period, growth of high-status populations enhanced rather than changed the suburb's high position. Residents used their resources to enhance the status of the suburb through advantages such as superior schools and facilities, and thus they protected their own investment.

This view of persistence has been challenged by Harvey Cholden, who suggests that suburbs, like city neighborhoods, have a life cycle of generally moving down over time (Harvey Cholden, Claudine Hanson, and Robert Bohrer, "Suburban Status Instability," *American Sociological Review,* Vol. 45, 1980, pp. 972–983). However, this decline in status may have been a function of rapid suburban growth in the period for which the study was done. Using a sample that included all suburbs in the United States having a population of more than 10,000, John Stahura found that as suburban growth rates slowed in the 1970s, there was a tendency toward crystallization of the differences between suburbs (John M. Stahura, "Suburban Socioeconomic Status Change: A Comparison of Models, 1950–1980," *American Sociological Review,* Vol. 52, 1987, pp. 268–277). Thus, unless circumstances dramatically change through factors such as unexpected rapid growth or government policies, it does not appear that there will be major changes in the status-ranking of suburbs.

Affluent suburbs are particularly likely to hold their status over time. One way they are able to maintain their position is by using their considerable resources to control who can move into the suburb (John

R. Logan, "Growth, Politics, and the Stratification of Places," *American Journal of Sociology*, Vol. 84, 1978, pp. 404–415). This can be done through high tax rates or by passing zoning regulations that mandate certain size homes and/or large lot sizes. Such practices have the effect of excluding the nonwealthy. Upper-income suburbs, thus, use their political knowledge and power to protect and enhance the value of their investment.

This political-power model is usually associated with scholars taking a conflict perspective, while the status-persistence model is usually associated with those holding an ecological model. However, in this instance both approaches seem to reinforce rather than contradict each other. Older and more affluent suburbs have had the greatest success in maintaining their favored position. There also appears to be regional variation. Specifically, in the north and midwest, involuntary annexation of suburbs had ceased by the beginning of the twentieth century, while in some of the south, and especially in Texas, annexation is still possible. Thus, one would expect to find the greatest number of affluent suburbs practicing exclusionary zoning in the north and midwest.

Exclusionary zoning is not a recent development. Zoning has been used by suburbs since the 1920s as a means of keeping out undesirable activities, housing, and people. An excellent example of a contemporary system is affluent Hoffman Estates, northwest of Chicago. To upgrade its image, it hired an additional fifteen building inspectors to clamp down on owners of lowrent apartments ("A Tale of Two Suburbs," *U.S. News and World Report*, November 9, 1992, p. 34). A strict adherence to the letter of the housing code makes it difficult to make a profit renting to lower-income populations. This was the intent. However, even more important than keeping undesirables out is attracting new high-status residents. Here a self-fulfilling prophesy seems to occur for affluent suburbs. A suburb having an established reputation as a high-status area employs its social prestige to attract new high-status residents. Realtors also play a major part by steering high-income newcomers toward what are perceived as being the more prestigious areas. Reputation creates a reality, which in turn reinforces reputation. In this fashion a suburb such as Lake Forest on Chicago's North Shore has maintained its upper-status position for well over a century.

Location, Age, and Ethnicity

When Burgess posited his concentric zonal pattern of metropolitan growth, he suggested that socioeconomic status was directly related to distance from the center of the city. Centrally located space goes to those functions that can use space intensively and are willing to pay the costs (William Alonso, "A Theory of Urban Land Market," in Larry Bourne, ed., *Internal Structure of the City: Readings in Space and the Environment*, Oxford University Press, New York, 1971, pp. 154–159). Costs include not only purchase price, but also taxes and factors such as congestion, pollution, noise, and so forth. As a consequence, central land was most expensive and peripheral space less so. This means that those affluent families living further out can afford more space. Thus, there is a tendency for an inverse relationship between the value of land and the status of those who occupy it.

In the inner ring adjacent to the city, the oldest suburbs often had the bulk of their housing completed prior to World War II. Many of these inner-ring suburbs are composed of substantial homes built originally for upper- and upper-middle-class occupancy. Some of these older suburbs still maintain their elite status. Outer-ring suburbs have almost all been built in the postwar era of mass suburbanization, and they differ substantially in socioeconomic status. They tend to vary based on type of housing, characteristics of the residents, and direction from the city.

Within the metropolitan area different ethnic, religious, and racial groups often suburbanized in specific directions. In Atlanta, for instance, blacks went south and whites went north. Ethnic groups also followed specific patterns. In Chicago over the past century, Polish-heritage populations have moved from the near-north side to the northwest side and into northwest suburbs such as Niles. The Jewish housing pattern was roughly similar, with upper-middle-class Jews moving into northwest suburbs such as Skokie and wealthy Jews moving north to Glencoe and Highland Park. Italian-heritage populations, on the other hand, moved progressively west, and in time into western suburbs such as Melrose Park. WASPs, by contrast, moved up the North Shore to Evanston, Wilmette, and Winnetka. Thus, the pattern of ethnic inner-city neighborhoods was in modified form carried to the suburbs.

OTHER TYPES OF SUBURBS

Minority suburbs are discussed in detail in Chapter 8, Minorities in Suburbia, and it would be redundant to spend more paragraphs on middle-class suburbs, since much of this book revolves around describing that model. There are, though, a few types of residential suburbs that deserve special notation. A number of these variations follow.

The above large home is located in Radnor Township outside of Philadelphia. During the last century the Philadelphia Main Line became synonymous for an affluent upper-class suburban life-style. Advertisments for contemporary suburban subdevelopements often try to suggest they have a similar exclusivity.

High-Income Suburbs

High-income suburbs are not new to the urban scene. As noted in the earlier section on romantic suburbs, the nineteenth century saw many examples of exclusive suburbs designed as refuges for the wealthy. Then as now upper-status suburbs usually feature large, imposing homes built on extensive properties that are screened off from casual external observation by shrubbery and trees. Generally, such suburbs have been located at the outer suburban edges, but there are some clear exceptions, such as centrally located Grosse Pointe, bordered by Detroit, and Beverly Hills, surrounded by Los Angeles. Beverly Hills is now undergoing a building boom which, since the community has no open land, means that older mansions are being torn down so newer mansions can be constructed on the same sites.

However, what gives most upper-status suburbs their character is not so much their housing style as the style of life and patterns of social interaction among the residents. Demographically, high-income suburbs tend to have an older median age population and a low proportion of women employed in the labor force. Population turnover, except by death, is low. Particularly in the east and midwest, the older elite suburbs were, and in many cases still are, socially closed WASP communities. Social life in earlier decades traditionally centered heavily around a few mainline churches. In more recent decades it has been more likely to focus on membership in an exclusive country club.

Older elite suburbs have never been believers in multiculturalism. Wealth is required for entry, but *nouveau riche* outsiders are not considered suitable for membership either in the clubs or the community. Racial minorities have been welcome only as servants. Those whites having southern or eastern European ethnic heritage are also automatically disqualified for residency. So have been Jews and Catholics. When the Kennedy family bought a large home in Hyannis Port, Massachusetts, several neighbors moved out on the grounds that the community was surely going downhill if Catholics were allowed to move in. Opposition remained even after John Kennedy became President of the United States. Similarly, the richest suburb in the country, Kenilworth, on Chicago's North Shore, had, until fairly recently, a reputation for discouraging Catholics or Jews as residents. Homes simply would not be sold to those who did not have the proper Anglo-Saxon Protestant heritage. Those Catholics and Jew who were excluded responded by founding their own exclusive suburbs and country clubs. For example, Jewish families who were not welcome in other North Shore suburbs responded by developing Glencoe and Highland Park as wealthy Jewish suburbs.

In newer upper-income growth suburbs, such as South Barrington, northwest of Chicago, ethnicity and religion tend to have lesser relevance so long as one has sufficient cash. Similarly, in the rich suburbs of Texas and southern California, background is even less important. One's heritage is secondary to one's bank balance. For instance, elsewhere in the world Jews and Arabs may have been in deadly conflict, but in Beverly Hills wealthy Arabs and wealthy Jews lived as neighbors. Another change is that wealthy suburbs are no longer automatically communities of single-family homes. Luxury high-rise condominiums are increasingly found in newer suburbs for the well-to-do.

A Note of Caution

As a final note, there is a tendency to equate the high costs of housing in an area with the affluence of the residents. This is generally the case, but it can be misleading insofar as it might suggest that counties with high housing costs, such as those in southern California, necessarily also have the highest percentages of affluent householders. In fact the 1990 census indicates that the counties having the most affluent householders are still concentrated on the east coast. Of the twenty countries having the greatest proportion of population with households earning $100,000 or more in 1989, fully half were found in the suburban ring of the New York consolidated metropolitan area (Judith

Residences are now marketed as recreational as well as residential environments. Sun Village in Albuquerque, New Mexico, is typical of contemporary suburban developments where major emphasis is placed upon the package of external amenities such as swimming pools and sports facilities.

Waldrop and Linda Jacobsen, "Affluent Americans," *American Demographics,* December 1992, p. 38). Leading the list is Westchester County, New York, with 18 percent of its households having incomes of $100,000 or more. Just behind are Morris, New Jersey; Fairfield, Connecticut; and Nassau, New York. Another three counties, Montgomery, Maryland; Fairfax, Virginia; and Howard, Maryland are in the Washington, D.C.-Baltimore suburban ring. Only six counties among the top twenty are west of the Mississippi. Marin and San Mateo counties in the San Francisco metropolitan area were numbers 5 and 16, respectively. Santa Clara County (San Jose) was number 19, and Orange County, in southern California, just made the list as number 20.

Working-Class Suburbs

Prior to the mass suburbanization following the second World War, working-class suburbs were almost certain to be older industrial or factory suburbs. An example would be Cudahy, south of Milwaukee, which was established when the Milwaukee city government refused to allow Patrick Cudahy to build a stockyard and slaughterhouse within the city. As a consequence, the meat packer established a new suburb outside the city limits, which he named after himself. Another example would be the working-class suburb of Cicero, west of Chicago. Cicero achieved national notoriety during the

Contemporary suburbia has an all but universal appearance. These suburban single family homes are located on the outskirts of the Denver metro area. However, take away the mountain foothills in the background, and the homes could be anywhere in the United States.

1920s as the headquarters of Al Capone's operations when a short-lived reform administration in Chicago temporarily forced the organization to move to the suburbs. Most prewar working-class suburbs, however, were simply factory towns. They were in no way distinctive. Plain but generally well-kept houses with small yards were the norm.

Following World War II the GI Bill allowed blue-collar workers as well as the traditional middle class to successfully apply for long-term mortgages. Growing prosperity also made it possible for working-class workers to purchase a family automobile. At the same time new interstate and other road networks made new suburban locations a reasonable alternative for aging inner-city factories. Industries could relocate beyond streetcar lines without fearing they would be unable to recruit a work force. As a result, factories and labor forces decentralized. It is sometimes forgotten that the new postwar working-class suburbanites that followed the factories to the suburbs were not fleeing decaying city neighborhoods. More often than not, they were somewhat reluctantly leaving tight ethnic neighborhoods with high levels of social interaction.

As discussed on page 87 under the myth of suburbia, Bennett Berger studied the life-style of some one hundred blue-collar Ford assembly workers and their families who were forced to move from Richmond, California, to the suburb of Milpitas, California, in order to work at the new automobile plant (Bennett M. Berger, *Working Class Suburbs*, University of California Press, Berkeley, 1960). What Berger found was that suburbanization had little or no effect on the workers' style of life. They didn't see the move in terms of social mobility; they had no great hopes of getting ahead in their jobs. They had no illusions of wealth; their wage level was dependent on the union contract. As a consequence of becoming suburbanites, they didn't change their political affiliation (81 percent Democrat), go to church more, or join community organizations. They participated only minimally in formal groups. What they did do is continue their traditional working-class pattern of tight, informal socialization with long-term friends and neighbors. While they enjoyed the creature comforts of suburban living, they remained peer-group- and ethnic-group-centered. In brief, they lived life patterns quite similar to those workers living in blue-collar central-city neighborhoods. Their new suburban homes were not seen as way stations on the road to social mobility, but rather as permanent places of residence.

Now many of these postwar blue-collar suburbs are experiencing the same downward economic pressures suffered by central cities. Declines in nearby heavy-industry and manufacturing jobs mean that those living in older inner-ring suburbs have long commutes to service jobs in outlying edge suburbs. Ironically, the automobile factory that triggered the move Berger described was itself closed for being technologically out-of-date. Commercial tax bases are also eroding in working-class suburbs. Meanwhile, new outlying areas boom. Thus, class divisions between suburbs are becoming sharper rather than blurring. Additionally, older working-class suburbs, with their low-cost housing, have been most likely to attract minority families escaping the city. The deterioration of job prospects for blue-collar workers in a postindustrial economy suggests that such workers may now find themselves trapped in declining working-class suburbs. These suburbs lack the affluence of other suburbs, and even the basic amenities of the central city.

NEW DEFINITIONAL SYSTEMS

Since defining a modal suburbanite or a modal suburban life-style is becoming less and less possible, one way out of the difficulty is not to even try. Rather than seeking overall similarities, business-oriented researchers now more often focus on the differences that will aid politicians and marketers to fine-tune their advertising campaigns to meet specific needs and markets. A marketing research firm by the name of Claritas has developed a system that identifies every ZIP code area in the country into one of forty different types of communities on the basis of the dominant economic, family-life-cycle, and ethnic-racial characteristics of households and of the physical characteristics of the areas (Michael Weiss, *The Clustering of America*, Tilden Press, New York, 1988).

In effect, Claritas has tried to create ethnographic areas, what Chicago School sociologists of the 1920s referred to as "natural areas." They have done this using sophisticated statistical cluster-analysis techniques. This application of cluster analysis had resulted in a methodological advance toward explaining the relationship between physical space and social behavior. Claritas's areas have become a virtual Bible for market researchers, but thus far they have had less use by academics, who are concerned more with universality of standards and, thus, generally require somewhat more rigorous scientific standards than those required by business firms.

The strength of the system is that it provides fairly detailed information on areas as small as ZIP codes. The primary limitation is that some of this detail may be spurious. This is because postal ZIP codes are sometimes anything but homogeneous, and the cluster-analysis technique gives the average characteristics for the area. Therefore, if population or housing characteristics are diverse within the area, there is a serious risk of committing the "ecological fallacy" of attempting to predict the behavior of individuals from the characteristics of an area. The more homogeneous the ZIP code, the greater the validity of the coding. Of the forty life-style communities Claritas identifies, a dozen have a suburban location. Roughly going from upper income to lower, these areas and their characteristics are:

Blue-Blood Estates. The wealthiest neighborhoods of largely suburban homes

Furs and Station Wagons. Newer-money metropolitan bedroom suburbs

Pools and Patios. Older upper-middle-class suburban communities

Gray Power. Upper-middle-class retirement suburbs

New Beginnings. Outer-city or suburban areas of single complexes, garden apartments, and well-kept bungalows (single or childless)

Two More Rungs. Comfortable multiethnic suburbs

Blue-Chip Blues. More affluent blue-collar suburbs

Young Suburbia. Outlying child-rearing suburbs

Young Homesteaders. Exurban boomtown of younger mid-scale families

Levittown, U.S.A.. Aging postwar working-class tract suburbs

Rank and File. Older blue-collar industrial suburbs

Norma Rae-Ville. Older industrial suburbs and mill towns, primarily in the south

Not surprisingly, the highest-income suburban areas are all predominantly white. However, the community areas differ in terms of age, income, and life-style. The strength of the Claritas system is its explicit highlighting of community differences. Mass-mailing retailers can be expected to use increasingly refined versions of the above to target specific subpopulation markets. Obviously, contemporary suburbia, even in its residential manifestations, is far from one homogeneous area.

EXURBS AND RURAL SUBURBS

The term "exurb" refers to the type of upper-middle-class settlement that has taken place in outlying semirural suburbia—the area beyond the second ring of densely settled subdivisions. Fringe exurban areas have more widely separated homes, often with woods between, and the homes tend to be large and expensive. Sometimes exurbanites settle around old villages or small towns. Exurbanites, as a rule, are affluent, well-educated professionals. Sometimes these individuals work in fields such as communications, advertising, and publishing, which allow them to work at home and avoid daily commuting. The use of PCs with modems and fax machines means they can remain in touch through offices in their homes. If their base is New York, they may live in Fairfield County, Connecticut, or northern New Jersey; if the office is in Philadelphia, then Bucks County, Pennsylvania; and if in San Francisco, then Marin County, California.

Unfortunately, the study of exurbia that gave these areas its name, *The Exurbanites,* presents a rather shallow caricature of suburban lifestyle (A. C. Spectorsky, *The Exurbanites,* Berkeley, New York, 1957). Exurbanites were portrayed as hyperactive, upwardly mobile strivers who have left city streets for tri-level houses. The picture is of people desperately trying to find meaning in their lives by moving out of the city. Working in highly competitive industries where the standards for judging performance are subjective and fickle, they seek solace by escaping the city. Basically, exurbanites are displaced cosmopolites living in the twentieth-century version of what a century ago were called romantic suburbs. They are urbane seekers of the American Dream who seek to reside in rustic settings. They want to move out of the city but not away from its advantages and services. Living such a semi-country life puts a strain on the budget and creates pressure to have a standard of life one can't afford. According to the stereotype, it also puts considerable pressures on wives, who find themselves locked into a schedule of maintaining the house and providing shuttle service for children and commuting husbands while attempting to maintain their own careers and interests.

If the above sounds familiar, it may be because this general outline has served as the plot for dozens of novels, television soaps, and movies. The difficulty is that it is often taken as a scientific reflection of reality rather than inventive fiction. Solid research is scarce; but at least based on demographic characteristics, there does not seem to be support for the belief that exurbanites are significantly different from other same-status suburbanites. In fact, exurbs have a way of turning into reluctant suburbs as more and more people move into the same area, all seeking to escape the urban pace.

Even harder to pin down are those places beyond the exurbs that are *not* oriented toward a major city. While definitionally these areas may still be within a metropolitan area, the orientation of residents may be more rural than urban. Housing in these in-between areas that are not truly rural, but are probably never destined to become suburban, is sometimes of marginal quality. Some of those living in such "ruban" areas are barely getting by economically in spite of low housing costs and taxes. It is not uncommon for ruban residents to commute long distances to work at low-income jobs. They are anything but affluent suburban commuters.

Adding to the confusion over what is suburban are some outlying college towns that the census has defined as metropolitan but that are not urban in character. One of these is Centre County, Pennsylvania, which is the home of Pennsylvania State University. Because of its population, Centre County is a metropolitan area named State College, but it is clearly neither urban nor suburban. The county includes a widely dispersed and mixed population having a wide range of interests and occupations. There are 165 acres for every person in the metropolitan area (John Herbers, *The New Heartland: America's Flight Beyond the Suburbs and How It Is Changing Our Future*, Times Books, New York, 1986). The consequence is a metropolitan area that is known for its hiking trails, numerous lakes, trout streams, and mountains.

In practice, even residential suburbia, to say nothing of the outer cities to be discussed in Chapter 11, has become remarkably diverse. So diverse, in fact, that just calling an area "suburban" doesn't really tell us much anymore. As suburbia has come to house and employ the largest segment of the American population, the characteristics that define a "typical suburb" and "typical suburbanites" have become even more attenuated. The next chapter, on minorities in suburbia, indicates the distance that is often found between our perceptions and contemporary suburban reality.

CHAPTER 8

Minorities in Suburbia

NEW REALITIES

INVISIBLE SUBURBANITES

Minorities in many respects remain invisible persons when it comes to suburbs. In spite of considerable research over the past two decades on the suburbanization of minorities, the popular assumption remains that all suburbs are segregated, and that suburbanites, by definition, are pale-skinned. Minorities, and especially African Americans, are expected to be city dwellers. The common assumption seems to be that black suburbanites are exceptions to the urban norm and, in any case, few in number. The media, whether through news magazines or television, involuntarily contribute to this stereotype by almost invariably presenting blacks as living in the inner city. It is often forgotten how large and diverse is the African American population. As of 1990, African Americans totaled some 30 million people—almost exactly one-eighth of all Americans. The American black population is larger than the entire population of Canada. Of the 30 million blacks in the United States, the 1990 census indicates that 17 million live in central cities, almost 5 million live in rural areas, and over 8 million live in suburbs (U.S. Bureau of the Census, "The Black Population of the United States: March 1990 and 1989," *Current Population Reports,* P-20, No. 448, August 1991, Table 15, p. 66). This means that *one of every three* blacks living in a metropolitan area is a suburban resident. The 1990 census reported forty metropolitan areas where there were at least 50,000 black suburbanites. This is well beyond tokenism. African American suburbanization is substantial and widespread. Today, black suburbanism is a social reality; it is not simply a footnote to white suburbanization.

Amount of Black Suburbanization

That blacks are suburbanizing in increasing numbers is clear to anyone doing research on the topic. As noted at the beginning of this section, for every two central-city black residents, there now is one suburban resident. As a consequence, black suburbanization is a major contemporary population trend. By 1990, Washington, D.C., alone had 620,000 black suburbanites, while Atlanta had 463,000 and Los Angeles 401,000. These substantial figures indicate that those who still speak of "token suburban integration" have not kept up with the changes of recent decades. Between 1980 and 1990 Atlanta added a quarter of a million blacks to its suburbs. Washington, D.C., added almost as many, and Miami added 100,000 black suburbanites (William O'Hare and William Frey, "Booming, Suburban, and Black," *American Demographics*, September 1992, p. 33). Nor is this simply overflow from the central cities. In metropolitan areas such as Washington, the major growth of African American suburbanization has not been in the older inner suburbs but rather in the newer developments on the suburban periphery.

Between 1986 and 1990, some 73 percent of black population growth occurred in suburbs. It also needs noting that while the number and proportion of black suburbanites has been growing, the pattern is not entirely new. Over a decade ago the 1980 census indicated that as of that date, 23 percent of American blacks were already suburbanites (compared to 57 percent being city dwellers). By 1990, 27 percent of all African Americans were suburbanites (William P. O'Hare et al., "African Americans in the 1990s," *Population Bulletin*, Vol. 46, No. 1, 1991, p. 9). The paragraphs that follow will discuss the characteristics of this population, and whether these suburban blacks are rich or poor, live in married-couple or single-parent households, and whether or not they live in racially segregated areas.

Thus, the first step in any discussion of black suburbanization is simply to recognize the existence of millions of suburban African Americans. This is not as common as one might suppose. Even highly acclaimed historical works on suburbia, such as Kenneth Jackson's *Crabgrass Frontier*, largely ignore African Americans. It discusses blacks only by lamenting how racist patterns and practices have kept the suburbs white (see Kenneth T. Jackson, *Crabgrass Frontier*, Oxford University Press, New York, 1985, p. 287–290). Sociologists also have

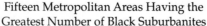

Fifteen Metropolitan Areas Having the
Greatest Number of Black Suburbanites

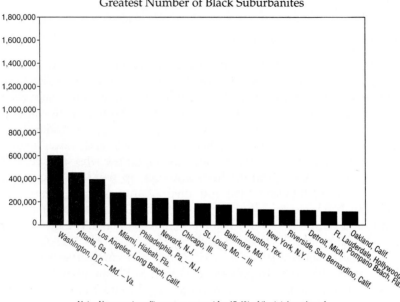

Note: Above metropolitan areas account for 45.4% of the total number of
suburban blacks in the United States. (Compiled from 1990 census data.)

often been slow to acknowledge change. For years there was a reluctance to acknowledge substantial black suburbanization and subsequently a reluctance to recognize that black suburbanization was more than the spillover of city-ghetto overflow into older inner-ring suburbs. As a consequence, the changes of recent decades, and the extent of black suburbanism, is sometimes underplayed. Part of the difficulty comes from using old data from earlier decades. Until the 1990 census data were released, the census data used for most studies of black suburbanization came from the 1980 or earlier censuses, and thus, reflected patterns based on data coming from the 1970s or even earlier decades. Thus, findings sometimes were both accurate and out-of-date, since in suburbanization, as other areas, a great deal has happened since Richard Nixon was president.

In general, black population growth is occurring where white growth is occurring. Regionally, this means the fastest growing black suburbs are in the sunbelt. The four most populous states for blacks (California, New York, Texas, and Florida) are the same as the top states for whites. The fastest growing suburbs for blacks during the last decade were in California's Riverside-San Bernardino and San Diego metropolitan areas, which saw their black populations double. Houston and Dallas also saw their black suburban populations double. In some cases the black suburban growth far outpaced total metropolitan-area growth. Chicago's metropolitan-area population barely changed from 1980 to 1990 (there was a 0.2 percent gain), while the suburban black population grew 65 percent (O'Hare and Frey, 1992, p. 36). Overall, blacks still have a lower proportion of their population in suburbs than do whites, but the rate of black suburban growth is higher. For example, Gwinnett County, Georgia, just north of Atlanta, saw its population double during the period 1980–1990 because of both job growth and the availability of affordable housing. During this same period, the black population in Gwinnett County increased 344 percent. As of the 1990 census, some 9 percent of the county's residents were black.

Historical Patterns

Until the twentieth century the African American population in the United States was overwhelmingly rural and southern. On the eve of the Civil War, the south was rural, with, as of 1860, only 8.6 percent of the total population living in cities. Slavery was essentially a rural institution founded on a plantation economy, and plantation owners vigorously opposed the use of slaves in urban manufacturing. Laws were passed in the attempt to restrict the number of slaves in cities, and, as a consequence, the urban black population actually declined in most southern cities prior to the Civil War. Slaveholders feared that slaves' relative freedom of life in the cities would undermine the south's "peculiar institution." In this fear they were quite justified. In urban areas the system of slaves being hired out or even hiring themselves out and sharing the income with their nominal owners led to a modification of the system. In effect, through such contractual agreements, the slave "purchased" some degree of freedom. According to Frederick Douglass, the major black figure of the Civil War period, such an urban slave was "almost a free citizen" (Richard C. Wade, *Slavery in the Cities: The South 1820–1860*, Oxford University Press, New York, 1964).

Prior to the Civil War not all blacks were slaves. As of 1860 roughly one of every eight American blacks was a "free Negro" or "free person of color." The great bulk of those free persons of color were urban, and most lived in border states. It is usually not known that when the war began, Richmond, Virginia, the capital of the Confederacy, counted one-fifth of its black population as "free persons of color." Moreover, one-quarter of the city's black population, including some slaves, owned their own modest homes. By comparison, at the outbreak of war, the northern states had only limited populations of freed blacks. In the north, as in the south, the only black suburbanites were usually those living in the poor shantytowns on the city's fringe.

The initial expectation after the Civil War was that blacks would flood out of the rural south. It didn't happen. Even the extensive political and social changes wrought by Reconstruction did not change the overwhelmingly rural and southern pattern of black residence. Social relations remained castelike, with blacks not in competition with whites for jobs or status. Thus, there was no need to segregate the races in terms of housing (J. John Palen and Leo Schnore, "Color Composition and City-Suburban Status Differences," *Land Economics*, Vol. 41, 1965, pp. 87–91). A common southern pattern was for whites to occupy the big house on the street while blacks lived in small structures facing the alley. As of 1910 nine of ten blacks still lived in the south, and three-quarters of all blacks were rural.

What did change black residence patterns was the first World War. The outbreak of war in 1914 cut off the supply of European immigrant labor just at the time factories were being flooded with war orders. New labor sources had to be found. One method was increasing the use of women workers. The second was to recruit labor from the rural south. Northern factories sent recruiters south offering one-way train tickets to those, black as well as white, who would sign up for factory jobs. In the early years of this century, life had been getting harder for rural blacks with the mechanization of agriculture, the spreading destruction of cotton crops by the boll weevil, and new Jim Crow laws that brought increasing segregation and racial repression. These factors provided a strong push that, when combined with the pull of northern jobs, initiated a mass migration of rural southern blacks to the urban north. The World War I decade (1910–1920) saw the five states of the deep south "black belt"—South Carolina, Georgia, Alabama, Mississippi, and Louisiana—lose over 400,000 blacks to out-migration.

The migration continued during the 1920s, with high black growth rates for major northern cities. New York (114 percent), Chicago (113 percent), Detroit (194 percent), and Philadelphia (64 percent) showed the heaviest growth (Daniel M. Johnson and Rex R. Campbell, *Black Migration in America*, Duke University Press, Durham, N.C., 1981, p. 78). Harlem, which was already crowded in 1920, added five times more residents during the decade. The Depression years of the 1930s saw migration slow and then shoot up dramatically during the World War II years because of the needs of war industries and the implementation by President Roosevelt of an executive order mandating fair employment policies. The aftermath of the war saw the urban relocation of blacks continue. By the time the migration to northern cities had substantially run its course in the late 1960s, over 5 million blacks had left the south for northern cities. Chicago now housed more blacks than all of Mississippi, and the New York metropolitan area had more blacks than any state of the old south (Thomas F. Pettigrew, *Racially Separate or Together?*, McGraw-Hill, New York, 1971, p. 3). This movement to urban places provided the population for consequent black suburbanization.

Early Forms of Black Suburbanization

Between the 1920s and the end of the second World War, the very limited amount of black suburbanization generally took one of two forms. The first was the all-black suburb. Almost all of these suburbs were poor, and the majority were unincorporated. In the south, it was common for nonwhites to live in small hamlets and less-developed areas on the city's periphery. These low-income shantytown neighborhoods often even lacked community water and sewage and were suburban in name only. While such small communities were technically *in* the suburbs, socially and economically they were not *of* the suburbs. An example of this type of suburb was the black suburb of Kinloch, 6 miles outside of the city limits of St. Louis. Kinloch, surrounded by more affluent white suburbs, did not become incorporated until 1948. It was typical of early black suburbs insofar as because of a limited tax base, it had poor schools, potholed roads, and minimal governmental services. The roads from Ferguson, the suburb east of Kinloch, actually stopped short of Kinloch at an overgrown easement only to start up again on the Kinloch side of the border (John Kramer, "The Other Mayor Lee," in John Kramer, ed., *North American Suburbs*, Glendessary Press, Berkeley, Calif., 1972, p. 186). As late as 1970 some of these black "suburban" neighborhoods could be seen south of Washington, D.C., across the district line.

During the interwar period, some solid working class-black suburbs also existed, such as Robbins, southwest of Chicago. At this time the Federal Housing Administration (FHA) directly supported segregated housing by refusing to make loans in other than all-one-race areas. Until 1950 FHA regulations specifically prohibited making loans that would permit racial integration. "The Federal Housing Administration's official manuals cautioned against 'infiltration of inharmonious racial and national groups,' 'a lower class of inhabitants,' or 'the presence of incompatible racial elements,' in the new neighborhood" (Charles Abrams, *The City Is the Frontier*, Harper and Row, New York, 1965, p. 61). Thus, federal policies prohibited loans that would encourage the integration of neighborhoods. During World War II, the

FHA consistently refused to insure war-housing projects for black workers (Robert C. Weaver, *The Negro Ghetto*, Harcourt, Brace and Co., 1948, pp. 217–222). The formal regulations weren't changed until the Kennedy years of the early 1960s, and the policies really didn't change until the Open Housing Act of 1968 barred housing discrimination. However, the outlawing of discriminatory policies didn't eliminate informal practices of racial steering, where blacks were shown housing only in areas already having black residents.

The second form of black suburbanization prior to World War II included small communities of blacks found in the most elite suburbs. Blacks living in such suburbs were not equal-status homeowners. Rather, in the vast majority of cases, they were servants. The 1930 census showed, for example, that along Chicago's prestigious North Shore, 5 percent of Glencoe's and 4.3 percent of Kenilworth's residents were African American. The majority of these were live-in servants (Michael H. Ebner, *Creating Chicago's North Shore*, University of Chicago Press, Chicago, 1988, pp. 234–235). Over time some of the servants and household workers purchased or built small homes in the less desirable sections of the community. Such black populations contained the seeds of social change. For example, Evanston, on Chicago's North Shore, as of 1930 listed 7.8 percent of its population as black. Evanston as of that date already had a separate aspiring middle-class black neighborhood for those working on the North Shore. Over time this nucleus would grow to be a substantial portion of the Evanston community.

Post-World War II Patterns

The 1950s and 1960s may have seen an emptying out of the cities, but this pattern was largely restricted to white families. Numerous forms of institutional discrimination insured that racial segregation would persist. Real estate practices, lending policies of banks and savings and loan institutions, governmental policies, and the beliefs of individual homeowners all contributed to practices of legalized segregation in the south and *de facto* segregation in the north. As blacks seeking employment moved to metropolitan areas, they were segregated within selected areas and neighborhoods within the central cities (Karl E. Taeuber and Alma F. Taeuber, *Negroes in Cities: Residential Segregation and Neighborhood Change*, Aldine, Chicago, 1965). As whites departed the city, more previously white neighborhoods were opened to black occupancy, but although the ghetto expanded its borders, it remained a segregated area. Government policies also directly encouraged racially restrictive areas. In the suburbs the FHA proposed racially restrictive protective covenants that stopped racial integration in order to prevent "declining property values." The 1947 FHA manual stated that

> If a mixture of user groups is found to exist, it must be determined whether the mixture will render the neighborhood less desirable to present and prospective occupants. Protective covenants are essential to sound development of proposed residential areas, since they regulate the use of the land and provide a basis for the development of harmonious, attractive neighborhoods (Quoted in Gwendolyn Wright, *Building the Dream: A Social History of Housing in America*, MIT Press, Cambridge, Mass., 1981, pp. 247–248).

The elimination of these legal barriers made no difference to the lives of most blacks. In 1948 the Supreme Court, in *Shelley v. Kraemer*, ruled that racially restrictive covenants were not unconstitutional, but that they were no longer enforceable through the courts. This had little practical impact, and until 1968 the FHA continued to accept written and unwritten restrictive covenants. The FHA and VA subsidization of mass suburbanization was almost exclusively for whites; there were only a handful of postwar suburban black housing developments. Institutional housing discrimination remained. Realtors would not show suburban housing to blacks, and homeowners would not sell to them.

Additionally, even without explicit racially restrictive covenants, there were a host of exclusionary zoning practices. These included density controls on the number of units on a piece of land, minimum lot and housing sizes, housing codes, prohibitions of trailers, and other policies that were intended to exclude low-income populations in general and blacks in particular.

Blacks that did suburbanize during the 1950s and 1960s generally had as their destinations either long-standing working-class black suburban communities or spillover communities that occurred when black city ghettos expanded beyond city boundaries into aging inner-ring suburbs (Harold M. Rose, *Black Suburbanization: Access to Improved Quality of Life or Maintaining the Status Quo?*, Ballinger, Cambridge, Mass., 1976). Prior to the 1970s black suburbanization occurred overwhelmingly within already black communities. In effect, the United States had a dual housing market in which realtors and financial institutions steered blacks into suburbs that were no longer desirable to whites. The dual housing market was used to contain and control black suburbanization within less suitable areas. Further, blacks purchasing homes in the black suburbs paid a "race tax" that ranged from 10 percent to 25 percent. This was the additional amount blacks had to pay for comparable housing over what whites would pay. Not surprisingly, under these handicaps, the rate of black suburbanization increased only minimally in the immediate postwar period. As of 1960, census figures indicated that suburbs were 4.6 percent black; for 1970, the rate barely changed to 4.7 percent. Moreover, most black suburbs were far from being the promised land. According to Logan, the reality of black suburbs was that, "The average black suburb is poor, fiscally stressed, and crime-ridden, compared to other suburbs" (John R. Logan, "Realities of Black Suburbanization," in Roland Warren and Larry Lyon, eds., *New Perspectives on the American Community*, Dorsey Press, Chicago, 1988, p. 235).

The postwar years were difficult ones for the civil rights movement. Civil rights activists of the 1940s and 1950s were still battling against lynchings and trying to get black children access to equal education. The movement did not have the luxury of concerning itself with opening suburban housing. Metropolitan blacks overwhelmingly worked and lived in the central city, and urban blacks had more practical survival concerns than seeking to move to white suburbs. Moreover, with whites leaving the cities, more and better-quality urban housing was opened for blacks. For the average urban black worker who lived every day with racial discrimination, what happened in the suburbs was more of a theoretical than a practical matter.

The civil rights focus on obtaining equal access to education culminated with the landmark 1954 *Brown v. Topeka Board of Education* ruling. A decade later followed the passage of the 1964 Civil Rights Act and the 1965 Voting Rights Act. With the passage of these acts, the attention of the civil rights movement shifted from education and personal civil rights to a concern over housing discrimination. The 1968 Civil Rights Act, more commonly known as the Fair Housing Act, for the first time outlawed overt forms of housing discrimination. Title VIII focused on eliminating racial discrimination in housing. While enforcement penalties were weak, the Fair Housing Act, for the first time, threw the weight of the federal government behind equal housing access.

While there is a general consensus that as a result of the act, the level of discrimination against minorities has declined, there is far less agreement that this has been accompanied by substantial reductions in racial segregation (Richard A. Smith, "The Measurement of Integration Change through Integration and Deconcentration," *Urban Affairs Quarterly*, Vol. 16, 1991, pp. 477–499). The year 1968 also saw federal attempts to move poverty-level families into the private housing market. The Housing and Urban Development Act provided direct home ownership subsidies to low-income home buyers. Thus, as the 1970s dawned, the possibility of racial minorities achieving suburban home ownership for the first time became a real option.

Housing Fraud: Using the Poor

The 1968 Housing and Urban Development Act was important for its implementation set for decades the attitudes and beliefs of citizens and policymakers regarding the feasibility of the federal government aiding the working and welfare poor to purchase their own housing. The assumption was that most of those aided by the act would be minorities, and thus the act would foster integration. The Housing and Urban Development Act was designed to turn the economically marginal into responsible, tax-paying homeowners. It had a rehabilitation section that applied largely to the cities, and a new-housing section that had a more suburban application. The purpose of the act was not so much to open the suburbs to the black middle class but to make home ownership open to all, regardless of income. The Housing and Urban Development Act was, in many respects, a response to the urban riots that racked American cities in the late 1960s. Following the assassination of Dr. Martin Luther King, Jr., in 1968, rioting broke out in some one hundred and twenty-five cities, and the period that followed came to be known as "the long hot summer." The Urban Development Act was rapidly passed, with the expectation that by providing the hope of home ownership it would relieve urban pressure. The emphasis was on immediate action, with less attention given to careful monitoring of the program. There was considerable political pressure from the Johnson White House to get the program going. It was thought that problems could be corrected later.

The positive side of this fast start-up was that for the first time, the weight of government attention was focused on the housing needs of poor urban minorities. Particular attention was directed at rapidly expanding the number of low-income minority home purchasers. Integration *per se* received less attention than using federal subsidies to turn the urban poor into homeowners with a stake in the system. The downside of the fast start-up was that no one was monitoring the effects of the program and controlling the cash flow. In hindsight, what occurred was quite predictable. The program was exploited, often criminally, by those who knew how it could be manipulated—not the poor, but the private-sector banking and real estate professionals, who saw the program as a money tree. As expressed by the director of HUD's Chicago office: "Every unethical, unscrupulous real estate broker and lender, many of them so slimy they crawled out from under a rock, looked at this program and said, 'What a gold mine out there'." As usual, the poor were the victims.

Basically, what occurred was criminal collusion between real estate speculators, banks, and FHA employees to sell supposedly rehabili-

tated properties at high prices to marginally qualified low-income minority purchasers, with the expectation that the buyers would default
so the FHA would have to take back the loan and the unsalable property. The scheme worked as follows. A real estate speculator bought a
run-down home at a low price and then put in a few cosmetic repairs
such as a cheap paint job. A low-income buyer who marginally qualified for the program was then found, and the appraiser was paid to
considerably overestimate the value of the property. The bank then authorized the loan; the FHA or VA insured the mortgage at the inflated
price; and the speculator made a fast profit minus the bribe. The new
homeowner soon found the property was unlivable and defaulted on
the mortgage.

The ideal purchaser from the speculator's and banker's viewpoint
was someone so economically marginal that he or she was likely to default. (Until almost the final days of the program, even those with no
income but welfare qualified as purchasers.) The bank then foreclosed
and turned the property over to the FHA, who paid off the overpriced
mortgage. Since the more properties sold, the greater the profits, federal monies were, in fact, used not to provide housing, but to provide
real estate speculators and banks subsidies for destabilizing neighborhoods. The majority of the supposedly rehabilitated 235 properties
were eventually abandoned by their low-income purchasers, and these
deteriorating properties greatly added to the stock of abandoned city
housing. Eventually, several hundred persons were convicted of fraud,
but by then the program had been misused to create huge amounts of
abandoned housing. As a consequence, the federal government found
itself by the mid-1970s to be the nation's largest holder of foreclosed
and unsalable slum properties. The federal government, in effect,
found itself financing the creation of urban wastelands. Callous greed
destroyed what was potentially a good program.

The suburban version of the program involved not rehabilitation
of existing properties, but the building of new homes, usually in outlying locations. Unfortunately, the new-homes program had problems
similar to the urban program. Homes were built at high cost to the taxpayers but with a quality of construction often below industry standards. There was little monitoring of the performance of developers.
Since the new subsidized homes were of a clearly identifiable style and
almost always of poorer construction than other homes in the neighborhood, existing homeowners almost always saw the building of subsidized homes nearby as a threat to their property values.
Unfortunately, they were correct in this belief. Shortsightedly, the program did not budget funds for garages or landscaping. More importantly, the low-income buyers were marginal purchasers with no finan-

cial cushion. To qualify for the program, the buyer had to have a very low income or be on public assistance. Such purchasers soon found themselves saddled with lemons requiring considerable expensive work. (A student of mine who purchased one of these homes in suburban Milwaukee County found, among other things, that his kitchen drainpipes had been installed with an upward tilt.)

Minorities also often found that their new suburban homes were located in areas far from services or employment. Physical isolation compounded social isolation. The houses were distant from established black neighborhoods, black churches, black stores, and black friends. Subdivisions in which the new housing was constructed invariably did not have public transportation and rarely had stores within walking distance. Low-income residents quickly discovered that car ownership was essential for their survival. Without at least one dependable auto, they were stranded miles from friends and services. As the physical problems with the homes became more evident, and the economic and social costs of living became clearer, the political support within the black community for constructing additional suburban subsidized housing rapidly declined. A companion piece of legislation, the Title 236 program, provided rent subsidies for the poor so they could move out of public housing. The suburban effects of this program were minimal, however, because of the scarcity of suburban rental housing for which low-income blacks could qualify (Kevin M. Fitzpatrick and Sean-Shong Hwang, "Bringing Community SES Back In: Reanalyzing Black Suburbanization Patterns, 1960–1980," *Social Science Quarterly*, Vol. 71, 1990, pp. 767–773). By 1974, when President Nixon, with the connivance of Congress, terminated support for the subsidy programs, there were few voices raised in protest. Only the construction companies and a handful of die-hard supporters felt the program deserved to survive. The tragedy was that a well-meaning program to turn low-income renters into homeowners died, not because it was misused by the recipients, but because the program had become a bureaucratic disaster that exploited the poor to enrich banks, builders, and speculators.

One consequence of the failure of these housing programs was that the African American community would become increasingly divided between the suburbanizing middle-class blacks and central-city blacks, who became more isolated in the old core neighborhoods of economically weakening central cities. The 1970s ended the black exodus from the south and initiated the middle-class black exodus from the cities. As black middle-class role models began to exit the city, the social fabric of central-city life began to deteriorate. Those leaving also took with them stable mainstream institutions and the informal job network (William J. Wilson, *The Truly Disadvantaged: The Inner-City Underclass, and Public Policy*, University of Chicago Press, Chicago, 1987). During the 1970s the South Bronx lost 37 percent of its population, and the once vibrant southside ghetto of Chicago lost 38 percent of its population. With the suburbanization of successful role models and jobs, the result was a growing economic and social marginalization of those left behind.

William Julius Wilson argues that:

> Social isolation deprives residents of certain inner city neighborhoods not only of the resources and conventional role models, whose former presence buffered the effects of neighborhood joblessness, but also of cultural learning from mainstream social networks that facilitate social and economic advancement in modern industrial society (William Julius Wilson, "Poverty, Joblessness and Family Structure in the Inner City: A Comparative Perspective," University of Chicago Family Life Conference, presented paper, 1991).

Thus, the central city has had to cope not just with the shift from an industrial-based to an information-based economy, but also with the resultant loss of entry-level blue-collar jobs. The inner city also has lost its middle-class role models and their important informal job networks.

Changing Seventies

By the 1970s the postwar pattern seemed set. Whites, for a variety of racial, educational, life-style, and tax reasons, would continue to outmigrate to the suburbs. Racial minorities, on the other hand, with few exceptions would become ever-more concentrated in the cities. The assumption that this is the inevitable future continues to be "popular wisdom" today, in spite of a quarter of a century of white inner-city revitalization and gentrification and black suburbanization (Dennis E. Gale, *Washington, D.C.: Inner City Revitalization and Minority Suburbanization*, Temple University Press, Philadelphia, 1987). During the 1970s it became increasingly apparent that in spite of the fact that both scholarly and popular attention were focused elsewhere, there were major changes in minority suburbanization. The fair housing legislation of 1968 legally opened the suburbs to middle-class minorities. While racial steering still occurred, the housing legislation meant that black suburbanization was no longer *de facto* restricted to predominantly black suburbs. The result was the beginning of a black middle-class exodus to the suburbs. Not only did the suburban black population grow faster than that in the cities; nationally, the rate of black suburbanization was twice as fast as in the previous decade. During the 1950s and 1960s, the percentage of blacks who lived in suburbs barely changed. The 1970s marked a real turning point, with the black population living outside cities growing faster than that within. In contrast to earlier decades, the 1970s showed the black suburban population increasing three times as rapidly as the white suburban population (Larry Long and Diana DeAre, "The Suburbanization of Blacks," *American Demographics*, September 1981, p. 16).

Washington, D.C., for example, saw its black population decline 17 percent during the decade. By contrast, suburban Fairfax, in Virginia, saw a 119 percent increase in its black residents, while the percentage increases for suburban Montgomery and Prince George's counties in Maryland were 136 and 170 percent. By 1980 the latter county had 248,000 black residents (Gale, 1987, p. 114). Moderate- and middle-income minorities were leaving the city for the suburbs. For upwardly mobile blacks, as for whites, owning a home in the suburbs became a symbol of success in climbing the economic ladder (Morton D. Winsberg, "Suburbanization of Higher Income Blacks in Major Metropolitan Statistical Areas," *Urban Geography*, Vol. 10, 1989, pp. 172–177).

However, while the legal restriction of middle-class blacks to urban ghettoes was no more, housing discrimination remained. *De jure* housing discrimination on the basis of race was no longer operative, but *de facto* discrimination, particularly on the individual level, remained a fact of life. Nonetheless, in spite of *de facto* discrimination, there was an opportunity for middle-class blacks to leave the ghettos, and those middle-class families who could afford to do so left the cities and moved into suburban neighborhoods. The leavers sought better housing and better educational opportunities for themselves and their children. As a consequence, middle-class black rates of suburbanization accelerated at the same time as white suburban growth rates were declining (John R. Logan and Mark Schneider, "Racial Segregation and Racial Change in American Suburbs," *American Journal of Sociology*, Vol. 84, 1984, pp. 874–888; John M. Stahura, "Changing Patterns of Suburban Racial Composition, 1970–1980," *Urban Affairs Quarterly*, Vol. 23, 1988, pp. 448–460). According to the Bureau of the Census figures, the white suburban population increased 13.1 percent during the decade of the 1970s, while the black population increased 42.7 percent. The white suburban increase was exactly half the 26.1 percent figure of the 1960 to 1970 period and only a fraction of the rapid growth of white suburbanites in the 1950s.

Black suburban growth during the 1970s was not just a regional phenomenon; it took place in all areas of the country. A pattern seemed to be developing in which black population shifts trailed white changes by a decade or so but followed the same general patterns. One example of this black population shift was that several of the cities having the largest black populations, such as Philadelphia, Washington, Cleveland, and St. Louis, saw their black populations actually decline. During the 1970–1980 decade, blacks departed from Washington, D.C., at twice the rate of whites. Moreover, those departing were disproportionately people in their twenties and thirties with young children. One consequence of the upswing in black suburbanization was that by 1980, blacks numbered 12 percent of the national population and represented 6.1 percent of the suburban population. By 1990, the African American figure had increased to 6.6 percent. Therefore, it is still the case that blacks are underrepresented in suburbs. Also, this underrepresentation is not just because of income or educational differences. Research by Reynolds Farley using 1980 census data indicated that "blacks of every economic level are highly segregated from whites at the same economic level" (Reynolds Farley and Walter Allen, *The Color Line and the Quality of Life in America*, Russell Sage Foundation, New York, 1987, p. 148).

CONTEMPORARY DEVELOPMENTS

The Chicago School urban ecologists of the 1920s believed that social distance was reflected in spatial distance (Robert Park, "The Urban Community as a Spatial Pattern and a Moral Order," in E. W. Burgess, ed., *The Urban Community*, University of Chicago Press, Chicago, 1926). The level of segregation would thus be reflected in the social distance between groups. Thus, as segregation decreased, the integration of social groups would increase. The data are fairly definite in suggesting that this is what occurred with white ethnic populations, although for some groups it was considerably faster and easier (Stanley Lieberson, *A Piece of the Pie: Black and White Immigrants Since 1880*, University of California Press, Berkeley, 1980). For European ethnic populations, as generations increased, and income, educational level, and occupational status rose, they increasingly blended into the general American population. For example, as recently as the end of the second World War one could map out distinct ethnic neighborhoods for groups such as the Irish. Today, with the exception of a few historical holdovers such as south Boston, there no longer are any demographically distinct Irish neighborhoods. Richard Alba argues that what is emerging is a new ethnic group—"one based on ancestry from *anywhere* on the European continent" (Richard Alba, *Ethnic Identity: The Transformation of White America*, Yale University Press, New Haven, Conn., 1990, p. 3).

The major exception to the relationship between rising socioeconomic status and declining spatial segregation has been African Americans. Historically, rising income and education has not, over time, been more or less automatically translated into declining segregation, as has been the case with European or even Hispanic immigrants (Douglas Massey and Nancy Denton, "Trends in Residential Segregation of Blacks, Hispanics, and Asians: 1970–1980," *American Sociological Review*, Vol. 52, 1987, pp. 802–845). Nor did segregation decrease as generations in the United States increased. For blacks the fact of race traditionally has overridden other variables. For decades research has shown that suburban blacks were more likely to live in suburban municipalities that had lower income, less adequate housing, and strained local finances (Mark Schneider and John R. Logan, "Racial Segregation and Black Access to Local Public Resources," *Social Science Quarterly*, Vol. 63, 1982, pp. 762–770). At least until the 1980s the pattern was of residential segregation increasing in the north and declining in the south (Linda Brewster Stearns and John R. Logan, "Racial Structuring of the Housing Market and Segregation in Suburban Areas," *Social Forces*, Vol. 65, 1986, pp. 28–29).

Movement of blacks to the suburbs does not automatically increase interaction between the races if there is a dual housing market that shunts blacks primarily into already black communities. There is clear evidence that the housing market has been structured to provide different housing opportunities for whites and blacks. However, there is less institutional discrimination in suburban rental housing than in owner-occupied housing (Stearns and Logan, 1986, p. 39). In terms of suburbs, the crucial question is whether individual suburbs increasingly have been integrating black and white residents, or whether black suburbanization simply means more and larger segregated black suburbs.

Invasion-Succession?

Do changes in the number of suburbanizing African Americans represent increased housing integration, or merely the growth of all black suburban areas? A related issue is whether the government's goal should be racially integrated neighborhoods or freedom of choice for blacks to live where they choose. Some minority scholars suggest that the latter, rather than the former, has always been the black priority (W. A. Leigh and J. D. McGee, "A Minority Perspective on Residential Racial Integration," in J. M. Goering, ed., *Housing Desegregation and Federal Policy*, University of North Carolina Press, Chapel Hill, 1986, pp. 31–42). Researchers refer to suburbs where one racial group replaces another as "displacement" or "succession" suburbs. The northern version of succession typically involves blacks overflowing in substantial numbers from the central city into older and less desirable inner-ring suburbs. White residents then, in turn, depart for newer suburbs further out. This type of central-to-periphery racial movement fits the ecological invasion-succession model of urban change first proposed by Chicago School sociologists in the 1920s. Black suburbanization of this type does not indicate racial integration, but rather the expansion of the ghetto across city lines. The period of integration this type of suburbanization encompasses is only the interval between the arrival of the first blacks and the departure of the last whites. Research examining the period before the 1980s indicates that the pattern of black spillover into older and less desirable inner-ring suburban housing has empirical validity (Stahura, 1988, pp. 448–460). Areas that were most prone to turn over racially were those in close proximity to all-black areas. Thus, a 1978 HUD study interviewing blacks and whites confirmed that little actual residential integration had occurred (*1978 HUD Survey on the Quality of Community Life: A Data Book*, U.S. Department of Housing and Urban Development, Washington, D.C., 1978). Whites continued to show reluctance to move into areas they viewed likely to be incorporated into black ghettos. A real fear was that inner-ring suburbs into which blacks disproportionately were flowing would undergo the same economic difficulties and population declines that plague central cities. The assumption was that blacks would remain concentrated in the inner suburbs abutting central-city black ghettoes.

Current Patterns

However, the 1980s and 1990s have showed a different pattern. Overall suburbs are becoming more diverse racially, and spillover is not the major pattern in the metropolitan areas having the largest black populations, such as Washington, Atlanta, and Los Angeles. Here there appears to be more of a "leapfrog" effect (Morton D. Winsberg, "Flight from the Ghetto: The Migration of Middle Class and Highly Educated Blacks into White Urban Neighborhoods," *American Journal of Economics and Sociology,* Vol. 44, 1985, pp. 411–421). Also, the old classic model of the racial tipping point has less validity (Nancy A. Denton and Douglas S. Massey, "Patterns of Neighborhood Transition in a Multiethnic World: U.S. Metropolitan Areas 1970–1980," *Demography,* Vol. 28, 1991, pp. 41–63). Rather than invasion-succession, with one group totally supplanting another, the more common pattern is now one of stable multiracial neighborhoods. Research on patterns of neighborhood racial succession indicate, "the succession model may be more

With a third of all metropolitan area African Americans now living in the suburbs, the old image of suburbs being "lily white" no longer fits the facts.

limited than popularly believed" (Barrett A. Lee and Peter B. Wood, "Is Neighborhood Racial Succession Place Specific?" *Demography*, Vol. 28, 1991, p. 37). Although the classic invasion-succession model is still commonly accepted by much of the population (and some scholars), it largely ceased to have empirical validity as the major model of African American suburbanization by 1980. Old beliefs die hard, however. As will be discussed later in this section, the all-black suburbs of today tend to be not poor but middle-class or even affluent communities. Their racial makeup is a matter of deliberate choice by those moving in.

The traditional southern version of the displacement model now is also largely history. It was the invasion-succession model in reverse. Rather than blacks moving into previously all-white areas, middle-class whites moved to outer areas and, by so doing, displaced low-income blacks who were living in black neighborhoods on the city fringe. As was noted earlier, it was a common residential pattern throughout much of this century for southern cities to have poorer blacks residing in marginal areas on the urban periphery. Those living in such fringe areas often mixed some rural farming with urban wage labor. The data indicate that the older southern pattern of middle-class whites displacing poor blacks has become less common (Avery Guest, "The Changing Social Composition of Suburbs, 1950–1970," *Urban Affairs Quarterly*, Vol. 14, 1978, 195–206). The southern pattern of movement of whites into black suburban areas now appears to be part of history. Invasion-succession models of any form, although still widely used, are now largely outdated.

Parallel Growth

The alternative to the succession model is that of "parallel growth." What this model suggests is that suburbs show both white and black population growth without either group displacing the other. This appears to have been the more common pattern for recent decades. Both blacks and whites have been suburbanizing for decades, with comparatively less racial turnover when compared to the pattern in central cities. Even twenty years ago, when black rates of suburbanization were already exceeding white rates, there was no major pattern of succession of suburbs from white to black occupancy. Why didn't suburbs turn over racially, as was occurring in city neighborhoods? Why were most suburbs different?

A couple of factors are relevant in explaining the difference. Rapid racial displacement of whites didn't occur in suburbs partially because of the more dispersed suburban pattern of detached, single-family housing. There is also some evidence for increasing white acceptance of open housing. However, doubtlessly, the major reason for the lack of racial replacement was that whites were also suburbanizing in massive numbers. For example, some 11 million whites moved to the suburbs between 1970 and 1980. Since whites constitute roughly 85 percent of the population, it is inevitable that as long as whites continue to live in, and move to, suburbs, the majority of suburban areas will continue to retain their predominantly white complexion.

An analysis of Bureau of the Census Annual Housing Survey data by Daphne Spane and Larry Long indicates that by 1980, four patterns in black suburbanization had emerged (U.S. Bureau of the Census, "Black Movers to the Suburbs: Are They Moving to White Neighborhoods," *Special Demographic Analyses*, CDS-80,4, Washington, D.C., December 1981). First, suburbanizing blacks were moving to predominantly white areas rather than to black suburbs. It was not simply the black ghetto flowing across the city line. Second, the higher the income and the education level of the black in-movers, the more likely they were to move to white suburbs. Third, in-moving blacks had higher socioeconomic status than blacks already living in the suburbs, but they tended to move to less prestigious neighborhoods than did in-moving whites. Finally, both white and black suburbanites were more likely to rate predominantly white suburbs higher than mixed suburbs. It is speculated that the higher rating reflects the higher level of amenities and services found in predominantly white suburbs. Data from the 1990 census confirm these trends. In metropolitan areas with a population of at least a million, black suburban families had an average income of $32,000. (O'Hare and Frey, 1992, p. 32). This was 55 percent higher than the average income of central-city blacks in the same metropolitan areas.

Mortgage Fund Availability

One method of restricting African American access to suburbia is through the limiting of mortgage money for minority applicants. There is no question that overall, blacks have lower rates of obtaining mortgage financing than whites. Nationally, as of 1991, banks rejected black applicants twice as often as white applicants. And it is not simply a question of creditworthiness, since high-income black applicants were denied credit more often than low-income whites. These findings have been documented using the nation's banks' own lending records ("Blacks Get Fewer Mortgages," *Washington Post*, November 1, 1992, p. 1). Mortgage financing is still not race neutral.

Interestingly, however, suburban lending patterns apparently differ from the older city patterns. Research done in the Milwaukee metropolitan area indicates that in city neighborhoods increases in neighborhood integration correlate with decreases in the amount of housing financing available, but mortgage-lending patterns in suburban areas are more complex (Gregory D. Squires and William Velez, "Neighborhood Racial Composition and Mortgage Lending: City and Suburban Differences," *Journal of Urban Affairs*, Vol. 9, No. 3, 1987, pp. 217–232). In the suburbs, independent of other applicant and neighborhood characteristics, there was an actual increase in banks lending funds as the minority population increased up to 10 percent. In other words, independent of other factors, more mortgage funds went into integrated as compared to all-white neighborhoods. However, as the minority percentage passed 15 percent, the pattern changed, and mortgage funds available for loans began to sharply decrease. Equitable distribution of mortgage loans occurred most frequently in communities that had approximately 10 to 15 percent minority population. This suggests that while racial bias continues to persist in mortgage markets, the pattern is more complex than in the past. Funds appear to be more available in one-race or moderately integrated suburbs than in areas undergoing substantial increase in minority population.

Reasons for Moving to Suburbs

The reasons for accelerating black suburbanization are similar to the reasons for white suburbanization. Blacks, like whites, move to the suburbs for a better life for themselves and their children. Urban areas often have poorer schools and more serious problems with public safety. Washington, D.C., for instance, saw its black population drop by 49,302 persons between 1980 and 1990. Many of those who left wanted to stay but found life in the District becoming too difficult. As expressed by Arthur Gay, 54, who left in 1988: "I'd love to move back into it and be a part of it. I moved there at age 20 and I lived there 31 years. But there would have to be a big change." He said his once-pleasant apartment was sold to new owners who didn't seem to care, and then his wife was mugged. The final decision to move came in 1988, when he was awakened by gunfire at 2 a.m. Outside his kitchen window, a thirteen-year-old boy had been shot. "He was shot by his 9-year-old cousin who lived the next entrance from me. What happened is the 13-year-old took drugs from the 9-year-old without paying, chased him around the corner and shot him" (Steve Twomey, "District Black Flight Points to Crime, Cost," *Washington Post*, February 18, 1991, p. A14). The outflow of middle-class taxpayers, of course, exacerbates the problems of Washington and other cities by putting an even heavier tax burden on those that remain behind. Problems with deteriorating buildings, drugs, crime, cratered streets, declining schools, and increasing taxes continue to force middle-class blacks to depart for safer, if possibly less interesting, communities.

Nor is the black exodus to the suburbs restricted to older east coast cities. Census figures show that during the 1980s, about 75,000 blacks moved out of south Los Angeles, the site of the 1992 riots. Many of those leaving relocated to the so-called Inland Empire. While the south Los Angeles black population dropped 20 percent, Riverside and San Bernardino counties more than doubled their black population, to approximately 170,000 residents. Terry Nunley, who now lives in Moreno Valley, decided to leave the day he picked up 20 dollars from an automated teller machine and a man sidled up to him, flashed a pistol, and demanded, "Give it up." In his words, "I don't feel any responsibility to return to L.A.: I feel a responsibility to my family. It's a purely individual move. A guy pulled a gun on me, I'd had it, so I left. That's it." ("L.A.'s Loss: 'Black Flight'," *Los Angeles Times*, Aug. 13, 1992, p. A1).

It also has to be remembered that ties to older black city neighborhoods are remote for those generations of younger blacks that have had no experience with living in central cities. Black college students, for example, are increasingly suburban-born and suburban-bred. For these black suburbanites in their teens and twenties, the central city is every bit as foreign and strange as it is for their white cosuburbanites.

The proportion of blacks in suburbia will continue to increase for the foreseeable future. This increase will parallel a slower white rate of increase. African American population growth in suburban counties has occurred nationwide and is not confined to any particular region of the country. The 1990 figures, when compared to those for 1980, also indicate that black suburbanization has gone well beyond the token level and represents real change from earlier decades. Black suburbanization is now a substantial demographic pattern. It is also reasonable to anticipate no substantial suburban racial turnover or succession to occur. The lack of racial turnover is because of three factors: continued white suburbanization, the dispersed, less intensive land use pattern of suburbs, and some increases in racial integration.

Middle-Class Exodus

The above does not mean that racial equality is here. What it indicates is that the lives of middle-class and lower-class blacks are increasingly dissimilar. The 1980s saw the move of middle-class blacks counterbalanced by increasing poverty for lower-class central-city blacks. Attention of scholars and policymakers during this period was increasingly focused on the problems of the semipermanent urban underclass (William J. Wilson, *The Truly Disadvantaged*, Oxford, New York, 1987). However, while the 1990 census showed the overall black median income to be only 56 percent of white income, this is not the case with suburbanizing black families. Those moving to the suburbs are not single-parent, low-income welfare families. They predominantly are middle-class, married-couple families. Black married-couple families, by 1990, had 84 percent of the income of white married-couple families (Bureau of the Census, "Income, Poverty, and Wealth in the United States: A Chart Book," *Current Population Reports*, Series P-60, No. 179, Government Printing Office, Washington, D.C., 1992, p. 6). This compares to 76 percent in 1975. By comparison, over two-thirds of black female-headed families were below the poverty level.

In 1990 families headed by younger college-educated blacks had 92 percent of income parity with whites. These latter young families represent the blacks most likely to move to the suburbs. In the Virginia suburbs outside Washington, D.C., black median incomes rose faster than white in Alexandria, Fairfax, Loudoun, and Prince Williams counties ("Middle Class Gets Strong Foothold in N. Va.," *Washington Post,* May 5, 1992, p. 1). In all cases, black incomes were only 82 to 88 percent of those of local whites, but black suburban incomes were still considerably higher than the national median household income. The median 1989 black household income in Prince William County was $42,160 and that in Fairfax County $41,657. For the same year, the national median household income for all races was $34,210. It is apparent that while differences still remain as of the 1990s, blacks moving to suburbs increasingly resemble their white neighbors. This increasing similarity can be viewed as good or bad, depending upon how one views suburbia, but it is what is taking place.

Predominantly One-Group Suburbs

It is no secret that most suburbs are predominantly white. Racial and ethnic preference for own-group suburbs still persists for white, black, and Hispanic populations (W. A. V. Clark, "Residential Preferences and Neighborhood Racial Segregation: A Test of the Schelling Segregation Model," *Demography*, Vol. 28, 1991, pp. 1–19). Even when options are available, some choose to live in ethnically homogeneous areas. For example, some second- and third-generation American-born Jews who are nontraditional in their religious observances still choose to maintain their identity by moving to predominantly Jewish suburban communities (Gerald L. Showstack, *Suburban Communities: The Jewishness of American Reform Jews*, Scholars Press, Atlanta, 1988). The same is true for other groups, including middle-class African Americans.

While minorities generally are more open to integration and diversity than are whites, this does not mean that all middle-class black families want to integrate residentially. There is increasing evidence that some blacks, in seeking the suburban dream, are deliberately forgoing the American dream of an integrated society. New black suburbs, such as Rolling Oaks in the Miami area and Brook Glenn and Wyndham Park outside Atlanta, represent for many African Americans an affirmative decision to live in a predominantly black suburb. This is not a case of a suburb turning over racially, but of blacks by choice moving into new affluent black suburbs. Prince George's County, Maryland, just outside of Washington, D.C., has for a number of years had a black majority, and many of these suburbanites live in affluent communities and subdivisions that are predominantly black. The median black household income in Prince George's County in 1989 was a comfortable $41,265. Some 47,000 of the black households in the county had 1989 incomes of $50,000 or more (Judith Waldrop and Linda Jacobsen, "American Affluence," *American Demographics*, December 1992, p. 34). Black suburbanites living in such areas often say they find it more comfortable to live with other black neighbors. As put by one professional woman, "When I'm socializing with people who are not African American I have to do a lot of explaining. It's stressful because you know it's your responsibility to educate whites who have a sincere interest in understanding an issue. But it's more like work when you should just be socializing" (David J. Dent, "The New Black Suburbs," *New York Times Magazine*, June 14, 1992, p. 23).

For most black suburbanites, however, class is more important than race in determining one's neighbors. Race is still a core variable in American society, but as William Julius Wilson documented over a decade ago in his book *The Declining Significance of Race*, for much of the black (and white) middle class, race is increasingly being supplanted by the social-class variables of income, education, and occupation (William J. Wilson, *The Declining Significance of Race*, University of Chicago Press, Chicago, 1980). Others suggest that while there is a dramatic increase in the numbers of the new black middle class, racial discrimination continues to be a significant factor (Bart Landry, *The New Black Middle Class*, University of California Press, Berkeley, 1987). However, as we approach the turn of the century, the variables of social class are increasingly becoming the crucial variables affecting housing decisions. While middle-class neighbors of any race are becoming increasingly acceptable, lower-class neighbors are not.

General Pattern

Overall the pattern is one of both some optimism and some discouragement. A quarter of a century after the 1968 Fair Housing Act, racial segregation is decreasing; whites accept open housing in principal. Neighborhood or suburban racial changeover is no longer triggered by the presence of minority residents, but whites still exhibit reluctance to move into predominantly minority areas. The old racial segregation is largely becoming history, but racial steering by real estate agents and discrimination against minorities by banks and financial institutions still persists (A. B. Shlay, "Not in That Neighborhood: The Effects of Population and Housing on the Distribution of Mortgage Finance within the Chicago SMSA," *Social Science Research*, Vol. 17, 1988, pp. 137–163).

Over the decades suburbs have taken much criticism as being the recipients of white flight and the last bastion of the lily-white community. As indicated in this section, the data show a much more complex racial mosaic. Suburbs are becoming more multiracial and multiethnic. Ironically, as we enter the new century, the suburbs have the opportunity to achieve what the cities largely have failed to accomplish: truly racially integrated communities.

MANAGED INTEGRATION

Often popular as opposed to scholarly writings on racial integration of suburbs seem to fall either into a Pollyannaish "what we need to do is to communicate more and try to understand each other," or a pessimistic "American society is essentially racist, and real change is impossible." Harvey Molotch's 1960s research on the south shore community inside Chicago influenced thought on integration for many years (Harvey Molotch, *Managed Integration: The Dilemmas of Doing Good in the City*, University of California Press, Berkeley, 1972). His findings seemed to suggest that once racial transition had begun, no amount of local intervention could maintain the neighborhood as racially integrated. Racial residential turnover does not require white flight; all that is necessary is that an area attract more black than white newcomers. However, the study's assumption that dual housing markets make racial change inevitable has been challenged by examples of stable, long-term racially integrated suburbs.

However, given the economic and social pressures on such areas, it sometimes requires special efforts if racially integrated areas are to survive. Complicating the efforts of any particular metropolitan-area suburb to integrate is the fact that individual suburbs aren't islands. What occurs in the central city or adjacent suburbs has a major impact and may, in fact, outweigh the effort of any one area. What happens, for example, if a municipality makes every effort to follow the spirit as well as the law regarding open occupancy while neighboring municipalities continue to discriminate? Park Forest South, a suburb 30 miles south of Chicago, made every effort in the 1970s to integrate, while its neighboring suburbs of Homewood and Flossmore remained respectively 1 and 2 percent black. As a consequence, Park Forest South was rapidly resegregating as a predominantly black suburb, since it followed open-housing policies. And in a situation where only some suburbs welcome blacks, those areas that do so are likely to attract black purchasers who are likely to outbid whites who have alternative housing options.

One controversial practice to maintain racial diversity is the use of affirmative marketing ordinances, which have been denounced as reverse steering. Under such ordinances, special efforts are made to retain racial balance, which, in effect, often means directing advertising at potential white buyers and counseling blacks to move into predominantly white rather than already-black areas. At the core of the controversy is whether communities can or should take actions to keep their areas integrated. Given the complexity of the issue, it is not surprising that even civil rights organizations often come down on different sides of the debate. In the Park Forest South case, for example, the Chicago chapter of the NAACP and the Southern Leadership Conference joined with their old enemy, the real estate industry, in denouncing as racist the attempts to keep the suburb integrated by trying to attract whites. On the other side, the local open-housing groups and the national NAACP applauded the affirmative marketing ordinance as a "legitimate" means of achieving racial integration. They approved of the community's attempt to prevent resegregation. Although it is too late for Park Forest, the courts, in cases such as *South Suburban Housing Center v. Greater South Suburban Board of Realtors* (1988), seem to be increasingly supporting affirmative marketing as a means of racial stability (Richard A. Smith, "Creating Stable Racially Integrated Communities: A Review," *Journal of Urban Affairs*, Vol. 15, 1993, pp. 127–128).

In real life, such questions are not just matters of social philosophy but are invariably further complicated by economic and other issues. In the Park Forest South case, the television show "60 Minutes" also brought to light that the head of the Chicago NAACP and members of its board were real estate brokers who owned firms that directly profited from racial turnover. Members of the board emphatically denied any conflict of interest, but the whole controversy indicates just how complex such questions can become. The Supreme Court has not yet resolved the issue of whether integration is important enough as a social value to justify attempts to attract white in-movers in order to prevent resegregation. Until then, opinion will remain divided over the issue.

The Case of Oak Park

An often-cited successful example of how suburbs can maintain themselves as racially integrated communities is the suburb of Oak Park, immediately west of Chicago. Although legally a village, Oak Park is an urban-looking older suburb of some 60,000 residents with roughly half its population living in multistory rental units. The community also has many expensive and architecturally interesting homes. Frank Lloyd Wright lived in Oak Park, and the village prides itself on having several of his early homes. In spite of this, Oak Park, with its aging housing stock, seemed an inevitable candidate for racial turnover— particularly since the suburb directly abuts Chicago's lower-class West Side Ghetto. The West Side Ghetto has a reputation of being among the poorest and the most violent of the areas within the city. It was the major site of looting and burning during the 1968 Chicago riot, and the West Side Ghetto's reputation for poverty, drugs, and violence has increased since then. The Chicago neighborhood directly east of Oak

The old suburb of Oak Park bounding Chicago on the west is an example of how suburbs can both upgrade physically and integrate racially.

Park is known as Austin. Until the 1960s it had been considered one of the city's prime residential areas. As the West Side Ghetto expanded, Austin rapidly changed from upper-middle-class white to lower-class black. Austin is now 98 percent black. Austin's housing stock is primarily rental, and over the years it has experienced considerable physical deterioration. The area also is plagued by drug and crime problems.

Given these circumstances, it would have been reasonable to expect Oak Park to undergo rapid social and racial change. This expectation would be reinforced by knowing that Oak Park primarily had older rental housing of somewhat indifferent quality along its boundary with Chicago. Thus, Oak Park appeared to be a prime candidate for becoming part of the West Side Ghetto.

It didn't happen that way. Unlike the south shore neighborhood in Chicago, Oak Park controlled its own board of realtors, so it could act to prevent outside real estate firms from encouraging panic selling. The community also controlled its own schools, so school boundaries could not be arbitrarily changed. Instead of packing and fleeing, most residents decided to face integration head on. The community decided to actively encourage racial integration while at the same time maintaining its middle-class character. Carol Godwin argues that Oak Park was successful in so doing in large part because it controlled its own local institutions (Carole Godwin, *The Oak Park Strategy*, University of Chicago Press, Chicago, 1979).

To physically maintain the community, several million dollars of local government funds have gone into low-interest loans to remodel and upgrade apartments, particularly those near the Chicago city line. Ten percent of all apartment building flats are inspected every year, and a building must be brought fully up to code before it can be sold and title transferred. The village also invested in a new village hall and street shopping mall. In order to prevent attempts at panic selling, the community banned house-to-house solicitation of properties to be sold and also banned the posting of "For Sale" and "For Rent" signs. An Oak Park Community Relations Department was established to both monitor sales and rental trends and discourage all-white or all-black apartment buildings.

In 1978, with the assistance of the Ford Foundation, the community initiated a "moral homeowners insurance" to further discourage panic selling. Under the unique plan, homeowners who sign up for the insurance and who stay in the community at least five years are guaranteed that they can sell their homes for 80 percent of the difference between the appraised value and the selling price. The purpose of the insurance was psychological rather than economic, and in fact, the program has had only a few takers. Property values have been appreciating, and today concerns over panic selling are part of the past. Emphasizing diversity, the community welcomes all who want to live in an integrated community. To discourage all-one-race apartments on the community's edge abutting Chicago, the suburb began, in 1985, a unique plan that pays landlords to integrate their buildings. On a voluntary basis, a landlord can enter a five-year agreement to let the Oak

Park Housing Center serve as the landlord's rental agent. The landlord, on signing, becomes eligible for matching grants of up to $1,000 per unit to improve apartment interiors; there are larger grants for exterior renovations. The Housing Center, in turn, actively seeks black tenants for buildings that are predominantly white and white tenants for buildings that are predominantly black. If a suitable tenant cannot be found, the apartment can stay off the market for up to ninety days. Meanwhile, the landlord receives 80 percent of the last rent charged for the unit. The purpose is to integrate housing while upgrading the housing stock and protecting landlords against vacant units. The plan is supported through local taxes. Since the 1990 census shows the proportion of blacks living in the census tracts nearest to Chicago have increased their percentages to between 25 and 40 percent, the program has not been as successful as hoped.

In both of the goals of physically maintaining the suburb and encouraging integration, the community has been remarkably successful for a quarter of a century. Oak Park is currently a desirable housing area, particularly with young white home buyers seeking good-quality housing in a stable, racially integrated community. However, Smith argues that assumptions of Oak Park working as an integrated area may be premature. He points out that the black population grew from 11 to 18 percent between 1980 and 1990, and that an invasion-succession pattern seems to be emerging, and, "Indeed, Oak Park appears to be moving in the direction of transition" (Smith, 1993, pp. 127–128). Those who actually live in the community, however, are much more hopeful and optimistic.

Oak Park has been successful in both integrating and maintaining an aging suburban housing stock. However, Oak Park, with its strong middle- and upper-middle-class population, had more resources than many areas faced with racial turnover. The community also was one with a strong sense of citizen involvement. There is no question that Oak Park is a tightly managed community, and this does not appeal to some. The community quickly intervenes to prevent signs of building deterioration and to encourage racial diversity. The suburb tightly enforces building codes and also acts swiftly to prevent unethical or illegal activities by realtors, such as racial steering of blacks into all-black areas. Oak Park has been criticized for managing its housing stock and rental market to an extent not found in most American communities. It also is clear that the community is integrated racially, but not economically. Oak Park does not welcome poorer families that cannot afford middle-class standards. Still, Oak Park demonstrates that even an older suburb abutting a lower-class city neighborhood of extreme poverty can, at the same time, integrate racially and upgrade physically.

Outside critics may disapprove of the scope of housing controls in the community, but Oak Park has proven for a quarter of a century that managed integration can work.

HISPANIC SUBURBANITES

Overall Picture

Discussions of minorities often, in practice, are only discussions of African Americans, but in fact, blacks now comprise just under half (49 percent) of all American minorities. A more rapidly growing minority population is the Hispanic population. Nationally, there are some 22.4 million Hispanics, and they account for some 9 percent of the national population. If present growth trends continue, the Hispanic population will be the United States' largest minority—outnumbering the black population within a little over a decade. The Urban Institute projects that by 2010, the United States population will contain 39 million Hispanics, comprising 12.9 percent of the population. African Americans, by comparison, will constitute 12.5 percent of the United States population ("The Future Immigrant Population of the United States," Program for Research on Immigration Policy, Urban Institute, Washington, D.C., 1992). Between the 1980 and 1990 censuses, the United States non-Hispanic population increased 7 percent, but the Hispanic population increased a remarkable 53 percent (U.S. Bureau of the Census, "The Hispanic Population in the United States: March 1990, *Current Population Reports,* Series P-20, No. 444, 1990). These figures largely exclude undocumented aliens, which may add an additional 2.5 to 4 million persons. By comparison, there was a 13 percent increase for blacks and only a 4 percent increase for non-Hispanic whites. In California, where there was an explosive Hispanic population growth of 70 percent between 1980 and 1990, there were 7.7 million Hispanics in 1990, constituting just over a quarter (25.8 percent) of the total population.

Even if both legal and undocumented immigration ceased immediately, the Hispanic population would be expected to continue to grow. This is primarily because of two factors. The population age structure of the Hispanic population is far younger than that of the general population. The median age for Hispanics is twenty-six, while the median for non-Hispanics is thirty-three. This means a greater proportion of the Hispanic population is of child-bearing age. Second, Hispanic birthrates are approximately 50 percent higher than the United States average. Birthrates among Hispanic teenagers exceed those for African

Americans and are roughly three times those for Anglos. Thus, the expectation is that Hispanics will be an increasing proportion of the American population.

Approximately 43 percent of Hispanics were suburbanites according to the 1990 census. This was up somewhat from 40 percent in 1980. Since the Hispanic population grew rapidly during this period, the actual number increase was to 8.7 million from 5.1 million, or a 69 percent gain over the decade. Hispanics accounted for roughly a quarter (23 percent) of the total suburban population gain between 1980 and 1990 (William H. Frey and William P. O'Hare, "Vivano los Suburbios!" *American Demographics,* April 1993, p. 32).

Hispanics are highly concentrated geographically in a few states. Half the Hispanic population is clustered in California and Texas. Three-quarters live in those states, plus New York, Florida, and Illinois. Over 3 million Hispanics live in Los Angeles County alone, while the New York area has just under 2 million. Other large concentrations are in the Miami metropolitan area, with more than 950,000; the Chicago metropolitan area, with 735,000; and the Houston metropolitan area, with over 700,000. This geographic concentration, however, sometimes masks considerable difference within the Hispanic community. According to the Bureau of the Census, if one examines the Hispanic population, some 63 percent are of Mexican heritage, 11 percent are Puerto Rican, 5 percent are Cuban, 14 percent are Central and South American, and the remaining 7 percent are other Hispanic (U.S. Bureau of the Census, "The Hispanic Population in the United States: March 1991," *Current Population Reports,* Series P-20, No. 455, 1991). Hispanics living in California and Texas are overwhelmingly Mexican and Central American in origin, while those living in New York are Puerto Rican and those in Miami largely Cuban.

The eight metropolitan areas having the most suburban residents are all in the sun belt. Of these, five are in California, two in Texas, and one in Florida. By far the largest is the Los Angeles metro area, with over 1.7 million Hispanic suburbanites. During the 1980s more Hispanics moved to Los Angeles suburbs (600,000) than the total Hispanic population of any other area (Frey and O'Hare, 1993, p. 33). The dozen fastest-growing counties for Hispanics all are located in states of the sun belt. In fact, only four of the rapidly growing Hispanic counties are outside the south or west. Florida dominates the enumeration of fastest-growing Hispanic areas, having four of the top five and nine of the top twenty. Six of these are in central Florida, and three are in the rapidly growing Orlando area. Disney World and a host of other tourist attractions made this a prime location during the 1980s for those seeking jobs in service or retail trade. Of the twenty-five fastest grow-

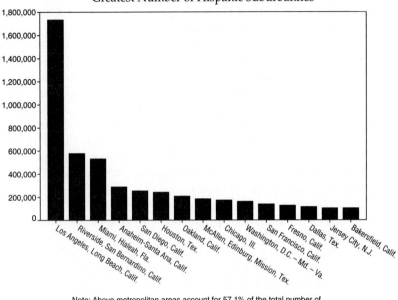

Fifteen Metropolitan Areas Having the
Greatest Number of Hispanic Suburbanites

Note: Above metropolitan areas account for 57.1% of the total number of
suburban Hispanics in the United States. (Compiled from 1990 census data.)

ing Hispanic counties, none are in the midwest, and only four are in the northeast. All the remainder are in the south and west sun belt. Hispanic growth and suburbanization is most prominent in those areas of the country showing the greatest economic growth. Future growth will continue to be disproportionately found in Florida and the states along the Mexican-United States border.

Socioeconomic Patterns

As a group, Hispanics are better off than blacks and worse than non-Hispanic whites. Government figures indicate that 25 percent of Hispanic families fall below the poverty line, as compared to 9.5 percent of non-Hispanic whites and one-third of blacks (U.S. Bureau of the Census, "The Hispanic Population of the United States: March 1991," 1991). However, the variations within Hispanic groups are considerable, with Puerto Ricans earning slightly less than blacks, Mexican Americans earning slightly more, and Cuban Americans earning considerably more. The Cuban group includes many middle-class businessmen and professionals who left Fidel Castro's Cuba with marketable skills and professions. Cuban Americans, particularly in

Florida, tend to be very conservative politically, while Puerto Rican and Mexican populations tend to to vote heavily Democratic. In 1990 the median family income of Hispanic groups varied from $18,000 for Puerto Ricans and $23,200 for Mexicans to $31,400 for Cuban Americans. Suburban Hispanic household incomes were a third higher than those in central cities ($26,811 as opposed to $20,387). The income difference between urban and suburban Hispanics is even greater in the larger metropolitan areas. Exacerbating the differences are divisions between native-born Hispanics and those who are more recent immigrants. New Mexican immigrants sometimes refer to earlier, more settled immigrants as Chicanos. (A generation earlier, the Chicanos were the newcomers.) The newcomers and the older groups often speak different languages, eat different foods, dress differently, and have different political agendas and goals.

While suburban Cubans are often well-to-do and suburban Mexicans are increasingly indistinguishable from their neighbors, the stereotype remains of poor Mexicans and others entering the United States to serve as farm workers. The popular media—whether doing sympathetic portrayals of Hispanic migrant laborers, advertising for Colombian coffee using a peasant and burro, or discussing union attempts to organize California's farm workers—generally also portray Hispanics as agricultural workers. This is quite erroneous, for while some Hispanic immigrants may have rural roots, the Hispanic population is now 93 percent metropolitan. It is more concentrated in metropolitan cities and suburbs than the populations of either non-Hispanic whites or blacks, and some 90 percent of California's population with Mexican roots live in metropolitan areas. Los Angeles now has far more Hispanics than blacks. And the Hispanic population is rapidly increasing. Between 1980 and 1990, Los Angeles city alone added some 1.3 million Hispanic residents. A third of the Los Angeles metropolitan-area residents are Hispanic. Today, Los Angeles has more residents of Mexican ancestry than any other city in the Americas excepting Mexico City and Guadalajara.

Hispanics, unlike blacks, have faced wide variations in patterns of physical segregation (Frank D. Bean and Marta Tienda, *The Hispanic Population of the United States*, Russell Sage Foundation, New York, 1987, pp. 170–177). Historically, segregation was most common in border states such as California and, particularly, Texas. Outside of the border states, economics rather than ethnicity has played the major role in determining residential patterns. Housing segregation never became institutionalized elsewhere as it did in Texas and California. Evidence from school data appears to indicate increasing segregation for poor Hispanics in Texas and California (Karen DeWitt, "Rising

Segregation Is Found for Hispanic Students," *New York Times News Service,* January 9, 1992).

Poorer Hispanics, as is the case with blacks, tend to be segregated in the less desirable central-city areas. Affluent Hispanics, on the other hand, live in affluent suburbs and the more comfortable city neighborhoods. For Hispanics, suburban residence is associated with lower levels of segregation and greater association with non-Hispanic whites (Massey and Denton, 1987, pp. 802–825). The data show the same pattern of higher socioeconomic status associated with outlying residence as is found in the Anglo population. Suburbanization of Hispanics is strongly associated with higher income level (William Frey and Alden Speare, *Regional and Metropolitan Growth and Decline in the United States,* Russell Sage Foundation, New York, 1988, pp. 311–316).

ASIAN SUBURBANIZATION

Fastest-Growing Minority

Half (50.6 percent) of all those of Asian background in the United States are suburbanites, making Asians slightly more suburban than the white population. Asian Americans constitute the nation's fastest-growing minority population; nationally, the Asian population went from 3.5 million in 1980 to 7.3 million in 1990. That is a remarkable 108 percent increase in one decade. In California, the Asian population more than doubled, to 2.8 million, or 9.4 percent of the state population. Overall, the United States' Asian population is approximately 3.5 percent of the total population; but its influence extends beyond its small size. According to the demographer Berry Edmondson, the Asian population is projected to grow to 17.1 million by 2010 and 34.5 million by 2040. This growth will be because of a combination of above-average fertility rates and high rates of immigration. Asian Americans are a remarkably diverse group, including Chinese, Japanese, Vietnamese, Filipino, Korean, Indian, Iranian, and others. Nationwide, the largest Asian population group is Chinese (32 percent), followed by Filipinos (19 percent), Japanese (12 percent), and Koreans and Indians (each 11 percent).

Economically, Asians are America's most affluent minority group, with a median household income considerably exceeding that of other groups. Bureau of the Census figures indicate that the 1990 median household income for Asians was $36,748, compared to $31,435 for non-Hispanic whites, $24,156 for Hispanics, and $19,758 for blacks. Some 14.1 percent of Asians were below the poverty level, compared to

9.8 percent for whites, 25.3 percent for Hispanics, and 29.5 percent for blacks. A remarkable 35 percent of Asian households had 1989 incomes of $50,000 or more, compared to just 26 percent of white households (Waldrop and Jacobsen, 1992, p. 34). Within the Asian population, Japanese income levels are the highest, and the more recently arrived Vietnamese have the lowest. Asian American educational levels also are higher than those for the white population.

Housing Patterns

Geographically, the Asian population is concentrated on the west coast and Hawaii. As of 1990, two out of five (39 percent of) Asians lived in California. The Los Angeles metropolitan area has an Asian population of almost a million, while the San Francisco area has one approaching a third of a million. On the east coast, the New York metropolitan area has the largest Asian population, with 556,399 Asian residents. While there are specific Asian neighborhoods in many larger cities, these ethnic enclaves are more a consequence of selection than segregation. Asians have not been subject to the same exclusionary housing practices that have been part of the historical experience of African Americans.

Asian populations, particularly newer immigrants, do not always share cultural assumptions regarding cities and suburbs with other American citizens. Most white Americans take it for granted, for example, that couples with young children believe that suburbs, although they may have some limitations for adults, provide a superior environment in which to raise children. Chinese, on the other hand, tend to believe in the social advantages for children of more communal urban living. There exists a strong cultural belief in the superiority of urban environments. As expressed to the author by an executive in Taiwan, "I have to work in the suburbs, but we, of course, live in the city because it is better for the children." One can see this urban preference in Taiwan, where Taipei has miles-long evening rush hour traffic jams. The difference from the United States is that in Taipei, the evening crush of autos is driving home *into* the city, while the outbound expressway experiences only light traffic. Asians immigrating to the United States from Hong Kong, Singapore, or Seoul thus find American suburban life to be a substantial cultural switch.

Traditionally, one way newcomers have tried to lessen the shock of transition to a new country has been by moving into neighborhoods having substantial numbers of those from similar backgrounds. The history of large-city turn-of-the-century Irish, Jewish, Polish, and Italian neighborhoods is well known. Asians follow the same pattern.

Chinese residents doing Tai Chi in suburban Monterey Park, California.

In the Los Angeles area, unlike Washington, D.C., Koreans (at least until the 1992 riots) tended to locate in more central locations, such as Koreatown, while Chinese tended to settle more in suburban areas, such as predominantly Chinese Monterey Park. In southern California, some developers have become proficient in designing homes to meet the needs of particular Asian populations. For example, if one wishes to sell to Taiwanese or Hong Kong Chinese, it is important that the developer contract with a geomancer to make sure the home is properly aligned for good luck. The geomancer makes sure the developer avoids obvious building errors such as planting trees facing the front door that might block good luck from flowing into the house or building a house at the end of a road, which allows bad luck to flow into the house. Having front and back door in a line is also something the developer would avoid, since it allows luck to flow through the house. Most important, the builder would make sure none of his homes were built with four doors, since four is an unlucky number (when pronounced, it sounds like the word for death). Some Americans might consider such practices rather strange, but recall that in western cultures, 13 is an unlucky number. It is very rare to find an American hotel having a 13th floor; the floors usually jump from 12th to 14th.

American Asians have been suburbanizing in increasing numbers. Population surveys conducted by the Bureau of the Census indicate that almost half the Asians who immigrated to the United States from abroad between 1975 and 1985 bypassed the cities and settled directly into suburban and nonmetropolitan areas ("Suburbs Absorb More Immigrants, Mostly the Affluent and Educated," *The New York Times*, December 14, 1986, p. 1). The majority of these immigrants arrived speaking fluent English and holding advanced degrees. There is also a regional difference. New immigrants in the south and west are more likely to initially settle in suburbs than those settling in the east and midwest. For middle-class Asians, suburbia, rather than the central city's Chinatown, Little Tokyo, or Koreatown, is the likely location of first settlement. In Washington, D.C., for example, there is no Koreatown, and most Koreans live in suburban Montgomery and Fairfax counties. Some 20 percent of Montgomery County residents do not speak English as a first language. Only 800 of the 44,000 Koreans in the Washington area actually live in the District ("Area Koreans See No Need for Enclaves," *Washington Post*, January 11, 1992, p. E1). The main reason for suburban location is the quality of the schools, since education is of crucial importance to Korean families. Homes commonly are selected on the basis of their location in school districts having the highest SAT scores.

Overall, most Asian newcomers do not live in predominantly Asian suburbs. Newcomers are more likely to move to suburbs that have an Asian presence but are predominantly white. An exception is Monterey Park in the Los Angeles area which has become the first Chinese suburb in America. Monterey Park is projected to be 80 percent Asian in 2000, and the rapid transformation from a low density suburb to a high density "Little Taipei" has resulted in a host of growth and land usage conflicts that often take a racial cast (Timothy P. Fong, *The First Suburban Chinatown*, Temple University Press, Philadelphia, 1994).

Unlike poor blacks or Hispanics, who often find themselves locked into older central-neighborhoods, legal Asian and other foreign immigrants tend to settle immediately into those suburban neighborhoods where employment opportunities are greatest and incomes the highest. Census data indicate that legal immigrants, regardless of Asian (or Hispanic) origin or darkness of skin, have rapidly spread throughout middle-class suburbs and better-off urban neighborhoods. This movement of immigrants directly to the suburbs lends support to the belief that suburbs are now restricted more by class than by race. The suburbs are now more or less open if you have an acceptable level of income and education. Asian immigrants today increasingly bypass the traditional American pattern of settling first in the central city and then later moving to the suburbs. They start in the suburbs.

CHAPTER 9

Women and Family in the Suburbs

Beyond Myths

IDEOLOGY OF DOMESTICITY

The nineteenth-century ideology of female domesticity suggested women were particularly physically and morally equipped to nurture. As discussed in an earlier chapter, when this view was melded with the belief of the home being the "women's sphere," the result was a combination that gave moral support to mid-nineteenth-century middle-class suburbanization. Woman's place was in the home, and that home was ideally in the expanding suburbs. The home was to be a fortress and a refuge from the evils and vices of the city. The home, under the practical and moral guidance of the mother, was to be a sacred place in which family values could be promoted around the fireside. A middle-landscape between city and country that had trees and greenery but that was neither too wild nor too urban was the proper Currier and Ives family environment. While the city was reviled as the center of infamy and anonymity, the suburb, with its open lawns and clean air, was to provide a healthful, natural, and moral atmosphere in which to raise children and teach values. In an era when activities were divided between men's and women's spheres, the city was Gomorrah—a world of men, factories, crowding, and vice. The suburban home, by contrast, was sacred space in which, under the wife's tutelage, men would be encouraged to become more civilized and children would be raised in health and virtue.

According to Catherine Beecher, who wrote over two dozen works and was the most influential domestic instructor and advice-giver of the mid-nineteenth century, the rearing of children and management of the home were not simply domestic virtues, they were activities essential for the survival of the Republic (Catherine Beecher, *Treatise on Domestic Economy*, Marsh, Capen, Lyon, and Webb, Boston, 1841). She was writing for an essentially new constituency of middle-class non-farm women. This was an expanding group whose major responsibility was management of the home. Unlike farm wives, they had no responsibility for working with their husbands as partners operating a farm, nor did they have to labor long hours in the expanding urban factories and sweatshops, as did working-class women. As a rebellion against the suggestion that the women of the growing middle-class population had no real role, an ideology was designed that gave women a central place in national life (Kathryn Kish Sklar, *Catherine Beecher: A Study in American Domesticity*, Yale, New Haven, Conn., 1974, p. xiii). The home was to be the central linchpin about which all else revolved. In Beecher's words, "Surely it is a pernicious and mistaken idea, that the duties which tax a woman's mind are petty, trivial, or unworthy of the highest grade of intellect and moral worth. Instead of allowing this feeling, every woman should imbibe from early youth, the impression, that she is training for the care of the most important, most difficult, and the most sacred and interesting duties that can possibly employ the highest intellect" (Beecher, 1841, p. 144). She believed that through their nurturing role, women could exercise an influence on national character that would transcend class and location. Women would provide the social order holding together American democracy.

Proper management of the home and children was seen as the woman's responsibility, and since this was so crucial, it made her a full partner with her husband. Catherine's sister, Harriet Beecher Stowe, the writer of *Uncle Tom's Cabin*, went further. As Margaret Marsh notes, Harriet Beecher Stowe, "was among the earliest to make public her suspicions that women were neither men's inferiors nor their equals, but their betters" (Margaret Marsh, *Suburban Lives*, Rutgers University Press, New Brunswick, N.J., 1990, p. 32). Men, in her opinion, were basically weak and had to be "guided" and "taught" by women, who were stronger. The suburban home, with its emphasis on shared domesticity, was the ideal setting in which to engage in this instruction.

The nineteenth-century defining of the home's interior as woman's space had some very practical and positive consequences for home design. Kitchens, for example, were no longer simply basement rooms with open fireplaces. For the first time kitchens were designed taking into account efficiency, sanitary food preparation, and scientific housekeeping. Domestic engineering was to be utilized to create a profes-

The myth of happy suburban domesticity has its roots in the nineteenth-century romanticization of suburban life.

sional and elevating influence for the housewives and servants who used the space (Mary Corbin Sies, "The City Transformed: Nature, Technology, and the Suburban Ideal, 1877–1917," *Journal of Urban History*, Vol. 14, No. 1, 1987, p. 94). Clean surfaces, indoor plumbing, and proper light and ventilation were all part of the design. The result was a far more useful, comfortable, and rationally designed interior. This is not to say that most kitchens henceforth were well designed. Women would continue, until the present, to have the legitimate complaint that many kitchens were poorly laid out and "obviously designed by a man." The nineteenth-century breakthrough was the acceptance of the view that kitchens were a specifically designed space.

Domestic Engineering

As the new century opened, old Victorian social patterns were further substantially modified by a Progressive Era emphasis on the housewife as a "domestic engineer." This was consciously advocated by Progressives and middle-road feminists to elevate household activities to the realm of skilled domestic engineering in order to provide housewives both higher status and greater personal freedom. No longer could a middle-class woman know only how to manage servants; now she was a manager responsible for the "scientific management" of the home. This meant she had to know budgeting, sanitation, and the characteristics of foods (balanced meals); she had to be an informed consumer.

This emphasis on domestic science was reflected in schools and colleges, which established departments of Home Economics. The land grant colleges which had first brought professional programs such as dentistry and engineering onto campuses, were also in the forefront in establishing programs of home economics for the application of domestic science. (Following World War II, the idea of scientific management was further extended by universities into the realm of personal relations with the proliferation of courses on Marriage and Family.)

All the concern with domestic management was designed to increase women's freedom by making the home role more professional and less restrictive. Mary Pattison made this explicit in her influential *Principles of Domestic Engineering*, where she sought to make the home more efficient by standardizing household tasks into a science (Mary Pattison, *Principles of Domestic Engineering: or the What, Why and How of a Home*, Trow Press, New York, 1915). Through the use of stopwatch and charts plus several thousand questionnaires that had been distributed to New Jersey housewives, the efficient ways to cook, clean, and sew were detailed. The titles of some of the chapters give a sense of the scope of the work. Titles of chapters include, "An Auto-Operative House," "The Business of Purchasing," "The Regeneration of the Kitchen," "Personal Freedom," "Organization of the Family," "The Cultural Value of Housework," "The Organization of the Consumer," and "Housework and Democracy." The scientific management of the home was tied to progressive idealism. According to the book's final paragraph, "the truly progressive home is akin to democracy's method . . . Domestic engineering would encourage cooperation between men and women leading to personal freedom and personal independence." In the final words of the volume, "The new progressive idealism shows Democracy as a Religion, where men and women guided by God, united, shall work for its issues" (Pattison, 1915, pp. 302–303).

Shared Domesticity

As the above indicates, the beginning of the twentieth century saw the earlier Victorian ideology of separate male and female spheres well on the way to being replaced by a newer Progressive household ideology. This ideology was not one of separateness, but one of shared domesticity. For those in the rising middle-class professions, the family, not just the mother and children, was now seen as the basic domestic unit. In practical terms this meant that husbands, as well as wives and children, were expected to share common time and space. This sharing was also encouraged by physical changes in the middle-class home. Older homes had been divided by walls and doors into separate male rooms (the study) and female rooms (drawing and morning rooms). Drawing rooms, for example, were the rooms to which women withdrew after dinner so the men could have their port, cigars, and male conversation. (If the home were an elaborate one, the men might withdraw to a smoking room or a billiard room.) Design of the rooms was to reflect their usage. Smoking rooms were to be heavy and masculine, while furniture in the drawing room was to be light, elegant, and "ladylike" (Robert Kerr, *The Gentleman's House: or How to Plan English Residences,* Johnson Reprint Company, New York [1871], 1972, p. 107).

Regardless of its usage, each room was heated by its own fireplace or stove, which encouraged designing a house with small rooms that could be closed off from unheated areas. Even central heating contributed to the success of the ideology of sharing space and activity. Central heating not only brought a new level of comfort, it helped change family patterns. Central heating and the removal of compartmentalizing walls meant that family members could now pursue individual activities in common familial space. Here was an implicit acceptance that within the home, there was an interconnection between physical space and the moral environment. The social rationale was that open spaces promoted familial togetherness and communal activities. The larger family living room, in which all family members could gather, came to replace the parlor and reception rooms (Sies, 1987, p. 98). Housing was being designed to be less gender-specific and to reduce gender segregation. Better designed houses would produce healthier children and a happier more cohesive family.

The modern suburban home, by encouraging familial activity, thus could ennoble those who inhabited it. Floor plans specifically were designed to strengthen family togetherness. In the middle-class house of a century ago, father, mother, and children might still be doing separate activities, but they should all be gathered around the family hearth, not in separate partitioned rooms. Particularly in the evening, the family was expected to congregate informally in the living room. This image of living room family domesticity was widely portrayed in the home advertisements as well as the women's magazines of the day. It is also the picture of the "ideal" family publicized in the famous Dick and Jane elementary school readers. These readers, with their picture of father in his chair smoking his pipe, mother in her chair doing the sewing, and Dick and Jane playing on the rug with the cat, were still commonly in use until the 1960s. They provided the "official" middle-class view of proper family life. This image was echoed in the family-based TV shows of the 1950s and 1960s. (It might also be noted that following World War II, suburban homes underwent another physical metamorphosis. The living room grew smaller and took on the more formal aspects of the earlier parlor. Everyday family activity and living now took place in a new, more informal, and specifically named, "family room.")

By the turn of the century, the new open floor plans and the idea of shared domesticity had achieved widespread acceptance. The living room, according to early twentieth-century home magazines, was the symbolic representation of family togetherness. Frank Lloyd Wright would later claim the sole honor of removing the partitions and doors from first floors, but other architects were moving in the same direction (Marsh, 1990, p. 84). Wright, however, did move further than others in removing segregated small spaces by making the whole first floor excepting the kitchen into essentially one large room.

Family togetherness thus was not something invented after World War II and only found in postwar suburban housing developments, as articles written in the 1950s sometimes suggested. A century ago shared domesticity or togetherness had already found suburban acceptance. By the beginning of the century, it already had been accepted by suburban men that males had a role in the home and men even had limited domestic duties and responsibilities for children, such as reading them bedtime stories. A suburban man's place most evenings was at home with his family rather than out with his clubmen or colleagues. Marsh indicates that this emphasis on a limited sharing of domestic duties, rather than supporting early feminism, tended to blunt the power of feminist demands (Marsh, p. 84). It also should be noted that while the ideology of shared domesticity developed strong middle-class suburban roots, this ideology was not equally shared either by the very wealthy or by the working class. Both the rich and the urban working class continued to maintain sharper gender-defined roles both within their lives and within their homes. Upper-class men had their male club, and working-class men had the male-dominated saloon.

By the 1920s the suburban ideal of the domestic family unit of father, mother, and children had become a mass-produced commodity (Marsh, p. 84). Home ownership had become part of the American middle-class ideology. Having your own home, preferably in a convenient suburb, meant that you had arrived and were part of the American Dream. Popular magazines such as *Good Housekeeping* and *Ladies Home Journal* constantly stressed the advantages of suburban environments for the proper rearing of children. The suburban home, not the city apartment, was touted as the place where small children would

Post-World War II versions of suburban domesticity as portrayed in TV shows such as *Father Knows Best* strongly reinforced traditional family patterns and values.

find a "normal" and "healthy" environment. The suburbs were where mothers could safely let children outside to play. One now moved to the suburbs "for the children's sake."

Twentieth-Century Efficiency and Family Living

As noted above, the dawning of the twentieth century saw a major social attack on the formality and excesses of the Victorian era. In architecture, this was reflected in the supplanting of the elaborate Victorian dwelling with the simpler rustic bungalow (See Chapter 5 on prewar homes for more on the suburban bungalows.) The bungalow became the most popular suburban home built in the 1920s. The bungalow style stressed efficiency and simplicity. In spite of its name, the bungalow characteristically had a second floor housing a bathroom and all the bedrooms, and a full concrete-floored basement. Compared to the suburban homes of earlier decades, bungalows were generally smaller and constructed without formal features such as entrance halls or parlors.

What they did have, however, was a high degree of comfort and convenience. Not unimportant for newlyweds, the bungalow was also a less expensive first home and thus had a particular appeal to young couples. From the standpoint of the housewife, suburban bungalows took far less time and energy to care for than the larger, but far less modern, homes of their mothers. The bungalows had all the technological advances of the day and included luxuries only available to the well-to-do a generation earlier. The homes were built with modern indoor bathrooms, electric connections, gas connections for kitchen stoves, and central heating. For the latter, you could have steam, hot-air, or hot-water systems. Individual wood- or coal-burning room heaters or stoves were no longer seen; they had been superseded by coal-fired central-heating systems. In some cases the furnaces were even automatic oil-fired units. The "fireplace" in the 1920s bungalow living room was likely to be a faux fireplace with gas-fed logs. (During the 1990s gas-fired fireplaces again returned to favor.) New "scientific" labor-saving devices such as electric laundry machines, electric irons, electric vacuum cleaners, and even electric toasters all made middle-class women's lives easier. No longer did you have to daily strain yourself to feed wood or coal into the kitchen stove or room heaters. No longer did you have to have a washerwoman—or yourself—do the backbreaking work of heating water on the stove and then washing the clothes by hand in huge vats. For hot water you turned on the faucet; to wash the clothes you turned on the washing machine, which was now located in the bungalow's concrete-floored, electric-lighted, and centrally heated basement.

It is all but impossible for us today to imagine just how much time and heavy physical labor was an everyday part of housekeeping prior to the modern era. The new labor-saving electric appliances and more efficient kitchen designs of the smaller bungalow-style suburban homes of the 1920s did more than reduce heavy labor around the home. They also contributed to the ongoing social revolution in women's equality by providing middle-class women much more free time. The comparative efficiency of the new electric appliances removed some of the time-consuming drudgery from housekeeping and promoted the possibility of leisure time. Women's magazines of the day noted how modern young women living in such suburban homes now had the "free time" to devote to social activities, charity work, or other activities. They might even have a career.

The idea that it was possible to have both a home and a career first came into vogue for the middle-class at this time. Having a job outside the home was not the norm, but it now, theoretically, became an option. Middle-class ideology began to change so that a suburban woman's working at a career or job was not automatically assumed to be the consequence of the early death of the male breadwinner. "Modern" married middle-class women, even those with children, could have a career without automatically being considered negligent wives and mothers. This is not to suggest that the technology of the new housing determined family social and work patterns. Rather, it is to suggest that technological advances, by changing the nature of housework, made it easier for patterns of greater social equality between spouses to develop.

A more recent development has been the assumption by adult family members of home repair and improvement activities that were previously done by hired male painters, plumbers, and carpenters. A "do-it-yourself" generation has grown up with the assumption that everything from kitchen cabinets to decks to new bathroom fixtures can be self-installed. TV ads show couples putting in a new ceiling fan or installing new countertops after viewing the hardware warehouse video on how to do it.

On the positive side, there is a decreasing division between what is appropriate men's work and women's work. On the negative side, home improvement activities decrease true leisure time. Nonetheless, labor costs all but necessitate that suburban couples who wish to upgrade their homes will do much of their own work. It is taken for granted that they themselves will do much of the work in building a rec room or adding a bedroom. In this respect, the contemporary family unit has a commonality with early American families, who were expected to physically contribute to the construction and maintenance of their dwellings.

Feminist Views

For the half-century from 1920 to 1970, the popular magazines equated the suburban home with attaining the American Dream, but this clearly was not the view of feminists. Rather than seeing the suburban bungalow as an ideal, feminists of the era saw the wife's involvement in a self-contained home as a patriarch-designed regression. Thus, feminists were almost always antisuburban, tending to equate the suburban home not with more freedom, but with a patriarchal desire to confine women and children to an isolated home environment. The suburban ideal of domestic togetherness was viewed as a male device for keeping women in their domestic place.

To break this pattern, feminists of the late-nineteenth and early-twentieth centuries often advocated making housework, laundry, and cooking communal responsibilities (Dolores Hayden, *The Grand Domestic Revolution: A History of Feminist Designs for American Homes, Neighborhoods, and Cities,* MIT Press, Cambridge, Mass., 1981). This, they believed, would emancipate women from the daily drudgery that confined them to the house and its responsibilities. Utopian feminist communities, such as the early-twentieth-century Llano del Rio in southern California, often were designed without kitchens in the homes. Rather, the houses backed on a communal kitchen and eating area. Laundry, similarly, was done in communal rather than household facilities. The goal was to provide time for other activities. Somewhat ironically, this goal was accomplished for middle-class women by having lower-class women do the heavy washing, cooking, and cleaning. In that day and age, it apparently never occurred to the proponents of Llano Del Rio that class discrimination was being substituted for gender discrimination.

Contemporary feminist writings on ideal housing continue to stress the advantages of communal housing models. This is particularly the case with those favoring neo-Marxist models. Gender inequality is seen as an inevitable consequence of single-family suburban housing being built by men for men. Feminist writers generally view spatial structure as reinforcing gender inequalities, with the cities representing masculine centers of production and the suburbs feminine centers of reproduction (Linda McDowell, "City and Home: Urban Housing and the Sexual Division of Space," in Mary Evans and Clare Ungerson, eds., *Sexual Divisions: Patterns and Processes,* Tavistock, London, 1983, pp. 142–163). Suburban single-family home designs are part of a patriarchal family structure in which, "The dominance of the single-family detached dwelling, its separation from the workplace, and its decentralized urban location are as much the products of the patriarchal organization of household production as of the capitalistic organization of wage work" (Ann R. Markasen, "City Spatial Structure, Women's Household Work and National Urban Policy," *Signs,* Vol. 5, No. 31, 1980). Important non-Marxist feminists such as Betty Friedan have also been justly critical of a model in which women were to remain tied to the house as homemakers while men commuted to the real world of work in the city (Betty Friedan, *The Feminist Mystique,* Norton, New York, 1963). Only by entering the paid work force and establishing careers could women be liberated from the bondage of domestic servitude.

Attempts to design more women-centered housing continue to be a major concern. Ideally, such women-centered housing would be designed to prevent the isolation from public life that is seen to be integral to contemporary suburbs (Dolores Hayden, *Redesigning the American Dream*, Norton, New York, 1984). Feminist designs, harkening back to the earlier communal models, emphasize the importance of planning new communities that have shared communal services and facilities (Dolores Hayden, "What Would a Non-Sexist City Be Like?" *Signs*, Vol. 5, No. 31, 1980). However, survey research indicates most women continue to prefer private over communal kitchens and other facilities.

Patriarchal or Matriarchal Suburbs?

It is somewhat ironic that the contemporary concern over the patriarchal nature of suburbia is the exact opposite of the major criticisms made by popular antisuburban literature of the post-World War II period. The accusation made by critics of suburbia following the war was not that suburbs fostered a patriarchal traditional family, but rath er that the husbands' absence from the suburban home during the day led to a suburban matriarchy. This matriarchy, it was charged, was leading to a child-dominated society. The suburban way of life was said to lead to excessive, overprotective "momism." Suburban mothers were criticized for having excessive involvement in the raising of their sons, which was leading to the raising of a generation of spineless male offspring. These beliefs were not fringe views. It is worth noting that Philip Wylie's *Generation of Vipers*, which put the term "momism" into the language, had gone through twenty printings by the 1950s (Philip Wylie, *Generation of Vipers*, Ferrar and Rinehart, New York, 1942). Popular postwar criticism, as expressed by psychiatrists and others, was that suburban life, with its daytime absence of males, led to excessive independence and isolation of women. Female-oriented suburban life was, in turn, blamed for increases in adultery, alcoholism, mental illness, and divorce (R. E. Gordon, K. K. Gordon, and M. Gunther, *The Split-Level Trap*, Dell, New York, 1962). Such pop-psychology myths received wide dissemination and acceptance as factual descriptions of reality.

The 1963 publication of Betty Friedan's landmark, *The Feminine Mystique* (1963) turned the argument completely around. Friedan gave voice to the widespread angst of housewives, and she noted that it came not from having too much suburban free time, but from powerlessness. She agreed that the suburbs helped create a female culture, but it was not a culture of dominating momism, but rather one of essential exclusion from outside-the-home decision making.

Gender Housing Preferences

There have been discussions going back over a century as to whether suburban life was better for males or females. Actual studies done in the 1960s and 1970s tended to show that suburbia and suburban life favored males, with husbands being more pleased with suburban living than their wives. Gans, in his famous Levittown study, found, for example, that three out of ten husbands, but six out of ten wives, preferred to live in the city "if not for the children" (Herbert Gans, *The Levittowners*, Vintage Books, New York, 1967, p. 272). College-educated women with young children particularly felt the restrictions of being tied to the limited local community for intellectual stimulation. Studies generally found that husbands, because they left the community for work, had wider networks of friends and colleagues, while wives were more likely to be restricted to socializing with those in the neighborhood (Claude Fischer, *The Urban Experience*, Harcourt Brace Jovanovich, New York, 1976).

A major study of Toronto housing by Michelson found that women living in urban residential areas had greater satisfaction with their neighborhoods than those in more suburban locations (William Michelson, *Environmental Choice, Human Behavior and Residential Satisfaction*, Oxford University Press, New York, 1977). Women particularly liked the access to services and public transportation that urban areas afforded. In most writings, men were reported more likely to prefer suburbs since they provided escape from urban pressures and demands. (See, for example, Susan Saegert and Gary Winkel, "The Home: A Crucial Problem for Changing Sex Roles," in Gerda Wekerle, H. Peterson, and D. Morley, eds., *New Space for Women*, Westview Press, Boulder, Colo., 1980, Chapter 1.) A feminist's 1980 review of the literature on the effect of housing environments on women concluded that the burdens of isolated suburban life fell particularly heavily on women (Gerda R. Wekerle, "Women in the Urban Environment," *Signs*, Vol. 5, 1980, Supplement pp. 188–214).

However, times change. While one still hears references to women being isolated in suburbia without access to cars, culture, or community, this picture increasingly is a cliché of another era. In a time when two- and even three-car families are the norm, and when most women, including those with young children, are in the labor force, the image of the isolated suburban homemaker seems somewhat quaintly dated. The picture of the homemaker trapped all day in her suburban home and kitchen has more ties to the 1950s than to the realities of contemporary life. Today most women have careers or jobs outside the home.

Also, the preference of women for the convenience of the city over

The post-World War II "modern" kitchen
showed the full effects of "scientific" domestic
engineering and home economics, but it was
still quite clearly a woman's domain.

the space of the suburbs no longer applies. The data are rather overwhelming in indicating that most American women want detached,
single-family suburban homes. Daphne Spain found that responses of
32,000 households to the federal government's Annual Housing
Survey indicate that women equally with men share a preference for
suburban over urban housing (Daphne Spain, "An Examination of
Residential Preferences in the Suburban Era," *Sociological Focus,* Vol. 21,
Jan. 1988, pp. 109–117). Large majorities of both sexes prefer single-
family homes. Moreover, single women heading households, similarly
to married-couple householders, expressed the greatest satisfaction
with living in suburban housing (Daphne Spain, "The Effect of
Changing Household Composition on Neighborhood Satisfaction,"
Urban Affairs Quarterly, Vol. 23, No. 4, 1988, pp. 581–600). Christine
Cook similarly found that female single-parent householders express
greater satisfaction with suburban rather than city housing (Christine
Cook, "Components of Neighborhood Satisfaction: Responses from
Urban and Suburban Single-Parent Women," *Environment and Behavior,*

Vol. 20, 1988, pp. 115–149). Lower rates of crime, better schools for their children, and the generally more peaceful environment were the most common reasons given for preferring the suburbs. For women house-holders, the traditional urban advantages of access to public transit and shopping now appear to be more than offset by concerns over crime and poor-quality schools. Gender differences are becoming less and less relevant in predicting housing preferences. The Annual Housing Survey indicates both men and women now give similar reasons for moving to a particular area.

The similarity of views might, as Sylvia Fava suggests, reflect a generational change (Sylvia F. Fava, "Residential Preferences in the New Suburban Era: A New Look," *Sociological Focus*, Vol. 18, 1985, pp. 109–117). Unlike the suburbanites of the 1950s and 1960s, the majority of young adults now living in suburbs have grown up in suburbs rather than in central cities. Thus, they are most comfortable with the suburban environment in which they were raised. Also, massive changes in shopping and employment patterns over the past decades have resulted in the majority of these activities now being located in suburbs. (See Chapter 11: Outer Cities and the Malling of the Land.) Living in the suburbs is now the middle-class norm; it is living else-where that requires a specific decision. Often critics of suburban hous-ing and life-styles appear to be viewing suburbs through a different prism than that used by actual suburban residents. Today's suburban-ites are more concerned about matters such as commuting problems and getting more open time than they are about being trapped in their suburban houses. Having too much independent or leisure time with nothing to do is not a prime problem of women of the 1990s. Most sub-urbanites, male and female, would welcome having a few days alone at home.

CHAPTER 10

Contemporary Issues
and Problems

ZONING

As the material on planned nineteenth- and early-twentieth-century suburban communities indicates, the concept of communities that were economically, ethnically, religiously, and racially homogeneous is not a new idea. What made zoning significant was not that it attempted to control what people and land-use activities could occur in an area. What made it significant was that the land usage and occupancy was controlled by law. Although attempts at zoning had occurred earlier, zoning became a national force when the New York Zoning Resolution of 1916 was enacted. The original goal of land-use restrictions was to "lessen congestion in the streets" and to "prevent the intrusion of improper uses into homogeneous areas" (Dennis O'Harrow, "Zoning, What's the Good of It?" in Wentworth Eldridge, ed., *Taming Megalopolis*, Doubleday Anchor, New York, 1967, p. 762). Zoning, it was thought, would limit land speculation and congestion. Community after community across the nation quickly followed the New York model in enacting their own zoning regulations to prevent "improper" usages such as lower-class housing moving into homogeneous areas.

The goal was to segregate land usages and freeze "noncompatible" usages out of higher-status residential and retail areas. The 1921 Standard State Zoning Enabling Act was even issued by the federal government to encourage state governments to grant power to cities:

> For the purpose of promoting health, safety, moral and the general welfare of the community, the legislative body of cities and incorpo-

rated villages is hereby empowered to regulate and restrict the height, number of stories, and size to the building, and other structures the percentage of the lot that may be occupied, the size of the yards, courts, and other open spaces, the density of the population, and the location and use of buildings, structures, and land for trade, industry, residence, or other purpose (New F. Baker, *Legal Aspects of Zoning*, (University of Chicago Press, Chicago, 1927, p. 24).

In 1926, the Supreme Court ruled in *Village of Euclid v. Amber Realty* that zoning was a constitutional extension of local government's police power. Today Houston is the only major city in the country without zoning laws, and Houston is debating establishing zoning. In practice, Houston accomplishes the same restrictive goals through the deed restrictions placed on over two-thirds of the property in the city. These restrictions are virtually universal in well-to-do Houston neighborhoods such as River Oaks (Richard F. Babcock, "Houston: Unzoned, Unfettered, and Mostly Unrepentant," *Planning*, Vol. 48, March 1982, pp. 21–23).

Zoning was extensively used by suburbs to maintain social and economic segregation by "zoning out" what were viewed as incompatible usages. Private prejudice thus became enacted into public policy. Cities often inadvertently compounded the pattern of suburbia being the location zoned for upper-income residences by overzoning urban land for commercial and industrial usage. While this zoning made commercial landlords happy because it meant they could convert residential land to other usages, it ensured that those who could afford to seek protection from such change would look to the suburbs with their residential zoning.

During the post-World War II suburban boom, subdivision regulations became the principal means of promoting social homogeneity in newly developing suburban areas. Even developers committed to providing homes for working-class populations deliberately kept their developments racially segregated. The original Levittown, for example, had no black families among the 82,000 community residents as of 1960. (Today the community is heavily minority.) William Levitt, the developer, was quite forthright, stating, "We can solve a housing problem, or we can try to solve a racial problem. But we cannot combine the two" (Kenneth Jackson, *Crabgrass Frontier*, Oxford University Press, New York, 1985, p. 241). Zoning practices that suggested that homogeneity of people and land usage is always superior to heterogeneity did not come into serious national question until critiqued in 1961 by Jane Jacobs in *The Death and Life of Great American Cities* (Jane Jacobs, *The Death and Life of Great American Cities*, Random House, New York, 1961).

ANNEXATION AND CONSOLIDATION

Annexation

Throughout most of the nineteenth century, cities grew by expanding their population on the periphery beyond the city lines, and then by formally annexing the land on which the outlying population resided into the city. According to Muller, "Annexation of surrounding suburban territory, including absorption of already incorporated satellite municipalities, was the predominant method of city growth" (Peter O. Muller, *Contemporary Suburban America*, Prentice-Hall, Englewood Cliffs, N.J., 1981, p. 36). Some of these annexations were spectacular in scope. Philadelphia in 1854 grew from a compact 2 square miles to a then-huge 130 square miles by annexing the entire county in which it was located. In one step, Philadelphia gave itself room to grow for over half a century while quadrupling its population.

Chicago did much the same thing. Chicago, as its population expanded, annexed new territory several times during the nineteenth century. However, its biggest expansion came near the end of the century. In 1889 Chicago added some 133 square miles to its south side. The annexation went ten miles south to include the model company town of Pullman that George Pullman had recently built for his railroad car workers. Observers came from as far as England to view the model industrial community that Pullman had designed to banish worker discontent. (The town of Pullman became even more famous in 1894, when the National Guard was used to break one of the most bitter strikes in American labor history.) Also included in the south side annexation were the then-suburban communities of Hyde Park and Kenwood. These both quickly turned into urban neighborhoods with the extension of the elevated line built to bring visitors to the 1893 World Columbian Exposition, which was located nearby. The construction of the University of Chicago in Hyde Park also confirmed its urban character.

Consolidation

Consolidations, where existing communities joined together to establish a new larger unit, also did much to expand cities. The New York state legislature consolidated Manhattan with four areas to create New York City as we know it in 1898. This consolidation radically increased New York's size and population while marking the passing of Brooklyn's status as a separate municipality and the fourth largest city in the nation. The consolidation of Brooklyn into New York City also meant New York could collect taxes on both sides of the river; land values had gone up immensely because of the building of the Brooklyn Bridge. Other cities followed similar patterns of consolidation and annexation. Baltimore, for example, more than doubled its size in 1888. Other cities such as Milwaukee, Minneapolis, Detroit, Cleveland, and Pittsburgh similarly experienced substantial, if less dramatic, annexations of adjacent suburban land and populations.

By and large, citizen reaction to nineteenth-century annexations was positive. However, regardless of local opinion, the courts during the nineteenth century almost uniformly supported central cities' rights to annex outlying areas whether these areas were developed or not. In practice, before the turn of the century suburban areas were more likely to desire to get into the city than to fight to stay out of it. Suburbs generally sought annexation in order to benefit from the higher-level city services. Cities almost uniformly had superior fire protection, more comprehensive schools, and better-maintained roads. Also, joining the city gave access to the city's water supply and municipally owned utilities. Not only were city gas rates lower, often utility hookups were not available beyond the municipal boundaries. Cities were not above using the availability of utilities as a way of fostering annexations.

While there were always special regional cases, the general pattern was that those suburban residents most likely to favor annexation were newcomers who wanted to obtain municipal services. Newcomers were more likely to see the suburb as an extension of the city rather than as a separate municipality. Longer-term residents were more likely to favor a continued separate existence. Separation meant both fewer services and lower taxes. Thus, large landowners who were interested in holding their property rather than in dividing it for speculation often opposed annexation since it invariably would raise their taxes. On the other hand, business interests in the city were among the greatest advocates of consolidation, arguing that management of small suburban areas was inherently inefficient. Additionally, they saw annexation as promoting regional growth. In any case, in most states annexation took place by legislative or legal action that did not require the assent of those in the annexed area. Throughout the nineteenth century, state legislatures rather consistently supported city annexations regardless of the view of those in the annexed area. Today only in the sunbelt states of the southwest is annexation still a viable option.

The first suburb to successfully resist annexation was the wealthy suburban town of Brookline, 3 miles west of downtown Boston. The Massachusetts state legislature passed a bill in 1872 consolidating Brookline with Boston if voters in both jurisdictions approved. Those favoring annexation argued that Brookline's merger with Boston was inevitable and that merger would result in water, drainage, and sewage improvements (Ronald Dale Karr, "Brookline Rejects Annexation," in Barbara M. Kelly, ed., *Suburbia Re-examined*, Greenwood Press, New York, 1989, p. 104). Opponents argued the importance of maintaining Brookline's independence, and that those favoring annexation were land speculators. Strongly opposing annexation were wealthy Boston Brahmin families such as the Cabots, Lowells, Gardners, Amorys, and Sargents, who owned large tracts of low-taxed land in Brookline (Karr, 1989, p. 107). In 1873 Boston voted for annexation, but Brookline voted against. Thus, Brookline became the first example of what in the twentieth century would become a common pattern of high-income suburbs successfully resisting incorporation into their central cities.

By the early years of the twentieth century, courts generally had become more sympathetic to legally incorporated independent suburban municipalities preventing the extension of central-city legal boundaries. Similarly, legislatures were becoming less favorable to central-city annexation and more agreeable to suburbs seeking "home rule" as incorporated villages. Upper- and upper-middle-class influentials were beginning to identify more with suburbs than with the immigrant-filled central cities. Suburbs such as Oak Park, west of Chicago; Grosse Pointe, next to Detroit; and Shaker Heights, east of Cleveland, were successful in seeking home rule. In some cases the desire for suburban autonomy was directly linked to the desire to keep upper-middle-class areas from the political control of the Irish and other ethnic groups governing the core city.

Home rule was seen as a way of remaining free of the political bosses, graft, and corruption of the city. It also meant that WASPs could effectively exclude poor Irish, Italian, Polish, and Jewish immigrants from their schools. Immigrants, particularly those from southern and eastern Europe, thus could be kept from mixing with suburban children. Public education could be racially, ethnically, and religiously segregated. Oak Park, which became a separate suburb in 1901, boasted of its title of "Saint's Rest" because of the numerous large churches in the town (Carole Godwin, *The Oak Park Strategy*, University of Chicago Press, Chicago, 1979, p. 32). What was understood without saying was that these were Protestant churches. Catholics weren't welcome, and Jews were unthinkable. Oak Park was also a temperance community, a suburb that Ernest Hemingway, who grew up there, called a place of "wide lawns and narrow minds." Suburban incorporation also meant the community kept control over its land usage and most important, over its taxes.

The census of 1910 already indicated the pattern for the future. In the twenty-five metropolitan areas that were then defined by the census, a full quarter of the residents already lived outside the city core. Suburbia was a permanent part of the metropolitan area. By the time of World War I, the era of central-city annexation was essentially over. Today, of all the forty-eight contiguous states, only Texas, and to a degree Arizona and New Mexico, continue to follow the common nineteenth-century policy of easy central-city annexation. Although the consequences of hindering central-city annexation would not become clear to most observers until after World War II, by the time of World War I it was already clear that most new metropolitan growth would, by definition, have to be suburban growth.

GROWTH POLICIES

As suburbia has become transformed from an area that is overwhelmingly residential to one that includes commercial, business, and even industrial activity, suburban residents have become concerned as to how these changes impact their lives and communities. As growth has gone from in the city to outside the city, there is a belief that the general quality of suburban life is decreasing. While applauding increases in employment and greater shopping alternatives, suburbanites feel frustration over traffic congestion, environmental degradation, crime, and crowded schools. Often these problems are attributed to a too-rapid pace of community growth. The question of limiting, or even halting, growth is one that is being debated in high-growth areas, such as the west coast. The concern first arose in high-growth areas, such as Orange County, in Southern California; now, as Californians out-migrate to Oregon, Washington state, or New Mexico, the concern about too-rapid growth has become a political issue in those localities.

Local concerns over rapid growth fly in the face of the long-standing American creed that bigger is better. City boosters, as a matter of course, bragged that their community was better than their neighbor's because it was growing faster. The novelist Sinclair Lewis might ridicule Babbitt for his boosterism of Zenith, but Babbitt's belief in the virtue of growth was shared by most local politicians (Sinclair Lewis, *Babbitt*, Harcourt Brace, New York, 1922). Not to grow was to stagnate. In 1960, Mayor Daley of Chicago castigated the Bureau of the Census for releasing figures suggesting his city was no longer growing. Not to grow was somehow un-American. Now that is changing, and there are increasing calls for growth controls. Governor Ariyoshi of Hawaii stirred up considerable controversy when he called for Hawaii to slow its exploding population by banning in-migration.

Research indicates that suburban residents have strong concerns about current and future growth. Studying the response of citizens in Orange County, California, Baldassare found that over half of his sample cited environmental reasons such as traffic congestion and environmental deterioration as reasons for limiting growth. Economic reasons, such as maintaining property values and avoiding government spending and taxes, were listed by approximately a third of the respondents (Mark Baldassare, *Trouble in Paradise*, Columbia University Press, New York, 1986). While there is documented widespread support for slow-growth or growth-limit policies, there is little public support for no-growth policies (Mark Baldassare, "Suburban Support for No-Growth Policies," *Journal of Urban Affairs*, Vol. 12, No. 2, 1990, pp. 197–206). Suburban residents desire local officials and policy makers to put limits on population and economic expansion rather than to halt development. Both no growth and unrestricted growth are opposed by most suburbanites. However, desiring controlled growth and accomplishing it are not the same things. Research indicates that municipal zoning and other techniques to control growth have only a modest effect (John Logan and Min Zhou, "Do Suburban Growth Controls Control Growth?" *American Sociological Review*, Vol. 54, June 1989, pp. 461–471).

Organizations favoring growth limits, such as the Sierra Club, generally argue that uncontrolled growth will continue to destroy what remains of our physical and cultural environment. Thus, the indiscriminate gobbling up of land by developers and industries has to be controlled. Opponents of control, such as the National Association of Homebuilders, say that those already in an area have no right to infringe on what they see as the constitutional right to settle where one chooses. Other opponents, such as the National Association for the Advancement of Colored People, are less concerned with the developers' right to build and make profits than they are with a "pull-up-the-gangplank" mentality. The NAACP fears that environmental policies such as setting minimum lot sizes and requiring municipal water and sewage hookups rather than allowing wells and septic systems will increase prices and thus exclude poorer blacks. Zoning regulations have a history of being used for zoning for exclusion (Michael Danielson, *The Politics of Exclusion*, Columbia University Press, New York, 1976).

The legal question of whether communities can impose growth controls was settled for the time being by the case of Petaluma, California. Located roughly 35 miles north of San Francisco and on a new freeway, the community of 35,000 felt it was being overwhelmed.

Silicon Valley, approximately 40 miles south of San Francisco, is another of the suburban outer cities that is not found on most maps. However, it has the traffic congestion that is endemic to such areas.

Growth in Petaluma had reached 18 percent a year. Schools were in double session, water and sewage systems were at the maximum, and the community feared it was being swallowed by an unending number of new subdivisions. The city established a plan to limit building to 500 units a year, and developers and builders sued. By refusing to hear the case, the Supreme Court in 1976 rejected the builders' argument that growth limits unconstitutionally restrict people's right to live where they choose. The Supreme Court let stand the Court of Appeals ruling that the traditional local community responsibility for the public welfare was sufficiently broad to allow Petaluma to preserve its character and open spaces.

In practice the question of growth controls is moot for most suburban communities. Only a limited number of communities, almost all in environmentally attractive locations in the west and southwest, have tried to control growth. Many older suburban communities are more likely to share the central-city problem of how to attract growth, rather than how to limit it. Much more common among suburbs than growth limits is the requiring of builders to offer "proffers." These are fees to cover some of the cost to the municipality of providing local road, school, sewer, and water services. The argument is that new residences should be assessed some of the costs associated with servicing them, and that the cost of providing services for newcomers should not be borne solely by existing taxpayers.

CRIME IN THE SUBURBS

It is impossible to discuss suburban issues without some discussion of crime. Obviously, one of the more common explanations one hears for the movement to the suburbs or the unwillingness to move back into the city is urban crime. The built-in assumption is that suburbs are relatively free of crime while cities clearly are not. Neither of these assumptions is fully accurate. Some city neighborhoods have low crime, while some suburbs do not. However, overall suburban crime rates are only 28 percent of city rates. The popular perception also is accurate insofar as central-city crime rates are rising faster than suburban rates. The gap between cities and suburbs, thus, is increasing. As of 1989 the median rate of violent crime in the nation's fifty-two largest metropolitan areas having a population of over 750,000 was 1,347 per 100,000 (*Uniform Crime Statistics,* Federal Bureau of Investigation, Washington, D.C., 1990). (Violent crimes include murder, rape, robbery, and aggravated assault.) This was a reported crime jump of 33 percent from a decade earlier. By comparison, the suburban rate was a far lower 386, which was an increase of 14 percent from a decade earlier.

No one knows for sure why urban violent crime rates accelerated so rapidly during the 1980s. Some have suggested the younger-age population in inner cities is a major factor since violent crime is largely an act of the young. (Forty-five percent of all crimes except murder are committed by those under eighteen.) Others have pointed to depressed economic conditions for the poor, with shrinking job opportunities. Still others have suggested the increasing use of drugs, more use of more lethal weapons, family breakdown, and racial discrimination as reasons for the increase. Whatever the reason, the popular belief that cities, or at least some parts of cities, are increasingly dangerous places is, unfortunately, accurate. In 1942 New York City had only 44 murders for the year. Fifty years later the total was 2,007 murders.

As noted above, suburban crime rates are only a bit over a quarter of city rates, and they are increasing at a slower level, so the gap between city and suburb is widening. Suburban crime is much less likely to be violent crime. It has been calculated that someone living in Chicago is six times more likely to be murdered and seven times more likely to be robbed than a suburban resident (*Chicago Tribune,* January 6, 1975, p. 37). The most frequently reported suburban crime is bicycle theft. This is a problem if it's your new expensive mountain bike that is stolen, but it is not equivalent to being mugged at gunpoint.

Moreover, within suburbs, crime is not randomly distributed. Some suburbs have rates approaching those of the cities, while others have far lower rates. Generally, the crime rates are highest in older, inner-ring suburbs whose economic and social characteristics approach those of the central city. Older low-income suburbs and minority-resident suburbs tend to have the highest rates. Ten of such suburbs surrounding Chicago holding only 15 percent of the population account for 40 percent of the murders and over half the armed robberies. By comparison, the ten richest suburbs have burglary rates only one-third those of the ten poorest suburbs. Affluent residential suburbs are able to restrict unwanted activities and limit their minority, poor, and unemployed populations. By restricting the influx of outsiders, they, in effect, deflect crime to lower-income areas (John Stuhura and John Sloane, III, "Urban Stratification of Places, Routine Activities, and Suburban Crime Rates," *Social Forces,* Vol. 66, 1988, pp. 102–118).

Higher crime rates are also found in those suburbs that have facilities that attract criminals. Large shopping centers and business parks are sites of opportunity for robbery and even rape, but especially for automobile theft. It is hard to imagine a better site for an auto thief to operate than a large anonymous parking lot. The overall result is that while suburban crime rates remain well below urban rates, they are nonetheless growing. As business and commercial activities suburbanize, growth in crimes such as car theft can be expected.

GOVERNMENT FRAGMENTATION

The fragmentation of American political jurisdictions has reached the status of a contemporary cliché. Today it is impossible to find a metropolitan area anywhere in the United States that is not divided and subdivided in a multiplicity of political jurisdictions. For example, within Cook County, Illinois, is found not only the city of Chicago, but also some additional 129 cities, towns, and villages (Barbara Page Fisk, ed., *Key to Government in Chicago and Suburban Cook County,* University of Chicago Press, Chicago, 1989, p. 1). And Cook County is just one of the several counties making up the Chicago metropolitan area.

Across the land the Bureau of the Census counts some 83,186 local governments (Bureau of the Census, *Statistical Abstract of the United States: 1991,* Government Printing Office, Washington, D.C., 1991, Table No. 487, p. 297). Included in this total are 3,042 county governments, 19,200 municipal governments, 16,691 township governments,

14,721 school district governments, and some 29,532 special district governments for areas such as fire protection, housing, and natural resources. The various special districts may be restricted in scope, but many of them are crucial to the maintenance of metropolitan-area services. Nor are all the special districts small in size or budget. Some are huge. Among the largest special districts is the New York Port Authority, which covers both New York and New Jersey and has over 9,000 employees and yearly revenues of $1.5 billion. Other large special districts are the Chicago Sanitary District, which has revenues approaching $400 million, and the Chicago Transit Authority, which runs the area's bus and rapid transit systems and has a yearly revenue approaching $1 billion.

As was noted in the earlier section on annexation, prior to the turn of the twentieth century, annexation was commonly used by larger municipalities to incorporate and contain all residential and commercial growth within the boundaries of the central city. However, for large east coast and midwest cities, substantial annexation of developed outlying areas has not been feasible for three-quarters of a century. In the contiguous United States, large-scale annexation of populated areas remains possible only in the southwest, where liberal annexation laws remain on the books. Elsewhere, annexation as a major means of urban growth is largely a matter of history. Joint city-county consolidations are also rare, numbering only a dozen or so in the United States (John C. Bollens and Henry J. Schmandt, *The Metropolis*, Harper & Row, New York, 1981, p. 211). With a limited number of exceptions, such as Dade County, Florida; Nashville, Tennessee; and Indianapolis, Indiana, there have been no successful moves toward consolidations for decades. By contrast, in Canada, metropolitan Toronto has had a successful two-tier system since 1953. Ottawa and Quebec also use federated systems.

In the United States it traditionally has been the pattern for city voters to approve regional government while suburban jurisdictions reject the consolidation. Opposition commonly was strongest among affluent homeowners, probably because of their concern over losing both local control and low taxes. More recently, however, strong opposition to consolidation also is coming from city officials. Elected officials whose racial or ethnic groups have finally achieved city power generally have no interest in diluting their influence in a larger regional unit. City officials also rightly feel that their chance for reelection would be significantly diminished if they had to run for office with a wider regional constituency. Additionally, over the years the expansion and upgrading of county-based services and the widespread use of special-service districts has significantly raised the level of suburban services. Today suburban services are often better than those found in the city. Thus, the suburbs have little to gain from consolidation. As a consequence, there is virtually no current pressure in the United States from either cities or their surrounding suburbs to adopt systems of regional government.

The proliferation of decentralized localized units has been blamed over the years for a myriad of problems—sometimes fairly and sometimes not. There is little question that suburbanites have no great interest in sharing the urban-area responsibilities for welfare and social service costs of the poor. Higher taxes to be used for redistributive purposes enjoy little support. Nor have suburban jurisdictions always been prompt to pay their share of metropolitan spillover costs for maintaining museums and public facilities shared by all the community. Research done in the 1970s indicated that suburbs enjoyed a net gain from the city public sector (Brian J. Berry and John D. Kasarda, *Contemporary Urban Ecology*, Macmillan, New York, 1977 pp. 214–226). However, times change. The imposition of commuter income taxes in some cities and, more significantly, the major economic shift of employment to the suburbs has weakened one of the strongest arguments of the 1960s and the 1970s regarding suburbs being parasites of the city. At that time it was argued that suburban commuters, through their use of city roads and facilities, raised the cost of urban municipal services. Today only a minority of commutation is to the central city; the majority is suburb to suburb. An ever decreasing minority of suburbanites actually commutes into the central city for employment or other purposes. Most suburbanites make minimal use of central-city services. City dwellers are increasingly likely to commute to suburbs for employment, shopping, or entertainment.

For those looking for signs of governmental fragmentation, there are numerous examples. Local governmental units do not always act in concert or even in a state of benign distrust. Jurisdictional debates, inefficiencies of local units, questions of competency of local officials, and budget demands that exceed resources all create local conflicts. Local organizations often have competing agendas and business demands, and the interests of residents often collide. Political disputes in an era of diminished resources often conflict in what is increasingly perceived as being a zero-sum game (L. Thurow, *Zero Sum Society*, Basic Books, New York, 1980). Local residents often also are unhappy with local political officials.

However, it would be a mistake to interpret this as a general dissatisfaction with smaller decentralized units of government. The majority of suburbanites believe that decentralization is not a disadvantage, but rather, one of the strengths of the American system. Research consistently shows that people prefer smaller governments. Polls continually indicate that taxpayers feel that local governments spend tax monies more wisely than do state governments. The larger and more distant federal government is felt to be the least efficient. Suburban populations feel that larger units are bureaucratic and inefficient and strongly prefer small local over regional governmental units (Mark Baldassare, "Is There Room for Regionalism in the Suburbs?" *Journal of Architectural Planning Research*, Vol. 8, 1991, pp. 222–234). This is a version of the "small is beautiful" argument. Local governments are felt to be more responsive to citizen needs and concerns, and this results in a higher level of citizen satisfaction (E. Ostrom, "The Social Stratification-Government Inequality Thesis Explored," *Urban Affairs Quarterly*, Vol. 19, 1983, pp. 91–112).

Thus, in spite of the concern among academics over too many local governmental units, the current system appears to work in a fashion that satisfies most residents and users. It is also the case that suburban areas do seem to foster greater political involvement by citizens. As put by Scott Greer in discussing political participation in the St. Louis area, "In general it seemed that familistic neighborhoods, with their dense networks of neighboring and voluntary organizations, did produce more involvement and informed political action" (Scott Greer, *The Urbane View*, Oxford University Press, New York, 1972, p. 97). The bottom line is that most suburbanites are more satisfied with local governments than with larger units, and there is little pressure for, or possibility of, changing the existing system.

A NOTE ON POLITICAL REPRESENTATION

As a consequence of the population shift to the suburbs, there also has been a corresponding political shift. Even as central-city neighborhoods cry out for more political influence and financial aid, the reapportionment following the 1990 census has transferred power away from central cities toward the suburbs. Some congresspersons who previously represented city districts found themselves, as of 1992, campaigning in districts that run into the suburbs. Philadelphia, for example, lost over 100,000 residents between 1980 and 1990, resulting in two of its three districts being extended into suburban Delaware County. Overall, this has led to some lessening of support for central-city concerns and a greater "suburban" emphasis on fiscal conservatism and balanced budgets. Representatives who suddenly find themselves answerable to suburban voters have a tendency to move politically from being urban liberals toward being more suburban law-and-order candidates. Some think this will benefit the Republicans, but Democrats seeking election in the new districts have shown an ability to adjust their rhetoric to their new constituencies.

Also producing real change is more active enforcement of the Federal Voting Rights Act, which requires states to consolidate African American, Hispanic, and other minority voters into districts where their group is the majority. The goal is to dramatically increase minority representation. However, one consequence of concentrating minority members in a few districts is that the remaining districts become more white and, often, more conservative. Jerry Hagstrom argues that the result is that there will probably be fewer representatives who have any accountability to a minority community (Jerry Hagstrom, *Beyond Reagan: The New Landscape of American Politics,* W. W. Norton, New York, 1988). He believes that more conservatives will be elected, whether Republican or Democrat. The fear is that those elected from the new overwhelmingly white districts will be able to disclaim any responsibility for urban problems on the grounds that minorities now have their own representatives. Whether this will occur in practice is still uncertain, but even with a Democrat in the White House, urban districts clearly lack the major clout they had during the earlier Kennedy and Johnson years. Suburbia now holds the majority of the voters, and that means suburban interests cannot be ignored by politicians seeking reelection. Politicians can be expected to follow the votes.

CHAPTER 11

Outer Cities and the Malling of the Land

OLDER PATTERNS

In discussing what is now occurring in the suburbs, it is necessary to occasionally take a glance back at the central city since comparisons between the two highlight the changes in the latter. As has been detailed previously, the downtowns of American urban areas came into their glory during the first half of the twentieth century as *the* retail trade and business locations of choice. Downtown was where all the major department stores were located. As of 1950, Chicago's Loop contained not only the huge Marshall Field store but also, a block away, Carson, Pirie, Scott. In addition, there were the other large department stores of Mandels, Sears, and The Fair. All of these department stores occupied multistoried buildings. Field alone occupied a full city block, with an additional five-story Men's Building annex across the street. Additionally, the downtown was filled with scores of restaurants and coffee shops catering both to business people and housewives who dressed up to make an event out of shopping downtown. Certainly, if one were interested in serious shopping in Chicago—or New York, or Philadelphia, or Boston, or Washington, or Detroit, or Minneapolis, or Omaha, or Dallas, or Seattle—one went downtown, usually by public transit.

As we approach the turn of the century, the above description reads like something from another time and place. Across America, downtown and peripheral suburban areas have switched identities. The old pattern has been turned inside out. Concentrated and centralized cities have been supplanted by dispersed and polynucleated sub-

181

urban malls and office parks. Downtowns that once were dominant in retail trade find themselves struggling not for dominance, but for survival. Numerous cities such as Baltimore, Detroit, and Omaha no longer have even a single downtown department store. The dispute of the 1970s and 1980s as to the comparative economic strength of downtown or peripheral suburban locations as centers for the purchase of consumer goods is over. Downtowns lost the competition. Central business districts now account for less than half of all sales in personal and household items, and yearly this share decreases. Downtowns, with some exceptions, such as part of Manhattan and North Michigan Avenue in Chicago, are no longer prime locations for major new retailing activities. Some of us who love the old downtowns wish this were not so. Along with downtown Chambers of Commerce we would like to see new retailers occupy the buildings abandoned by the large department stores. Unfortunately, this isn't going to occur. Central-city festival marketplaces provide wonderful urban vitality and a means of attracting tourists, but they are not where someone goes to buy shoes, a business suit, or a VCR. For the foreseeable future, large-scale retailing ventures will have suburban post offices. New office space is also most likely to be suburban. Deconcentration is the contemporary reality.

The above picture is often taken as a sign that central cities have lost their economic function. This picture is not just an exaggeration, it is wrong. What has occurred is that for decades downtowns have been shifting their economic emphasis. Even a brief drive through most American downtowns reveals not only areas where large department stores have closed or are closing, but also areas of numerous new high-rise office buildings. Downtowns have been changing their economic function. While they have declined as the major centers for household and personal purchases, they remain important business addresses. For thirty years, central business districts have been the sites of new office building construction. From the 1960s to the 1990s, older cities such as New York and Chicago have increased their central office space by more than two-thirds. Other places, such as Atlanta, Houston, and Los Angeles, have created new skylines by doubling their space and then doubling it again. Newer sun belt cities have experienced even greater central business district growth. Looking at the new skylines does not suggest the image of immediate economic decline.

Suburban decentralization during postwar decades has been selective. Back-office clerical jobs initially showed more inclination to relocate in the suburbs than activities such as finance, legal services, advertising, management, medical centers, educational institutions, and government. Such activities often remained in the central city because they are service-oriented and need access to one another. Management, finance, and law cannot afford to become isolated from the informal information networks regarding business patterns, competitors, and government policy that occur when there are a number of firms in the same business located in the same spatial area. Business may be conducted and information exchanged over lunch. Back-office operations easily can be decentralized, but management cannot as easily afford to be isolated from informal information networks. Fax machines or telephones are less useful than personal contact in conveying the important business gossip of the street.

Traditionally, the spatial ecology and design of high-rise downtown buildings also has favored the space-intensive needs of business and management. On the other hand, retail trade, manufacturing, and wholesaling have higher space-per-employee requirements. These needs can effectively be met by horizontal one- or two-story suburban buildings. Managerial, governmental, legal, and professional activities, on the contrary, are highly space-intensive and can effectively be stacked, layer upon layer, in high-rise office buildings (William Parker Frisbie and John D. Kasarda, "Spatial Processes," in Neil Smelser, ed., *Handbook of Modern Sociology*, Sage, Beverly Hills, Calif., 1988, p. 636). Thus, while suburban office parks grow, the central business district still remains a prime location for certain types of office space. Even in an era of computer-based information systems and fax machines, face-to-face contact remains a crucial, if intangible, business asset. As long as this remains the case, central cities will have an economic role.

MULTINUCLEATED EDGE OR SATELLITE CITIES

Contemporary Decentralization

There is general agreement that contemporary urban decentralization has developed beyond the traditional urban-suburban dichotomy. The old idea of the urban core surrounded by a ring of suburbs no longer neatly fits what we see when we travel to, or through, America's metropolitan areas. The traditional picture of metropolitan areas owes much to the 1924 Burgess Zonal Hypothesis which saw metropolitan areas growing from center to periphery through a series of concentric rings (Ernest Burgess, "The Growth of the City: An Introduction to a Research Project," *Publications of the American Sociological Society*, Volume 18, 1924, pp. 85–97). In this model, commercial and retailing activities were concentrated in the Central Business District (CBD). Surrounding the downtown were the industrial, warehousing, and tenement areas. The next ring out was predominantly working-class residences, followed by a ring of middle-class homes, and finally a band of suburbs. These latter were seen as being primarily affluent residential areas whose function was limited to serving as bedroom communities. Needless to say, these suburbs were seen as socially being inhabited by upper-middle-class WASPS (White Anglo-Saxon-Protestants). These suburban enclaves of single-family homes banned not only the less affluent and ethnically unacceptable, but also most industry and commerce (Michael Ebner, *Creating Chicago's North Shore*, University of Chicago Press, Chicago, 1988). For employment and for shopping for consumer goods, one commuted to downtown.

For the middle of the twentieth century, the above was not an unreasonable picture. Its fit was particularly good when one looked at the larger and older metropolitan areas of the north and midwest. Even the first couple of decades of mass suburbanization following World War II only modified the picture. Suburbia became more middle-class and even more socially diverse than critics of suburbia recognized. Nonetheless, suburbia still was primarily a residential rather than a commercial or economic location. There were, however, some pioneering industrial and commercial developments that foretold what was to come. As early as 1957 some ninety-nine new commercial and business facilities had located along what was to become Boston's famous circumferential high-tech expressway, Route 128 (A. J. Bone and Martin Wohl, "Massachusetts Route 128 Impact Study," *Highway and Economic Development*, Bulletin 227, 1959). As a sign of what was to come, some seventy-plus of these businesses had relocated from sites closer to downtown Boston.

The Economy Goes Suburban

The nationwide suburbanization of economic activities meant the old dispersed suburban-sprawl pattern was transformed to one of suburban subcenters. Relocated shopping and businesses would cluster around major highway junctions, leading to the development of minicenters that would attract new economic activities. By the 1980s a multinucleated or multicentered pattern of outer cities had developed—one that has been referred to somewhat fancifully as "the galactic metropolis" (Pierce F. Lewis, "The Galactic Metropolis," in Rutherford Platt and George Macinko, eds., *Beyond the Urban Fringe: Land Use Issues in Non-Metropolitan America*, University of Minnesota Press, Minneapolis, 1983, pp. 23–49). As the geographer Peter Muller noted back in 1981, "The recent emergence of the multicentered metropolis of realms has ended the usefulness of conventional core-periphery models" (Peter Muller, *Contemporary Suburban America*,

Prentice-Hall, Englewood Cliffs, N.J., 1981, p. 8). An example of how the old pattern has changed is G. H. Bass and Company, maker of Bass and Weejun shoes, who, in 1993, moved their corporate headquarters to be near the Maine Mall, the largest shopping center in the state. "The draw," according to Bass's vice president of human resources, "is the mall's strategic location. We wanted a place near the turnpike and the airport" ("Bass Moving Headquarters," New York Times Service, *Richmond Times Dispatch,* May 9, 1993, p. K5). The new headquarters near the mall is within a mile of the Maine Turnpike, Interstate 95, and Portland Jetport. Outer shopping complexes are now not only attracting consumers, they are magnets for corporate office parks. The mall has become the new town center around which business offices cluster.

Today's new multinucleated outer cities tear up the old definitions as to what is urban and what is suburban. The suburbs have become urban. Places that once were bedroom suburbs now attract commuters. The suburbs' share of the employment pie has been dramatically increasing. A look at what has occurred in Washington, D.C., for example, is instructive. As of 1970, the District held almost half (46 percent) of the metropolitan-area jobs, while suburban Virginia and suburban Maryland each held 27 percent (Stephen Fehr, "N. Va. Replaces D.C. as Area Job Center," *Washington Post,* Dec. 22, 1992, p. A14). While Washington, D.C., unlike most central cities, gained 78,000 jobs during the period 1980 to 1990, the city's proportion of metropolitan-area jobs declined. By 1990 northern Virginia actually had the highest proportion of Washington-area workers, at 36 percent. Next was suburban Maryland, at 33 percent, while the District's share had dropped to 29 percent. In other words, even in the nation's capital, with all its government jobs, some seven out of ten Washington-area workers are employed in the suburbs. Jobs as well as people have suburbanized. Moreover, most of those still working in the city do not live there. Seven in ten people who work in the District do not live there.

As noted earlier, the most common commuter trip today is not from suburb to city but within the suburbs. The 1980 census showed that even over a decade ago, commuting from a suburban home to a suburban job already was more common than commuting from suburb to city. By 1980 some 33 million people were employed in the suburbs, up from only 14 million in 1960. There is no longer a metropolitan area composed of a central city hub and its outlying residential areas spread along the spokes. As noted above, the metropolitan area no longer has one core hub; it has become multinucleated. Among other things this means that road and rapid transit systems designed to move workers from the suburbs to the central city are becoming outdated. Population and job growth are occurring in areas where transportation facilities often are least developed. Although it stretches the language a bit, it is reasonable to hypothesize that the periphery is the new urban core. Places such as Irving, California; Oceanside, California; and Scottsdale, Arizona are no longer bedroom suburbs, but real cities in their own right. Such increasing economically and politically powerful outer cities can be found sandwiched between somewhat declining central cities and rural areas, both of which are losing their political and economic clout. The meat of the sandwich is suburban.

Economically, the suburban economy is increasingly a service-based economy. Moreover, the marketplace patterns that dominate local economies are largely determined at the national or international rather than the local level (Mark Schneider and Fabio Fernandez, "The Emerging Suburban Service Economy: Changing Patterns of Employment" *Urban Affairs Quarterly*, Vol. 24, June 1989, pp. 537–555). New commercial and corporate growth is often in the outer cities. Increasingly, the initial expectation is that a new corporate headquarters will have a suburban location. By 1990, once-bedroom communities such as Plano, Texas, outside Dallas, had become economic centers in their own right. The 1990 census showed Plano had 128,000 people. More important, Plano is the center of a complex of telecommunications plants, and the office development of Legacy Park is the national headquarters for five major corporations. Frito-Lay, Electronic Data Systems, Murata Business Systems, Southland Life Insurance, and the new headquarters for J. C. Penney are all in Legacy Park. Indicative of the change is that J. C. Penney moved its headquarters to Plano from New York City.

The 1992 movement of Sears' Merchandise Group from downtown Chicago to the outlying suburbs mirrors how that corporation is seeking to regain lost suburban shoppers. As was briefly noted in the Introduction, by moving to the suburbs, Sears is symbolically as well as practically attempting to regain its suburban base. Two decades ago Sears was the nation's largest retailer, and to express its dominant position, it moved its headquarters' operations to the world's tallest building, the 110-story Sears Tower. The Sears Tower topped the Chicago skyline, but while putting its headquarters in the urban clouds, Sears seemed to lose touch with the changing needs of its suburban consumers. In 1992 Sears moved its 5,000 Merchandise Group employees out from the Sears Tower to suburban Hoffman Estates, 35 miles to the northwest. Sears's new retailing headquarters, named Prairie Stone, projects anything but a city skyline. Built on a former soybean field, Prairie Stone includes more than 200 acres of reconstructed prairie and wetlands. The highest building rises six stories.

The company is reorganizing its business on the assumption that if Sears is to have a future, it will be in the suburbs, not the central cities.

THE RISE OF PRIVATE CITIES

Outer cities or suburban municipalities sometimes are difficult to define since they don't look like how we think cities should look; nor do they behave as we expect cities to behave. For starters, they sometimes lack any clearly definable borders. Unlike a legally defined city or suburb, there are no signposts to tell you when you have moved out of their jurisdiction. They lack definable borders. That is because they are not legal entities having municipal boundaries. Legally, they often are nonplace places, having names but not legal status as places. Having no legal boundaries, they may not even appear on some maps. They are "cities" not subject to their own municipal legislation, codes, or regulation. Shopping malls, business parks, single-family subdivisions, and garden apartment complexes all seemed to be jumbled together without plan or design.

Not being legal municipalities, these outer cities also have another strange characteristic for a city—they have no distinct elected government. Within these edge cities there thus seems to be no real civic order. They appear to be public places, but in reality, they are private. Tysons Corner may be larger and have more office space than Tucson, but it has no elected local government. Tysons Corner is legally just another part of Fairfax County, Virginia. In practice, however, it is far more. Tysons, like Dallas's Las Colinas, Los Angeles's Marina Del Rey-Culver City, Philadelphia's King of Prussia, or Boston's Burlington Mall, is in effect a city unto itself. What really makes these places break with the past is not that they are newer, shinier, or have more glass and marble. What makes them different is that they are private domains rather than incorporated legally defined areas. The old city downtowns, whether planned or unplanned, were public spaces. City downtowns were open to all. The rules governing public dress and behavior were the laws and ordinances passed by those public officials elected by citizens of the jurisdiction.

The outer-city malls, for all their open courtyards, fountains, benches, and play spaces, are fundamentally different. They are private property. They are not governed by elected representatives, but by executives appointed by corporate boards. They are governed not by public laws, but by corporate regulations. Fundamental questions, such as who can be in a mall and what they can or cannot do while they are there, are determined by corporate policy rather than ordinances passed by elected representatives. Thus, a mall can exclude those soliciting funds for cancer research, those proselytizing for a religious belief, those handing out literature for a political candidate, or those not meeting a required dress code (e.g., those not wearing shoes or street people wearing dirty clothes).

What applies to the malls of the outer cities or edge cities is even more the case for the business parks filled with state-of-the-art offices and facilities. The new outer cities are cities administered by decree. They are not controlled by citizens, not even nominally. Such places may be safe, but they are not democratic. In many ways, the edge cities' privatization of public space and activities represents a shift back to the medieval and Renaissance concept of a city as a collection of essentially privately managed places controlled by an oligarchy. The malls are, in effect, separate city-state controlled and administered by the decree of private boards. What is perhaps even more remarkable is that this shift from public to private control has occurred almost completely without public notice. It has certainly occurred without public discussion or debate. The once-public city has been privatized.

SHOPPING MALLS

If you had to pick one symbol that would represent contemporary suburban life, that symbol would very likely be the shopping mall. Malls have become a ubiquitous element of modern American life. You may love the malls or believe they are sterile and without soul, but it is impossible to discuss suburbia today without noting the importance of the malls not only for retail purchasing but also for social life. As the old downtowns decline, the malls have become the primary site where people rub elbows with other citizens. Shopping centers dispense everything from lottery tickets (Anne Gaboury, "Structures of Lotteries and Behaviors of Players," *Revue de Psychologie Appliquee*, Vol. 39, 1989, pp. 197–207), to sports demonstrations (David A. Feigley, "Public Relations Program for a Shopping Mall," *Journal of Physical Education and Recreation*, Vol. 51, 1980, pp. 28–31), to providing an off-campus site for college courses (Frederick Bein and James East, "Teaching Geography on Weekends at Shopping Malls," *Journal of Geography in Higher Education*, Vol. 5, 1981, pp. 169–174). Some shopping malls offer community activities such as bingo games once a week, periodic health services such as blood tests, and occasional entertainment such as Christmas or Easter shows. The malls, with their shops selling mass-produced standardized goods, may also be the site for "Arts and Crafts" shows that sell expensive handmade one-of-a-kind heirloom-quality items (Nita Bryant, "Contemporary Nomadic Traders: Observations of an Arts and Crafts Show in a Suburban Shopping Mall," Paper for Seminar on the Suburbs, Virginia Commonwealth University, April 12, 1992). Malls also serve a social function, particularly for adolescents and the elderly. Being a teenage "mall rat" is part of growing up in many parts of the country. What Main Street, the malt shop, and the diner were to the teenagers of the postwar period, the mall is to the preadults of the 1990s. The mall is a teenage hangout, a form of "third place" or "neutral ground," where adolescents can gather free of parental observation (Kathryn Anthony, "The Shopping Mall: A Teenage Hangout," *Adolescence*, Vol. 20, 1985, pp. 307–312; George Lewis, "Rats and Bunnies: Core Kids in an American Mall," *Adolescence*, Vol. 24, 1989, pp. 881–889). The malls have also become the place where seniors go to socialize and ward off loneliness, a phenomenon that has produced a new variation (and spelling) of an old term, "mallingering" (Dawn Graham, "Going to the Mall: A Leisure Activity of Urban Elderly People," *Canadian Journal of Aging*, Vol. 10, 1991, pp. 345–358). Early mornings, before the malls are open for sales, many malls are filled with "mallwalkers" getting their morning exercise in the safe, temperature-controlled, and traffic-free environment of the local regional shopping mall.

If you want to find Americans who grew up in the era before the malls—adults who as children rode the streetcar downtown to go shopping in department stores and who went to see cowboy movies at the local movie house on Saturday afternoon—you have to speak with those who are at least middle-aged. For those who entered their teen years since 1970, the shopping malls have always been there. Life before the malls is life from another historical era. The shopping mall became part of the American scene about the same time the war in Vietnam became a national obsession. If you are old enough to have gone to Vietnam or to remember friends going to Vietnam, if you remember marching in antiwar protests, or if you remember the summer of love in San Francisco, then you are the last of the premall generations. To those coming after, the America of the premall era is as distant as the Roaring Twenties. It is something that you know about not from personal experience but from seeing a TV show or movie.

Today suburban malls are so common, so everyday, that we take them for granted. We assume they are a natural part of any metropolitan landscape. In the words of Kowinski, "More than locations for consumption, malls have become the signature structure for the age. The mall is Our Town's year-round carnival, the cathedral of postwar culture, the Garden of Eden in a box" (William S. Kowinski, *The Malling of America*, Morrow, New York, 1985, p. 22).

However, enclosed malls with two to four anchor department stores, scores of specialty shops, fountains, food courts, and multiplex movie theaters have not always been synonymous with suburbia. Actually, they are a relatively recent innovation. The first modern shopping mall did not occur until Northgate, in 1950, on the edge of Seattle. It had an open pedestrian mall lined with shops and an anchor department store. Northgate, like malls to follow, was near a highway and had some 4,000 parking spaces. The first enclosed shopping mall was not opened until 1956—Southdale Center outside Minneapolis, designed by the architect Victor Gruen. Not until the early 1970s did the Rouse Company introduce the idea of the now ubiquitous food courts.

Earliest Shopping Centers

There is general agreement (or as much as occurs among academics) that the first project that can be called a planned shopping center was in Roland Park, Baltimore. Sources give both 1908 (J. Ross McKeever and Nathaniel Griffin, *Shopping Center Development Handbook*, Urban Land Institute, Washington, D.C., 1977) and 1896 (Kenneth Jackson, *Crabgrass Frontier*, Oxford University Press, New York, 1985) as the date of founding. Actually, the date is of only limited importance, since few persons today would count Roland Park's six stores as a shopping center. By general consensus, the first real shopping center, as we now understand the term, opened its first stores in 1923 in Kansas City. Country Club Plaza was built by the visionary developer Jesse Clyde Nichols to service his Country Club District—a development that eventually housed some 35,000 persons in fine homes spread over 10 square miles.

J. C. Nichols's Country Club Plaza shopping center, like his homes, was state of the art for the 1920s. It was the first mall designed specifically for the automobile, with off-street parking. Following the ideas of the British garden cities as earlier proposed by Ebenezer Howard, Country Club Plaza was to be the town center, not merely a collection of stores. Nichols set the pattern for the luxury malls of today by lavishly landscaping Country Club Plaza and providing fountains, flowers, and walks with benches. The whole complex was done in an elaborate Spanish-Moorish-Hollywood style using Spanish plaster and red tile roofs. As previously discussed, this was a style immensely popular during the 1920s. (Expressions of the Spanish-Moorish style can also be

Country Club Plaza, opened in 1923 southwest of Kansas City, is usually conceded to be the first of the modern shopping centers. Today it remains an upscale shopping destination.

seen in many of the limited number of surviving movie palaces from that era. The surviving Spanish-Moorish-style movie palaces are now mostly registered as historic buildings. Often they have been refurbished to serve as restored city-centerpiece cultural centers.)

Nichols's Country Club District tightly controlled what sort of businesses would be allowed into the plaza and where they would be placed. Most buildings were two-story, with the walking level occupied by shops and the second floor largely by the professional offices of dentists, doctors, and lawyers. From the first, Country Club Plaza was an economic and social success. It not only made a great deal of money, it also became an alternate to the downtown as a location for cultural as well as business activities. As such it was a harbinger of contemporary suburban malls.

Country Club Plaza was designed from the first to provide an emotional, cultural, and socializing center for the community. It was to become the suburban version of the village center. Planners saw the separation of pedestrian from automotive and truck traffic as providing far more than convenience and efficiency. Landscaped grassy areas, winding walkways, and play areas for small children were all to contribute to better civic life. Shopping centers were also to encourage civic pride through physical design. Planners saw them contributing to the development of a more orderly, harmonious, and artistic environment—an environment that was being at least implicitly contrasted to the chaos, disorder, and confusion many planners saw in the central city. Planned shopping centers dovetailed with planned recreational facilities and planned neighborhoods (Clarence A. Perry, "Planning a City Neighborhood from a Social Point of View," *Proceedings of the National Conference on Social Work,* University of Chicago Press, Chicago, 1924).

The enclosed malls of the 1960s and 1970s simply took this idea a step further, adding background music, fashion shows, local art exhibits, movie theaters, and food courts. For adolescents today, the enclosed malls play a central role in their social and recreational lives. For those of retirement age, the malls provide a temperature-controlled site for early morning exercise walking. For those in between, the mall seeks to provide a safe and predictable image of middle-class life. Thus, going to the mall has gone beyond just purchasing something; going to the mall has become an activity in its own right. When the Chesterfield Mall in my metro area of Richmond, Virginia, renamed itself Chesterfield Town Centre, more was involved than clever advertising. For better or worse, what was being expressed was a contemporary reality.

Interestingly, the future of shopping malls was not widely foreseen by developers or store owners of the 1920s, 1930s or 1940s. Country Club Plaza, though widely praised, was not copied. Although it influenced Highland Park in Dallas and River Oaks in Houston, it did not immediately become a model for the building of clone plazas across the nation. The concept of a shopping mall having numerous independent stores while the mall itself was under a solitary management was widely applauded as being the wave of the future. Yet new malls weren't built. Similarly, the advantage of the mall having its own free parking was already recognized in the 1920s as providing mall retailers a significant edge. Yet few such places were built. One could argue that the absence of copycat malls was because of the Depression of the 1930s, with its chilling effect on new retailing and business ventures. However, this view of the Depression as preventing mall development needs to be tempered by the fact that copycat malls also were not built in the second half of the 1920s—a period when the economy was experiencing what some thought to be an unending economic boom. Perhaps the whole concept was too revolutionary for retailers. Retailers tend to be conservative, and there seemed to be little need to change—particularly since centrally located department stores and those on public mass transit lines already were doing a solid business.

Living as we do in an era when shopping malls are ubiquitous, it is important to remember just how recent the malls are. At the end of

World War II, there still were only eight shopping centers in all of North America. They were, in order of date of establishment: Upper Darby Center, in West Philadelphia (1927); Suburban Square, in Ardmore, Pennsylvania (1928); Highland Park Shopping Center, in Dallas (1931); River Oaks, in Houston (1937); Hampton Village, in St. Louis (1941); Colony, in Toledo (1944); Shirlington, outside Washington, D.C., in Arlington (1944); and Bellview Square, east of Seattle (1946) (Jackson, 1985, p. 259). These would be in addition to Country Club Plaza. Not until the postwar suburban population and housing boom had been underway for two decades would the auto-oriented shopping malls come into their own.

The handful of mostly small outdoor shopping centers found after World War II increased to 2,900 in 1958 and 7,600 by 1964, when the first national census of shopping centers was taken. However, most of these shopping centers were of modest size. Homer Hoyt's now classic study found that as of 1960, there were under sixty shopping centers in the country having over 500,000 square feet of floor space (Homer Hoyt, "The Status of Shopping Centers in the United States," *Urban Land,* Vol. 19, No. 5, 1960, pp. 4–16). As of 1992, the National Research Bureau counted some 38,966 shopping centers of all sizes in the United States. Some 1,835 of these were larger regional malls having more than 400,000 square feet of retail space.

Along the way the humble strip mall has evolved into the huge megamall, Canada's West Edmonton Mall has over 800 shops and services; 110 restaurants and places to eat; 19 movie theaters; a Caesar's Palace bingo parlor; a 355-room hotel; and the world's largest indoor amusement park, with forty-seven rides and the world's largest (5-acre) indoor water park. The mall even has dolphin shows, a life-size replica of the Santa Maria, and four small yellow submarines for riding under the indoor lake. All of this occupies some 5.2 million square feet. Its developers claim the mall yearly attracts some 25 million visitors, making it the major tourist attraction in the provence of Alberta. Clearly, something monumental has occurred, not only in the malls, but also in how we live.

All this has occurred with remarkable speed. In an era when major cities no longer have a single downtown department store, it is easy to forget that until the 1950s, downtown was the only place department stores were located. (As always, there were exceptions, such as Marshall Field, in Chicago, which built branch department stores in the business districts of inner-suburban Evanston and Oak Park. Both these stores have been closed for a score of years.) Following the second World War, retailers felt the suburban fringe was a suitable location for smaller stores and specialty shops, but they did not view it as a viable location for major retailing. When postwar suburbanization resulted in subdivision after subdivision, there was no rush of major department stores to the suburbs. Major retailers played it very safe, slow, and cautious. Retailers wanted a guarantee that there were enough customers within the shopping radius before they would consider constructing a store. As a consequence, stores followed rather than led suburban development.

Strip Malls

The most common form of mall in America is the strip mall. Such malls are not enclosed, not architecturally innovative, and not especially attractive. What they are is practical. They are street-oriented, with the shops facing directly onto their parking lot. Most are of moderate or small size, generally having much less than 350,000 square feet of leasable space. What such shopping centers lack in beauty, they make up in utility. They are remarkably efficient and attract large numbers of shoppers. As of 1990, strip malls accounted for 87 percent of all shopping malls, and such malls produced half (51 percent) of all shopping-center retail sales (Chip Walker, "Strip Malls: Plain but Powerful," *American Demographics,* October 1991, p. 48).

While virtually everyone shops at strip malls, those shopping at the smaller rather than the larger malls are more likely to be women, to be married, to be homemakers, and to have children (Walker, 1991, p. 49). Since the 1960s, the convenience strip malls, with grocery store, drug store, and other shops have been joined by Kmart, Wal-Mart, and a host of similar discount stores. These latter are invariably located along well-traveled roads or highways. They emphasize price and convenience over style and ambience. Wal-Mart has a policy of locating on major roads near small or medium-sized cities. The company also consciously locates its malls just outside the city boundaries so that local taxes and zoning controls can be avoided. Such policies commonly put small locally owned stores out of business. Economically, the mass market malls also are putting heavy pressure on the generally more expensive regional malls that have the overhead of higher levels of service and concern for ambience. Further squeezing the big malls are off-price shopping centers and discount warehouses.

Enclosed Malls

Enclosed malls date from 1956, when Southdale Center opened in the Minneapolis suburb of Edina. While rather modest by contemporary standards, Southdale Center had two department stores rather than a single anchoring department store, and it had some sixty-one additional shops. Its climate-controlled environment was a clear plus for anyone who has ever experienced the biting arctic winds of a Minnesota winter. Nonetheless, there were initial doubts as to whether a mall that lacked the external landscaping, and the external appeal, of a Country Club Plaza would attract customers. After all, the enclosed mall figuratively turned its back on the street, presenting only acres of parking spaces to the outside. The skeptics who said shoppers would not come were wrong; for not only did Southdale Center attract throngs, it attracted throngs that purchased. Soon the enclosed-mall concept was being expanded and elaborated upon across the country. Even major malls that had been built as open-air malls, such as Mayfair, west of Milwaukee, were converting themselves to enclosed malls. The malls, with their controlled environments, were looking less and less like the downtown shopping areas they were displacing.

Where earlier strip malls had followed the population, the new enclosed malls became magnets attracting people, housing, and commercial activity. The malls became a catalyst leading the development of a new suburban area. When the Rouse Company in 1961 opened the Cherry Hill Mall in New Jersey, east of Philadelphia, it drew huge crowds of sightseers and shoppers (Muller, 1981, p. 124). Cherry Hill Mall became the equivalent of a downtown for a diffuse developing residential area. The mall was so important to the area that Delaware Township, in which it was located, decided to adopt the name of the shopping center (Howard Gillette, "The Evolution of the Planned Shopping Center in Suburb and City," *American Planning Association Journal*, Autumn 1985, p. 451). Thus Cherry Hill, New Jersey, was born. The fact of a comfortable middle-class suburb naming itself after a shopping mall is one of those small acts that signify a sea of change in attitudes toward suburbia. The defining characteristic of the area was no longer the homes or the neighborhood; it was the size and quality of the shopping mall.

Regional Malls

What distinguishes the regional centers from others is partially the elaboration of their design, but mostly it is their sheer size. Woodfield Mall, out beyond O'Hare airport in Chicago, was constructed in the early 1970s with four anchor department stores and 230 other shops on three levels providing some 2 million square feet of shopping space. All this was surrounded by almost 11,000 parking spaces. Its likes were soon being constructed across North America. Tysons Corner, in Fairfax County, Virginia, on the Washington, D.C., Beltway, has virtually become an edge city unto itself. Roosevelt Field, in Long Island, New York, serves a similar regional function, while Houston's Galleria, with its Olympic-size skating rink, two hotels, and nightclubs, in addition to all the usual regional mall glitz and shopping, has become a regional tourist attraction. The Galleria, built in 1970, was different from earlier malls in that it incorporated nonretail usages, such as its ice rink, directly into the design of the mall itself. Thus, malls began to take on more of the character of public places rather than just collections of stores. The move toward malls as entertainment centers was underway. This would reach it apex in the West Edmonton Mall and the Mall of America. The adding of food courts to malls in the 1970s further broadened the usage of malls as public places. It is virtually impossible to find a regional mall today that doesn't also include an extensive food court.

It was the belief of philosophers of urban planning such as Victor Gruen that shopping centers would lead to the enhancement of social and civic life. Shopping malls were to be suburban agoras. They were to serve as new climate-controlled downtowns offering a full range of social, cultural, and even artistic activities. As expressed by Gruen, "By affording opportunities for social life and recreation in a protected pedestrian environment, by incorporating civic and educational facilities, shopping centers can fill an existing void" (Victor Gruen and Larry Smith, *Shopping Towns USA: The Planning of Shopping Centers*, Reinhold, New York, 1960, pp. 22–24).

One doesn't have to seek far to find critics who lambast the plastic artificiality and social vacuousness of shopping centers. The idea that the malls would bring vibrancy and vitality to suburban life is now widely dismissed. Nonetheless, if the malls have not promoted high culture, some have at least provided a place for lively amusements. The Rouse Company's central-city developments of Baltimore's Harborplace, Boston's Faneuil Hall Marketplace, and New York's South Street Seaport have become major tourist sites in their own right. There is no question that the Rouse Comany's central-city shopping malls have done much to revitalize stagnant downtown areas in Baltimore, Boston, and New York. Each year these festival marketplaces attract more tourists than does Disneyland. However, during the 1970s and 1980s, more than one hundred new central-city malls were built, and many of these are plagued with empty spaces today. Not every downtown has the potential to attract tourists, or even residents. In any case, urban festival marketplaces concentrate on attracting middle-class or well-to-do shoppers. Meeting the needs of less affluent or poor city residents is not the purpose for which they were created.

Safety and the Malls

It is a basic tenet of any successful mall that it must exude an image of security and safety. For a mall to be successful, it must give those within a feeling of comfort, and that means providing safety and security. This is provided by physically excluding activities or people that might prove disruptive or disturbing. The city downtown may be famous for producing a sense of surprise and excitement, of not knowing what is around the next corner. This is not the goal of the mall. Shopping malls studiously avoid and ban the unpredictable.

What the downtown offers is excitement, what the mall seeks is predictability. Mall publicity and advertisements may speak of excitement, but it is an excitement that is totally managed and predictable. All activities are controlled and programmed. The malls, for all their open courtyards, fountains, benches, and play spaces, are private property. As previously noted, they are governed not by public bodies, but by private boards. Malls are ruled by regulations rather than laws. Unpredictability in any form is banned from malls.

If it might offend some shoppers, it won't be found at a regional mall. Walking through a mall one will not encounter a Hare Krishna dancing, or even a Jehovah's Witness passing out *The Watchtower*. Malls are very white-bread places—no politicians or political parties, no street people, no dirt or clutter, no art that in any way might disturb or offend, no live or recorded music that is not preapproved, and no charitable solicitations or sidewalk merchants of any sort that have not been preapproved. Volunteers cannot simply collect for cancer, heart disease, or disaster relief. Most malls even ban the Salvation Army from ringing its bells and collecting food and clothing for the poor at Christmas time. All this is not so much out of any sense of meanspiritedness, but because mall patrons have been taught to expect predictability and no hassles. State courts generally have supported the malls' contention that they can control, limit, or exclude activities within their confines. The major exception is California; there the state constitution grants extensive public-access rights within malls. The 1972 United States Supreme Court ruling of *Lloyd Corp. v. Tanner* held that banning political leaflets did not interfere with First Amendment free-speech rights. Currently, the issue is in flux; but most mall managements tend to go with the most conservative interpretations. Generally, managements are not opposed to charity, community, or even political activities so long as these activities do not cost them shoppers or profits.

What the malls seek to portray is an image of a secure environment into which the problems of the outside world do not intrude. Malls attempt to radiate an aura of safety. As private entities, malls can ban those activities and persons that are thought to be disruptive, distracting, or dangerous. Malls consciously promote the idea that they are safe places. To that end strangers are excluded. There are no street people or bag ladies in the malls because those loitering or improperly dressed are excluded. Similarly, teenagers who are unduly loud or abusive may find themselves directed to the exits and told not to return. One can even be asked to leave for not being suitably dressed. This can be done because the mall is private rather than public space. No one has a right to walk unhindered back and forth through a mall simply because he or she feels like walking.

Enforcing these regulations are the mall police. In terms of uniform, badges, weapons, and demeanor, the mall police look and act like a police force. However, they rarely are police officers. Rather, they are private security guards done up to look like police officers. Northland Center in suburban Detroit has fifty-two security officers who wear policelike uniforms and have authority to make arrests. This blurring of the distinction between police and security personnel is deliberate. Security guards in most states lack formal police powers. This means that in most states guards can't stop and search purse snatchers or shoplifters. Often they cannot go into the stores, but they merely patrol common areas. Their only arrest power in most states is that of a citizen's arrest. Basically, the security guards notify the real police and try to hold the suspect until they arrive. The major function of the security guards is public relations. They try to look like the cop on the beat, help find lost children, and try to deter crime by looking official. Seven out of ten mall crimes are shoplifting, while another 24 percent are auto break-ins and thefts.

To increase safety, malls are designed to avoid dark corners, and elevators are invariably glass-sided. The latter is not so riders can see out, but so others in the mall can see those inside. Women are far less likely to be sexually molested in glass-sided elevators. In terms of personal safety, by far the most dangerous area in a shopping mall is the parking area or deck. For this reason, parking areas are well lit. Large malls have highly visible official-looking security vehicles with revolving flashing lights on the roof cruising the parking areas. This is to deter crime, but even more to reassure customers that the "police" are on patrol.

While car theft is the most common problem to affect a shopper, robberies, assaults, rapes, and even murders do occur. Managements tend to do everything possible to keep problems with crimes of violence away from the public notice. Unless major public violence occurs, there is likely to be no comment on the evening news or in the local paper. Malls and their stores are major advertisers. When a series of robberies and rapes occurred at the major mall nearest the author's home, no notice of the crimes ever appeared in the local newspaper or on local news shows. Nor were warning posters placed on mall entrance doors. The image of safety and freedom from aggressive strangers is thought essential for a successful mall. Crime is bad for business and is something that happens in central cities. To acknowledge publicly that malls have violent crime would do damage to the illusion that both mall operators and patrons seek to maintain. Malls, however, have begun to indirectly deal with the subject by publicizing that they have security forces.

Megamalls

West Edmonton Mall

Some regional megamalls have become major tourist attractions. South Coast Plaza, in Orange County, California, south of Los Angeles, is the county's third-largest tourist attraction. That achievement is put into perspective when it is noted that the first and second attractions are Disneyland and Knott's Berry Farm. However, sometimes the entertainment function of the mall as an amusement center is made explicit. On the open prairies of Canada, the concept of the mall as a festival marketplace and a center of amusement has taken a colossal step with the development of West Edmonton Mall. Here the Ghermezian brothers have taken the concept beyond what anyone two decades ago would have imagined possible. For starters, the West Edmonton Mall is the size of 115 football fields and has parking for 20,000 cars. As noted earlier, inside this goliath of shopping malls are 800 shops, 110 restaurants, 19 movie theaters, and a Caesar's Palace Bingo Parlor. It also has the world's largest indoor amusement park with 24 rides and two 13-story-high roller coasters. It boasts a 5-acre lagoon with the world's largest wave machine, and 22 water slides. If you would prefer other amusements, there is an 18-hole miniature golf course, an NHL-size ice-skating rink, and the opportunity to cruise the bottom of the 20-foot-deep lake in one of four 25-person submarines. (This is more submarines than are found in the Canadian Navy.) Edmonton has only 790,000 residents, but the mall, during the after-Christmas sales, attracts as many as 250,000 persons a day. In 1990, some 20 million people visited the West Edmonton Mall. Canada for that same year had a total population of 26 million people.

Mall of America

In August 1992, the Ghermezian brothers opened a United States version of the above in Bloomington, Minnesota, outside of Minneapolis-St. Paul. Named the Mall of America, it covers 4.2 million square

Contemporary malls have gone far beyond simply being retail centers. With indoor roller coasters, beaches with wave machines, and submarine rides, they have become major amusement and tourist attractions.

feet and is larger in square footage than twenty St. Peter's Basilicas. Among other amusements, it has a Knott's Berry Farm Camp Snoopy, with 7 acres of amusement rides, shows, and restaurants. Among its 23 rides the amusement park has a half-mile-long roller coaster on rubber wheels, a log flume ride, and a carousel. In addition to over 350 stores, there are 14 movie screens and 46 places to eat. There is even a Hormel cookout area named Spamland. To keep Camp Snoopy green, it has been designed with 400 trees, 30,000 plants, a mountain, and a 4-story waterfall.

For adults there is not only a 14-screen cineplex, but also a comedy club, a country and western theme dinner club, and a sports bar. The later stays open until 1:00 A.M. The Mall of America has its own zip code, doctors, dentists, and police, plus a public school for the children of the mall's 10,000 employees. Plans call for 1,000 on-site hotel rooms by 1995 to handle the tourists coming by tour bus as well as private auto. Obviously, shopping centers have come a long way from being a collection of stores having off-street parking.

All this has been done to entice shoppers back into the large malls. The fact is that fewer people are spending less time wandering through the malls than was the case in the early 1980s. Habits have changed from traditional mall department stores in favor of one-stop malls (e.g., Kmart) and smaller strip malls. Catalogs have become a convenient method of browsing. The number of adults that frequently shop at malls declined from 42 percent in 1987 to 36 percent in 1991 ("Mall Shoppers Want the Basics" *American Demographics,* October, 1991, p. 16). Young adults are the malls' best customers, while only a quarter of those over sixty visit malls "often" or "very often." There is also a difference by gender, with about half of all women saying they enjoy going to the mall; this is true of only slightly over one-third of all men. The megaentertainment malls are designed to bring people to the malls by making it a fun experience. The success of the Mall of America in accomplishing this goal will determine whether it is a dying dinosaur or a model for the future. The first week the Mall of America was open, it had over a million visitors. Thus far it seems to be meeting its developers' expectations.

Where all of the above will end is a matter of professional controversy. Some believe that the megamall, like the mammoth or the brontosaurus, is the last gasp of a concept that has been pressed to excess. As of 1993, the West Edmonton Mall was suffering from a sour economy and its own gargantuan size (Anne Swardson, "Casting a Pall over the Mall," *Washington Post,* June 2, 1993, F1). What we can say with certainty is that the idea of the shopping mall has changed the face of North America. While the skyscraper was the image of the city of the early- and mid-twentieth century, the suburban shopping mall is the dominant symbol as the century comes to its end.

A SUBURBAN DOWNTOWN ALTERNATIVE: RESTON, VA.

Reston, Virginia, is one of America's first planned new towns (see the Chapter 12 section on new towns). Since its founding in 1961 by the visionary developer Robert E. Simon, Jr., it has evolved into a community of 55,000 people. Reston, 18 miles west of Washington, D.C., near Dulles Airport, is more than a giant affluent subdivision. Reston is a more-or-less self-contained new town, having its own employment, shopping, and neighborhoods. Reston also has been a pacesetter in both architectural design and socially responsible programs. And as of the 1990s, Reston has built something not found in other outlying subdivisions—a real downtown.

Reston Town Center is not the typical suburban shopping center. Rather, it is trying to be a real downtown, with a grid street system, two 11-story office towers, streets with wide brick sidewalks, a 514-room hotel, some forty or so retail stores, eight restaurants, and a movie theater. Unlike traditional cities, where the residential areas grew up around the city center, in Reston the outlying residential housing came first. The downtown was built some twenty-five years later. Only in the late 1980s did Reston fully come of age.

In building Reston Town Center, the Reston Land Corporation deliberately set out to avoid copying other suburban models. In particular, Reston did not want to replicate the office-parks-and-shopping-mall model of Tysons Corner, which is located between Reston and Washington down the Dulles Airport road toward the Beltway around Washington. Reston did not want something that looked like a shopping mall and closed at 9:00 in the evening. The Reston Corporation deliberately set out to create a downtown that would still be humane and lively at 11:00 p.m. as well as at 11:00 a.m.

Overall, the project, although not a full downtown in the traditional sense, is both economically and socially successful. Office rentals are solid, and condominiums are being built downtown, to be followed by the construction of a cultural center. However, Reston Town Center is, in some ways, a very atypical downtown. Being built in an automobile-dependent suburb, the center district was built with the assumption that most people would drive downtown. Thus, some 3,100 parking spaces were designed into the plan. Also, Reston's downtown is not only new and clean, it is remarkably affluent. Reston was not designed for poor inner-city residents. Unlike real cities, there are no big stores or discount stores offering cheap goods. There are no panhandlers or street people. Reston is one of Virginia's more affluent communities, and the Town Center reflects the interests and incomes of its residents; it has a clearly upscale image.

Reston Town Center, in this respect, may have the combination of characteristics most Americans seek in a city center. It has more real life and vitality than a mall, but more security, safety, and parking than the old downtowns. The crucial question regarding Reston Town Center is no longer whether or not it will be successful. It is. What is still unclear is whether it will become a prototype for other suburban-based downtowns or whether, like Country Club Plaza in the 1920s, it will remain a much-applauded but uncopied model. We don't yet know whether Reston Town Center will become a prototype for the new century or an interesting, but one-of-a-kind, experiment.

CHAPTER 12

Planned Utopias and Other Communities

PLANNED SUBURBS

The earliest planned suburbs, which have come to be known as romantic, or garden suburbs, emerged in the middle of the nineteenth century. These suburbs provided not just housing but planned communities in which homes were placed in a created landscape that was designed to embellish nature by the picturesque placement of greenery, trees, ponds, and parks. An informal, naturalistic environment was created, which was to improve upon nature. The romantic suburb came out of the same impulses that led to Frederick Law Olmsted's design for the naturalistic Central Park in New York and to naturalistic cemeteries designed with hills, trees, and curving roadways, such as Hollywood Cemetery in Richmond, Virginia. Implicit in the emphasis on nature was an American version of the neo-Platonic concept of nature being a source of contact with the divine and the world being a garden that needs to be improved (James L. Machor, *Pastoral Cities, Urban Ideals and the Symbolic Landscape of America*, University of Wisconsin Press, Madison, 1987, pp. 81–86). Olmsted's Central Park thus can be seen as a practical application of Ralph Waldo Emerson's belief in the necessity to "unite rural and urban in order to promote spiritual and social advancement" (Machor, 1987, p. 169).

Llewellyn Park

Foremost among the planned romantic suburbs was Llewellyn Park, started in 1853. Constructed in New Jersey a mile from the North

Orange railroad station, its location permitted property owners to commute 15 miles to Manhattan. The goal of the developer, Llewellyn Haskell, and his architect, Alexander Jackson Davis, was to build a private community of villas in a park-like setting. All this was to be situated in a scenic location in the foothills of the Orange Mountains. Llewellyn Park, planned to provide "country homes for city people," clearly was influenced by the image of the manor house situated in an English rural park. According to an 1857 advertisement, the community was located on, "a tract of land, containing about 300 Acres, [that] has been divided in Villa Sites, of, from 5 to 10 Acres Each. It was selected with special reference to the wants of citizens doing business in the city, and yet wanting accessible, retired, and healthful homes in the country, by the proprietor, who adopted this method to secure a select and good neighborhood" (*Orange Journal*, May 16, 1857, p. 3).

Within the community, nature was to be conveniently domesticated as if it were a personal garden. Thus, all commercial enterprises were banned, even food stores. The site was designed with 7 miles of curvilinear roads that followed the terrain. This was a major break with the straight-right-angle streets that then were nearly universally used. Curvilinear roads today are almost de rigueur for upper-middle-class subdivisions, but their usage traces back to Llewellyn Park. The community was also completely architecturally landscaped. In the center of Llewellyn Park, a naturalistic 50-acre "ramble" was placed. In the community, the natural effect was in no respects left to the chance work of nature. Llewellyn spent the then-huge sum of $100,000 to have ponds dug and azaleas, dogwood, holly, rhododendrons, and other wild-looking plants placed to highlight and augment the natural look (John R. Stilgoe, *Borderland: Origin of the American Suburb, 1820–1939,* Yale University Press, New Haven, Conn., 1988, pp. 53–54). However, these advantages of Llewellyn Park were not to be available to uninvited visitors. A stone gatehouse notified outsiders that this was a strictly private Garden of Eden.

Riverside

While Llewellyn Park was remarkable, it was well beyond the reach of any but the wealthy. As a refuge for the well-to-do, it could never have widespread application. Its very strength was its uniqueness. More influential on the future of American landscape and domestic architecture would be upper-middle-class planned suburbs. The Civil War created new fortunes, and the Victorian era that followed may have been constrained in areas of behavior, but it was flamboyant and ostentatious in housing design. Urban housing for those who could afford it often was built without restraint on the premise that more was always better. Surprisingly, this idolization of excess did not invariably affect suburban design. Some now-classic suburbs were built with restraint and taste during the latter half of the nineteenth century. One of these was Riverside, southwest of the Chicago city line. Riverside's principle architect was Frederick Law Olmsted, the designer of Central Park. The project was begun in 1868 and was to combine the best of city and country and exhibit "the best application of the arts of civilization to which mankind has yet obtained" (Olmstead quoted in Robert Fishman, *Bourgeois Utopias*, Basic Books, 1987, p. 128). What this meant in practice was that the suburb was to be a bridge between the city and the country—an urban community in a rural setting. One of the early residents of Riverside was the architect William Le Baron Jenney, the reputed inventor of the iron-girdered building frame, which made the building of skyscrapers possible. Jenney designed several homes in Riverside in addition to his own. The site of Riverside, unlike that of Llewellyn Park, was without strong scenic attraction; it comprised 1,600 acres of Illinois prairie (Fishman, 1987, p. 129).

However, the location did have two advantages. The first was that it was along the Des Plaines River, which could be worked into a landscape design. The second, and more crucial, was that Riverside was the first stop west from Chicago's center on the Burlington Route railroad. Thus, the site was a good location for an affluent commuter suburb. Since the community lacked its own business activity, its residents would, by necessity, be those who could afford the expenditure of money and time for commuting. This meant a homogeneous community of at least an upper-middle-class level (excluding servants). Diversity was not one of the developer's goals. (Contemporary planned communities, such as Irving, California, continue this tradition of socioeconomic exclusivity. See pages 215 and 216.)

Olmstead was given a free hand in designing Riverside, and today the community still reflects the genius of his decisions. Of the 1,600 acres comprising the site, some 700 were reserved for parks and open spaces. The most picturesque of the parks wound along the banks of the river, but there were also parks and commons areas situated throughout the project. As in Llewellyn Park, the street pattern was curvilinear rather than right-angle grids, but unlike Llewellyn, property lines between homes were clearly drawn. All houses had to be at least 30 feet from the street, and trees were to be planted along the road to shield the homes from traffic and observation. However, Riverside was clearly designed to be a suburb, not a rustic retreat. It was to marry the best of the city and the countryside.

Riverside was not designed to be a utopian experiment, but a profit-making land development project. However, before it could be finished, it encountered severe financial difficulties. Turning a profit ran into three obstacles. The first was that the development was located 9 miles from the center of Chicago, and in the early 1870s, that was well beyond the city. It necessitated railroad commuting anytime anyone needed or wanted to go to Chicago. The second and third problems were factors beyond the control of the Riverside Improvement Company. The great Chicago Fire occurred in 1871, which resulted in neither attention nor investment funds being available for a number of years for peripherally located projects. Then, the financial Panic of 1873 and the depression that followed completed the bankruptcy of the developer. Riverside only slowly recovered, but a century and some later it remains a well-designed and pleasant suburb—a tribute to Olmsted's farsighted vision in combining city and country. Riverside still puts to shame the surrounding more modern, but far less imaginatively designed, suburbs.

Railroad Suburbs

Fully designed and heavily restricted planned romantic suburb communities for the well-to-do proved to have but a limited appeal. Among the less successful projects was the large-scale planned suburb of Garden City on Long Island, 20 miles from New York. Started in the 1870s, Garden City proved to be dramatically economically unsuccessful. In part this was because initially, houses only could be leased—a provision having little interest to those who could afford to live far from the city in a manner they chose. Far more successful were the wealthy and upper-middle-class railroad suburbs built in most cities like beads along a chain on residentially attractive land along the railroad right-of-way. One of these was Overbrook Farms, a planned community begun in the 1890s along the Main Line of the Pennsylvania Railroad. It was a twenty-minute commute to downtown Philadelphia. In addition to fine homes, its residents enjoyed a planned suburb containing churches, a community center, and a shopping plaza. Although suburban in life-style, technically Overbrook Farms wasn't a suburb, since although surrounded by rural land, it was legally just inside the city limits. (Margaret Marsh, *Suburban Lives*, Rutgers University Press, New Brunswick, N.J., 1990.)

To writers and suburban advocates of the last quarter of the nineteenth century, the availability of rapid railroad commuting meant that the perfect balance of city work and rural living was now at hand. As expressed by an 1872 newspaper promotional pamphlet, *"North Chicago: Its Advantages, Resources, and Probable Future,"*

The controversy which is sometimes brought, as to which offers greater advantage, the country or the city, finds a happy answer in the suburban idea which says both—the combination of the two—the city brought to the country. The city has its advantages and conveniences, the country has its charm and health; the union of the two (a modern result of the railway), gives to man all he could ask in this respect. The great cities that are building now, all have their suburban windows at which nature may be seen in her main expressions—and these spots attract to them cultured people, with their elaborate and costly adornments (Reprinted in Charles Glaab, *The American City: A Documentary History*, Dorsey, Homewood, Ill., 1963, pp. 233–234).

Railway suburbs, such as those along the Main Line from Philadelphia and those up the north shore outside of Chicago, came to symbolize affluent commuter suburbs. That was the case in the 1890s, and it is still the case in the 1990s. In fact, the terms "Main Line" and "North Shore" have entered the language as symbols for a comfortable, well-to-do life-style. It is one of the limited number of cases where popular stereotypes and sociological reality neatly mesh.

Comfortable railroad suburbs such as Chestnut Hill, on Philadelphia's Main Line, or Lake Forest, 27 miles up Chicago's North Shore, suggested at least solid prosperity if not considerable wealth. From the first they also suggested old families and old money. Particularly along the east coast, the railway suburbs of Boston, New York, and Philadelphia were considered blue-blood. Lineages were important, as was having attended the right schools and belonging to the right clubs. As one moved further west in the nation, family mattered less and money mattered more. However, in all cases religion was expected to be establishment Protestant. Predictably, an English Gothic-style Episcopal Church was one of Chestnut Hill's first landmarks, while on Chicago's North Shore, Presbyterian Lake Forest College was Lake Forest's dominant landmark. It goes without saying that nouveau riche Catholic or Jewish families were decidedly not welcome in either suburb.

This, however, is not to say that the prosperous railroad suburbs were all one social class. They were not. The necessity for workers both inside and outside the homes meant that the communities also had a substantial servant and working class. Both Chestnut Hill and Lake Forest had Irish Catholic servants and laborers. The suburbs' location relatively far from the central cities meant that all those who tended the large lawns, cared for the horses and carriages, cooked the meals, cleaned and maintained the houses, washed and ironed the clothes, and cared for the children also lived in the community. Those who did not live under their employer's roof generally resided in the small houses clustered near the railway station and on the less desirable land running up and down the tracks. Some comfortable suburbs, such as Evanston, north of Chicago, even had a substantial population of blacks. By the second decade of the twentieth century, Evanston even had its own segregated colored YMCA, known euphemistically as the Emerson Street Department (Michael H. Ebner, *Creating Chicago's North Shore,* University of Chicago Press, Chicago, 1988, p. 211). While this population of servants and other workers counted demographically, they definitely did not count socially.

Designed Streetcar Suburbs

The naturally designed suburbs of the railroad era were followed by electric-trolley-era suburbs such as Roland Park, northwest of Baltimore (1891); Forrest Hills Gardens, built on a 142-acre farm in the outer reaches of Queens, New York (1909); and Shaker Heights, east of Cleveland (1905). The first two of these suburbs were designed in large part by Frederick Law Olmsted, Jr. Being more closely tied to access to the streetcar line, none of the three emphasized the open public green areas and rural ambience of earlier romantic suburbs. In practice as well as philosophy, they were not outlying bucolic communities, but true suburbs. Physically and socially, they were more closely tied to the city. Roland Park, for example, reflected more urban than rural traditions (Stilgoe, 1988, p. 259). Roland Park clearly was oriented toward downtown Baltimore. Roland Park, Forrest Hills, and Shaker Heights each would come over time to represent the affluent inner-ring urban-oriented suburbs of the pre-World War II era. To many they would become the quintessential American suburbs.

All three suburbs shared features such as strictly enforced building codes, including house-setback regulations, but they differed in the degree of developer control. Forrest Hills was designed by its backer, the Russell Sage Foundation, to be totally planned. This can be seen today in the community's buildings, with their solid masonry construction and red tile roofs. The Van Sweringens brothers, who founded Shaker Heights, compulsively oversaw the building of all the homes, mandating not only acceptable architectural plans but even what materials and color schemes could be used. All homes in Shaker Heights had to be designed by an architect whose plans were approved by the brothers. They advertised their control over the community as one of its major advantages. The brothers sought "tasteful" designs and banned any too original designs as undermining the aesthetic, and financial, stability of Shaker Heights (Stilgoe, 1988, pp. 242–244).

In Roland Park, on the contrary, house style was not mandated.

You could build your home in Dutch colonial, English Tudor, or any other style of your choice as long as you met the other community standards. Roland Park soon became incorporated into Baltimore, but it never lost its reputation as a somewhat reclusive upper-middle-class WASP enclave. Roland Park represented not just an area, but also a WASP way of life. The novelist Ann Tylor, in her best-sellers *The Accidental Tourist* and *Searching for Calib*, makes the character of Roland Park itself an essential ingredient of the novels. Tylor portrays Roland Park residents as living very much self-satisfied and self-restricted lives; they have little interest in going out of the neighborhood or in matters beyond Roland Park. This view of the culturally restricted nature of upper-middle-class suburban life may or may not be an accurate reflection of reality, but it has been the basis of many good novels. We discussed this idea of the social conformity of suburbia when looking at post-World War II suburbanization.

VISIONARY COMMUNITIES

Planned Utopias

Planned communities have a long, if not always successful, lineage in American urban life. They share with the romantic suburbs the belief that man can be made over by proper surroundings. Many of the nineteenth-century new town examples, such as New Harmony, Indiana or Salt Lake City, were founded with an ideological-religious emphasis. Other new communities began as company towns—but company towns that also had a visionary or social component. Lowell, Massachusetts, began in the early nineteenth century as an idealistic community with a paternalistic interest in its workers, but by midcentury it was just another New England mill town. The classic American attempt to create a totally paternalistic suburban community was Pullman, Illinois, which was at the southern extremity of the Chicago urban area. Pullman, founded in the 1880s, was designed with solid urban planning to be a complete community with well-managed services. George Pullman, of Pullman car fame, was the founder and sole landlord. His goal was to provide a community of solid housing and few temptations (saloons were barred) so that workers would remain productive. He stated that, "With such surroundings and such human regard for the needs of the body as well as the soul the disturbing conditions of strikes and other troubles that periodically convulse the world of labor would not be found here" (Stanley Buder, *Pullman*, Oxford University Press, New York, 1967, p. vii). He was a poor prophet, for Pullman is best known today for the famous bitter and violent strike that occurred there in 1894. The strike was only crushed when National Guardsmen were brought in as strikebreakers. Today Pullman is part of Chicago.

Nineteenth-century planned utopian communities, such as John Noyes's Oneida, New York, with its system of group marriage, or political-philosophical communities such as New Harmony, Indiana, generally had difficulty maintaining themselves. In addition to having ideological disputes, the communities were almost always undercapitalized. Alice Austin's early-twentieth-century attempt to create the feminist planned "Socialist City" of Llano del Rio in southern California suffered this fate (Dolores Hayden, *The Grand Domestic Revolution: A History of Feminist Designs for American Homes, Neighborhoods, and Cities,* MIT Press, Cambridge, Mass., 1981). After struggling for many years, the community went bankrupt in 1917. As noted earlier in the text, a unique feature of Llano del Rio was the building of homes without kitchens. Rather than having individual kitchens, the homes backed onto a communal eating area. This system was to save housewives from the drudgery of cooking.

The New Town Movement

At the close of the nineteenth century, revulsion against the evils of the city and reaction to the isolation of the suburbs led to attempts to build entirely new communities in which the benefits of both types of living could be realized. The resulting communities thus grew out of a much different orientation than had led to the building of the earlier upper-status romantic suburbs. These communities had much more of a reformist and middle-or working-class orientation. Our suburbs of today are a melding of the two traditions. The turn of the century new towns were to be planned communities with fully developed commercial, residential, and industrial sectors. Much of the concern with new towns was because of the visionary efforts of Ebenezer Howard in England. His new towns, which were called "garden cities," were to be self-contained communities of 30,000 residents (Ebenezer Howard, *Garden Cities of To-morrow,* Faber and Faber, London, 1902). There were to be totally planned communities surrounded by a "green belt" of open land. Howard was going to solve the problem of the cities by abandoning them for a fresh environment of self-sufficient garden cities. Howard and his Garden City Association started the first new town at Letchworth, some thirty miles by train from London, in 1902. After many financial troubles, Howard launched the second new town, Welwyn Garden City, in 1920. Today it is a pleasant small city.

Following World War II, in 1946, Britain passed the New Town Act, which made the building of new towns an official government policy in Great Britain. Since that time some thirty-four new towns have been constructed.

During the 1920s some of the leading planners in the United States organized into the Regional Planning Association of America in order to promote comprehensive planning and new towns. The most famous new town with which members were associated was Radburn, New Jersey, started in 1928 outside New York by the City Housing Corporation. Radburn is often considered the first of the American new towns. Designed by Clarence Stein and Henry Wright, the houses were arranged in superblocks that fronted on open parkland while automobiles were restricted to peripheral areas. The superblocks were to be free of traffic and congestion. Radburn was thus the first community specifically planned for controlling the problems of the "motor age." An extensive pathway system, for example, was designed to separate pedestrians from automobiles. For financial reasons, it was not possible to build the external protecting green belt, and there was no provision for industry (Clarence S. Stein, *Toward New Towns for America*, M.I.T. Press, Cambridge, Mass., 1957, p. 41). The English new town model of communal ownership and property leaseholds also was not followed, since it would not be accepted in the American environment. From the first, Radburn was an upper-middle-class suburb. Unfortunately for Radburn, the first homeowners moved into the community in May 1929, and the stock market collapsed half a year later. The community was begun stillborn.

Now largely forgotten except by urbanists, three government-sponsored new towns were built over half a century ago by the United States government. They were built essentially as experimental or demonstration projects during the great Depression of the 1930s. The new towns were authorized with the three goals of demonstrating the advantages of community planning, providing good housing at reasonable rents, and giving jobs to thousands of unemployed workers. The three towns constructed were Greenbelt, Maryland, outside of Washington, D.C.; Greendale, Wisconsin, southwest of Milwaukee; and Green Hills, Ohio, near Cincinnati. Although they lacked their own industries, all three were successful. However, Congress, responding to claims by the real estate industry that having government-built housing was socialistic and a danger to the free-enterprise system, passed Public Law 65 of 1949. This law decreed that all the homes and the surrounding green belt be sold. Since then, all new town developers have built their communities in the expectation of making money. They have not always achieved this expectation.

New Towns of the 1960s

The social unrest of the 1960s, combined with the physical decline of central cities and disillusionment over the proliferation of low-density suburbs, led American architects, planners, and policymakers to again look at new towns. With the central cities undergoing racial turmoil and social disorganization, there was renewed interest in trying to recreate the older Jeffersonian ideal of community by creating new towns. In a very American way, it was argued that new towns would provide not only new housing, but also a new social start. The postwar British new towns appeared to be social as well as economic successes, and American new towns, it was thought, would allow for the solving of the economic and racial problems of the city without creating more economically inefficient and socially isolating suburbs. As foreseen by urban planners and federal housing officials, new towns would provide a setting for a new beginning of planned communities that would provide the answer to suburban sprawl. New towns would offer both economic success and social justice in an environmentally attractive setting. New towns would give their residents "a second chance, a redemption, to live a new life unencumbered by the sins of the past" (William Alonso and Chester McGuire, "Pluralistic New Towns," *Lex et Science,* Vol. 9, No. 3, 1972, p. 76). As during the Victorian age, the problems of the city were to be solved by abandoning the city and starting over.

The 1970s New Communities Act provided government guarantees for up to $50 million of each developer's bonds to finance the building of thirteen new towns. This was because building a new town required heavy front-end outlays for land and infrastructure before even a single house could be built. Private lenders were very reluctant to commit long-term funding to what appeared to be marginal economic ventures. Because of the British experience, it was assumed it would take a decade and a half for new towns to become self-supporting. By 1974 a total of $252 million in federally guaranteed debitures had been issued. The first project to receive federal mortgage guarantees was the new town of Jonathan, to be built in rolling countryside some twenty-five miles southwest of Minneapolis. Jonathan received a guarantee of $21 million, but almost from the start the new town was in serious trouble. What was occurring in Jonathan was typical of the program as a whole. In 1973 the nation was hit with an oil crisis, and suddenly there was no market for homes in distant outer-ring new towns. At this crucial point the Ford Administration announced that all federal monies would be cut off, and new towns would be left to sink or survive on their own. None survived, except Woodlands, 30 miles north of Houston. It survived because its developer also had natural-gas holdings. The usual pattern was for HUD to foreclose on the out-standing mortgages on the project, after which what remained would be sold to a private developer. Central-city mayors, far from being sup-porters of the new towns, were also strong lobbyists against providing funding, believing that money going to new towns would be taken from them. They wanted the federal focus to be on saving the cities, not on looking for alternatives to the cities.

Reston, Columbia, and Irving

The withdrawal of federal support, while a major blow, did not totally destroy the idea of the new towns as an expression of the suburban dream. Several privately financed new towns managed to not only sur-vive, but prosper. Perhaps the best known among these are Reston, Virginia, west of Washington, D.C.; Columbia, Maryland, south of Baltimore on the way to Washington; and Irving Ranch, in southern California. Reston was initiated by Robert E. Simon, who, having just sold Carnegie Hall in New York, had a dream of building an urbane

By the early 1960s the New Town of Reston, Vir-ginia, with its innovative use of walkways and treatment of the environment, set a standard that has been met by few suburban communities.

community in the rural Virginia countryside. He wanted a place where people could enjoy both the cosmopolitan advantages of the city and the beauty of rural countryside. Both employment and recreational opportunities were to be found within the community. Simon purchased some eleven miles of Virginia countryside (6,800 acres) west of Washington, D.C., near what was to be the new Dulles Airport. The cost of the land was $13 million, but he put down only $800,000 of his money and persuaded the landowners to take noninterest-bearing notes for the balance. From its founding in the 1960s, Reston was an aesthetic success, but its early decades were economically rocky. Simon was more a philanthropist and visionary than a developer, and he refused to sacrifice community planning or his dream of social diversity in order to sell more homes. From the first, Reston had architecturally interesting contemporary homes, something that was alleged to have slowed sales. Simon was forced out in 1967 by Gulf Corporation, which, in turn, sold out to Mobil.

Reston is now an economically successful town of over 55,000 with a substantial number of corporate offices and other "clean" industries. Where initially most residents had to carpool or take a long bus ride to Washington, today 40 percent of the residents work in the community. Residentially, Reston has a mix of free-standing homes, town houses, and condominiums facing Reston's four artificial lakes. Reston Town Center, as was noted in the last chapter, is an attempt to build a real downtown. From the earliest days, Reston has had a distinct upper-middle-class-but-involved character. Housing ranges from $800,000-plus homes to government-subsidized apartments. The average home buyer is between thirty and forty years old, has two children, and has an income considerably higher than the national average. (The 1990 census identified a median family income of $60,000). Reston has several hundred units of federally subsidized housing, but attempts to place lower-income and higher-income housing side by side were abandoned as not being economically sound. Mixed-income housing was a desirable social goal, but Reston is a profit-making enterprise. One in six Reston residents is a member of a minority group.

Columbia, Maryland, some twenty miles north of Washington, was developed by James Rouse, one of the nation's most respected developers. Rouse managed quietly to buy or option some twenty-two square miles of land from 169 separate owners before plans for Columbia were revealed in 1963. Architecturally, Columbia looks more like a suburb than Reston, since builders of Columbia's various sections were given a free hand to build their most popular home models. The community has some 65,000 persons living in eight villages, and eventually Columbia will house some 110,000 people on its 15,600 acres. The investment in the community totals over $3 billion.

Like most new towns, Columbia is organized into neighborhoods of some 900 houses having their own elementary school, swimming pool, recreational center, and convenience store. Four neighborhoods are combined to create a "village" of 3,500, which has an intermediate school and a small plaza including a number of shops and a supermarket. Wooded areas and pathways run throughout the village. Columbia is racially integrated, with over one-quarter of the residents being black. Economically, although there are subsidized units, the community is middle- to upper-middle class.

Irving, California, began in the 1960s with a dedication to create a new town of 100,000 on garden city principles around a new University of California campus. It was designed without a downtown, but rather, it was to have shopping centers and business parks intermixed within what is primarily a residential community of single-family homes. Irving from the first was to be a geographically dispersed community. The Irving family owned some 64,000 acres of ranch land and orange groves, which meant Irving would cover nine times the land space of Reston, or four times that of Columbia. All the land was owned by the Irving family and its successor, the Irving Company. The company had a strong commitment to architectural design, a high level of amenities, and controls over the use of the landscape. Irving was incorporated as a city in 1971.

However, Irving, unlike its east coast siblings, had little interest in racial or income diversity. Simon and Rouse each had a strong personal and corporate commitment to creating communities with population diversity. Irving executives and planners had no interest in providing subsidized or lower-income housing (Martin J. Schiesl, "Designing the Model Community: The Irving Company and Suburban Development, 1950–88," in Robert Kling, Spencer Olin, and Mark Poster, eds., *Posturban California: The Transformation of Orange County since World War II*, University of California Press, Berkeley, 1991, p. 66). From the first, Irving was designed to be an expensive and elitist community. Low-income or even middle-income housing and residents have been rigorously excluded. In recent years Irving residents have voted for controlled growth and to protect the coast from development. In this, the residents were opposed by the Irving Company. Rapid suburban growth is not welcomed by the existing homeowners. Irving offers a high quality of life to its residents, but the benefits are restricted to those with substantially above-average incomes or wealth. As such, Irving is not a reasonable new town model for the rest of the country.

Some, in fact, argue that Irving Ranch is not a self-contained and self-sustaining new town, but rather simply a well-designed upper-income suburb. Regardless, problems of land acquisition coupled with now more restrictive environmental and planning regulations make it difficult to build new private projects of such size.

New Community Models

Today the idea of the planned community is undergoing a bit of a renaissance. This is not occurring as a consequence of government policy or action. Rather, new communities are being developed that are essentially privatized communities. They are new suburban full-service communities. One version of this is the community designed to recreate the urban village (Edward J. Blaely and David L. Ames, "Changing Places: American Planning Policy for the 1990s," *Journal of Urban Affairs*, Vol. 14, No. 3/4, p. 433). The ideal is to create a reasonable-cost community that is not just another subdivision, but has employment opportunities and a sense of place. One of these new communities is Rancho Santa Marguerita, in southern California. Hughes Aircraft provided the original employment anchor for a community that, as of the early 1990s, had some 3,500 jobs and 15,000 residents living in 4,600 homes. Being able to live near one's employment substantially cuts commuting time, which, in the Los Angeles basin, can take an hour and a half each way. In Upstate New York, the Sterling Forest Corporation is similarly attempting to, over the next quarter century, build a community of 35,000 people in clusters of five villages. The goal is to have local employment for 20,000, and three-quarters of the land left as open space. However, protests by environmental groups concerned with building on steep slopes and wetlands, coupled with a sluggish economy, have slowed the proposed development.

Neotraditional Developments

The most discussed new communities are the so-called neotraditional developments. These are contemporary communities that are being designed for both mixed usage and walking, rather than solely automobile usage. Looking not to recent suburbs but to pre-World War II suburbs and small towns for their inspiration, the neotraditional developments ignore the planning orthodoxies of recent decades. Neotraditional planners design in both higher densities and mixed land usages in order to both reduce the need for auto travel and increase the sense of community (Susan Handy, "Neo-Traditional Development: The Debate," *Berkeley Planning Journal*, Vol. 6, 1991, pp. 135–144). The developers consciously are trying to design in the advan-

Seaside, Florida, with its nonautomobile streets and mandatory front porches and picket fences, consciously attempts to recreate the social patterns of a nineteenth-century small town.

tages and mood of earlier eras. Their model for an ideal livable community is the nineteenth-century small town, with its dense intermixture of small shops and homes. Thus, some of the most commented upon, and debated, new community developments at the end of the twentieth century are being built to approximate the character and amenities of the small town or village of a century ago.

New towns such as Seaside, on the Florida Panhandle, are designed with deliberately "old-fashioned" homes on narrow grid streets that encourage walking (Philip Langdon, "A Good Place to Live," *Atlantic Monthly* March 1988, pp. 39–60). Unlike the roads in typical suburbs, the roads here are deliberately kept narrow in order to discourage auto usage, and sidewalks are mandated in order to encourage walking. Rather than having zoning that requires rigid segregation of housing, manufacturing, and commercial activities, the towns are designed to encourage, rather than prohibit, the intermixing of people and activities (Andres Duany and Elizabeth Plater-Zberk, "The Second Coming of the American Small Town," *Wilson Quarterly*, Winter 1992, pp. 19–48). Master plan codes that call for separate shopping and housing pods are discarded in favor of designing on a more intimate scale a community that is both comfortable and interesting to the local residents. Certainly there is something both inviting and comforting about Seaside. Masshipee, on Cape Cod, and, less successfully, Princeton Forrestal Village, in Plainsboro, New Jersey, are examples of such attempts to repeat the nineteenth-century model of providing an inviting, livable, and walkable public environment. Forrestal Village is currently trying to recast itself as a factory outlet mall.

Critics are not so sure that high-density small towns are the answer. They question whether most suburbanites would be wiling to give up their low densities and large lots for some decrease in commuting time. Also, they say it is doubtful whether such small places with small populations could provide many jobs or sufficient services. Nineteenth-century town residents had to shop local. They didn't have the option of hopping in the car and driving to the mall for greater variety and cheaper prices. Seaside, for all its charm, is still more of a weekend retreat than a full-time residential community.

Surrounding the debate is the larger, if often unspoken, question as to how much behavior can be shaped or influenced by physical surroundings. Can architecture create the good community? Neotraditionalist developments are still too few and new to provide solid empirical answers. What is clear is that in questioning the accepted orthodoxies of suburban planning, the neotraditionalists are attempting to do for the suburbs what Jane Jacobs, in her classic, *The Death and Life of Great American Cities*, did three decades ago for city neighborhoods (Jane Jacobs, *The Death and Life of Great American Cities*, Random House, New York, 1961).

RETIREMENT COMMUNITIES

The fastest growing type of new community now being built is the retirement community. This is not surprising since anyone who reads a newspaper or pays Social Security knows that the elderly are the fastest growing segment of the population. Some 6,000 persons turn sixty-five every day, making older persons a substantial potential housing market. The elderly currently constitute 12 percent of the population; this is expected to rise to 17 percent by 2020 (Brad Edmondson, "Is Florida Our Future," *American Demographics*, Vol. 9, No. 6, 1987, pp. 38–43). The 1990 census reported 31.2 million persons aged sixty-five or over, a 22 percent increase since 1980. As of 1960, only a quarter of the elderly population lived in the suburbs. By 1990 this figure had grown to over 45 percent. More older Americans now live in suburbs than live in central cities or in rural areas. Some of the retirement communities are explicitly designed and advertised as such, while others are simply developments in recreational areas with lots of golf courses or a good fishing lake. Growth is taking place even in locations that are not true retirement areas. For example, Peachtree City, in fast-growing Fayette,

Georgia, grew from 2,000 residents to 22,000 in 1990 and expects to more than double that by 2000.

The postwar assumption that suburbs were for young couples and their children is another out-of-date myth. The assumption long has been that as those who moved to the suburbs in the 1950s and 1960s aged, they would sell their homes and move back into city apartments or condominiums. By and large, this has not occurred. The elderly are choosing to remain in the suburban homes they have occupied for decades (Kevin Fitzpatric and John Logan, "The Aging of the Suburbs, 1960–1980," *American Sociological Review*, Vol. 50, 1985, pp. 106–117). People are remaining in their suburban homes after the children leave, and even after their spouses die. This has resulted in suburbs being better integrated by age than anytime in the past fifty years. It also means that since most of the suburban elderly are not segregated in specific areas, it is more difficult to provide for their needs such as access to social services and public transportation. If an elderly widow or widower has restricted mobility and is no longer able to drive, he or she can become isolated.

Retirement communities offer another alternative for the elderly. While there have long been residences for the elderly, and even communities such as St. Augustine, Florida, where the elderly are a heavy proportion of the residents, the idea of an entire community restricted to only elderly residents is a post-World War II development. Retirement communities that attempt to provide needed physical and social services for sixty-something and beyond residents are now commonplace. According to an American Association of Retired People estimate, there were 2.5 million people living in retirement communities as of the early 1980s (Eleanor Furman, *Reitrement: You're in Charge*, Praeger, New York, 1984, p. 139). This number can be expected to dramatically increase as the new century opens and the baby-boom generation reaches retirement age. Increasing numbers of these retirees will be moving to self-contained gated communities with limited access to outsiders.

Probably the ultimate in the walled and self-contained retirement communities are the Sun Cities. Del Webb Corporation pioneered the building of what it calls "active adult communities" with the creation of Sun City outside of Phoenix in the 1960s. Completed in 1978, Sun City has 26,000 homes, eleven golf courses, and five recreation centers ("Del Webb Corp.: For Sun City Builder the Housing Market Still Glows," *Barrons*, August 31, 1992, p. 34). In terms of social class, the majority of residents are lower-middle or middle-middle class. There are no subsidies or other provisions for low-income elderly, and upper-income groups retire to more exclusive enclaves.

In addition to the original Sun City, there is a new Sun City West being built in Phoenix. More are located in Tucson, Las Vegas, and Palm Springs. Sun Cities differ from other facilities catering to older purchasers in that Sun Cities are not just neighborhoods or subdivisions for the elderly, but entire communities. Moreover, they are communities in which there is a minimum age limit of fifty-five for buyers. Younger people are expressly excluded. What Sun Cities sell is far more than housing; it is a life of golf, bowling, and crafts that is literally walled off from outside world problems. In the words of the Del Webb Corporation chief executive, "We are not a homebuilder. What we sell is a lifestyle" ("A Dare in the Desert: 5,500 Retirement Homes," *Business Week*, December 9, 1991, p. 94).

Resident status in retirement communities commonly is limited to couples where one spouse is at least fifty-five years of age. This affects not only the age composition but also the sex composition of the community. This is because women, on the average, live 10 percent longer than men. Higher mortality rates among males result in there being only seven males for every ten females over age sixty-five. A common pattern is for the longest-term community residents to be disproportionately widows. Young people are kept at a minimum by community regulations that ban other than short-term stays by adult children or other guests under the mandatory age. Young children or grandchildren are not welcome on other than a visiting basis. They cannot reside in the community. Such regulations not only maintain the homogeneity of the community, they also keep taxes low, since by banning young people, homeowners ensure they will not have to pay for building or staffing local schools or other expensive public services usually found in similar-size communities. These communities, isolated from urban areas, are insulated both from urban problems and from the responsibility to pay taxes for services to those not within the walled community. Community homogeneity also includes race. Nonwhite residents are a rarity in retirement homeowner communities.

This secure and nonthreatening environment has a particular appeal to some fixed-income middle- or lower-middle-class retirees. Sun City and similar retirement communities offer their residents a predictable and safe world of golf and crafts free from the problems, confusion, and variety that is a part of life outside the entrance gates. Problems, and the cost of paying for them, are kept outside. While the number of such retirement communities is growing, they have an appeal only to a minority of all elderly.

Few retirement communities are of the size of Sun City, but housing communities built exclusively for seniors exist throughout Florida and other sun belt locations. They usually are built in unincorporated areas in order to avoid taxes for nonresident services, and most offer a range of community activities and amenities in addition to housing. However, while retirees seek to limit their taxes, it is a mistake to think of areas with heavy retirement-aged populations as areas of economic decline. Just the opposite is the case. Economically, "places with fast-growing elderly populations are often better-off and healthier markets than those with slow-growing elderly populations" (Diane Crispell and William H. Frey, "American Maturity," *American Demographics*, March 1993, p. 33). Elderly in-movers may not be employed, but according to a 1992 analysis done for the Appalachian Regional Commission, "The average retirement migrant household's overall impact on the local economy is $71,600" (Crispell and Frey, 1993). Retirees bring economic resources and create new jobs. Estimates of the new jobs created by each retired in-mover range from one-third to one for each newcomer.

Retirement communities, in addition to having community centers, often include internal commercial districts that are designed to offer a range of products and services especially designed to fill the needs of older buyers. Oftentimes, extensive medical facilities are available, and one or more private hospitals is nearby. Increasingly, retirement communities also include living environments for aging residents who can no longer independently manage a home and require assistance ranging from semiindependent to nursing home care. Continuing-care facilities are increasingly being built into new retirement developments.

Retirement communities, with their generational exclusiveness, are likely to have some appeal to aging baby boomers, since boomers have long defined themselves explicitly on the basis of generational membership. As baby boomers age, the character of retirement communities inevitably will change. Some of these changes are easy to foretell; some are more speculative. One of the changes will be in the proportion of the retirement income coming from women's pension and work-related funds. Women of the boomer generation have more educational and work experience than earlier generations, and this is likely to be reflected in the organization of the communities. Economically, more retirees will have dual pensions from both partners working, but this will be partially offset by lower support from Social Security. It is virtually certain that boomers will be less able to rely on Social Security than has the current generation of retirees. On the other hand, they will inherit from their parents more substantially than any generation in history. The ethnic and racial diversity of retirement communities probably will also increase, reflecting the increasing ethnic and racial diversity of the country. Boomer retirement commu-

nities might also carry forward their reputed competitiveness and sta-
tus-seeking behavior. This would result in retirement communities
being far more competitively organized in terms of sports and even
crafts than is the case with current retirees who reflect more of the "togetherness" approach they practiced in the early postwar suburbs. In
any case, it is highly likely that boomers, who in many ways throughout their lives have defined themselves as a separate group, are likely
to have their own distinctive "sixty something" retirement communities.

CHAPTER 13

Quo Vadis?

CURRENT STATUS

As the previous pages indicate, the recent decades have seen North America transformed into a suburban continent. Suburbia is not only where most of us live, it is also where most of us shop, go out to eat, and catch a movie. It also is where most of us work. Overall, these changes have been accepted and even celebrated by suburbanites and lamented by architectural and social critics. Regardless, the suburban transformation is now clearly a social fact. Whatever one thinks about suburbs, it is now indisputable that they are no longer *sub*. Outer cities may sprawl over the landscape, but they contain all the functions of the older downtowns. Although it twists the language a bit, they have become outlying "central places" in their own right. Whether the outer cities are called edge cities, polynucleated cities, or technoblurbs, these outlying "urbs" now house more shopping malls, manufacturing plants, and business offices than do the traditional central downtowns.

The downtown retail outlets essentially suburbanized to the malls during the 1970s, leaving only skeletal remains in the once-dominant cores. The 1980s saw the dramatic proliferation of suburban office and manufacturing complexes—such that today, outer cities surpass most central cities in total business activity. Atlanta, site of the 1996 Olympics, is typical in that less than a quarter of the metropolitan area's office space is actually located in the impressive downtown skyscrapers. Transportation, and especially communication technologies, no longer favor centralization over dispersion. FAX machines and e-mail work equally well from suburban and urban locations. Whether one joins the writer Joel Garreau in applauding the spreading outer cities as the new American frontier (Joel Garreau, *Edge City*, Doubleday, New York, 1991, p. 4) or agrees with Kenneth Jackson in longing nostalgically for the return of the central city (Kenneth Jackson, *Crabgrass Frontier*, Oxford, New York, 1985, p. 302), the reality is that the major action is now in the suburbs. My personal preference for downtown department stores over suburban malls is not going to restore the former, or really affect the latter. Regardless of my preferences, suburbs will continue for the foreseeable future to increase their dominance.

Popular perception of the suburban residential and economic transformation lags behind reality. Even those who do their daily working, shopping, eating out, and seeking of entertainment in the suburbs still tend to think of suburbs as essentially single-family, white, middle-class, residential areas. As has been discussed earlier, there is a time warp in which our perception of suburbia is remarkably impervious to rejection, or even modification. Even those living in huge suburban garden apartment developments still think of suburbia as a land of free-standing homes on large lots. Stereotypical views regarding ethnic and racial changes taking place in suburbia are even more difficult to change. To date there is remarkably little acknowledgment of the increasing ethnic and racial heterogeneity of suburbia. Suburban-located minorities are viewed, and often view themselves, as exceptions to the rule. Change is often ignored or downplayed. It has not really registered, for example, that a third of all metropolitan-area blacks are already suburbanites, and that currently, three-quarters of all African American population growth is occurring in suburbs. The fact that many of these suburbanites are affluent seems even harder to accept. Generations that have been taught to view black suburbanization as ghetto spillover don't seem really comfortable with the idea of substantial middle-class black suburbanization. In spite of Washington, D.C., having over 620,000 black suburbanites, Atlanta now having almost 500,000, and Los Angeles having over 400,000, black middle-class suburbanization is sometimes even spoken of by social scientists as something of an exception to the pattern. It isn't; it is the pattern.

Even less attention is paid to the suburbanization of other ethnic populations. Hispanics, who are projected to be the largest American minority by the year 2010, accounted for a quarter of all suburban population gain from 1980 to 1990. Nonetheless, the image of the "typical" Latino is likely to bring up stereotypical pictures of migrant farm workers or central-city barrio dwellers. The reality is that 43 percent of Hispanics already are suburbanites, and the proportion is increasing. Asians, similarly, are often thought of as primarily residing in central-city Chinatowns, Little Tokyos, Koreatowns, or the like. Actually, half of those of Asian background in America are suburbanites—a suburban proportion higher than that found in the white population. It is clear that suburbia over the past few decades has changed not only its economic function, but also its population composition. What has been slower to change is our recognition of these developments.

WHERE WE ARE GOING

This leads to the inevitable question as to what lies ahead. Any such discussion of suppositions or suggestions has to be prefaced by noting that prognostication is a dubious art. Certainly, those experts writing at the end of World War II had no idea that suburbanization would become the dominant trend for the last half of the twentieth century. Rather, they saw a world in which the central city would only increase its economic and social dominance—that is, a world in which what had been happening would in linear fashion continue to do so. Obviously, that didn't occur, and plans made on that expectation quickly became worse than useless. Similarly, projections and arguments made in the 1960s and 1970s regarding the inevitable decline and even death of the city now seem overblown and overdramatic. Statements such as "The Newarks of America are forecasts of things to come . . ." fortunately have proven to be exaggerated (George Sternlieb, "The City as Sandbox," *The Public Interest*, Vol. 4, Fall 1971, p. 14). Similarly, expositions that, "There is something tragicomic about sitting around 'planning' to secure, extend, and improve what is about to be swept away" have proved to be poor prophesy (John Seeley, "Remaking the Urban Scene," *Daedalus*, Vol. 97, 1968, p. 1125). That so many fine scholars and practitioners would be so far off the mark has to give pause to anyone attempting to foretell future trends.

Another problem with predicting the future, especially the suburban future, is that one's ideology may play a powerful conscious or unconscious role in shaping expectations to what one wants to see, rather than what is likely to occur. This is clearly a difficulty. It is hard to concede that what one personally would like to see happen is probably not what is going to take place. The historian Kenneth Jackson, in his landmark work, *Crabgrass Frontier*, also encountered this problem. In his final section, on "The Future," he prognosticates that,

> I would argue that the long process of suburbanization, which has been operative in the United States since about 1815, will slow in the next two decades and a new kind of spacial equilibrium will result early in the next century. Quite simply, there are powerful economic

and demographic forces that will tend to undercut the decentralizing process. . . . As the suburban world begins to experience unmistakable signs of decay, both central cities and rural areas are making a comeback. Although statistics of population, jobs, and income do not support the thesis that a back-to-the-city movement has reversed the century-and-a-half old suburban trend, the gentrification of older neighborhoods may be the harbinger of major demographic changes in the next two decades. . . . Thus, the United States is not only the world's first suburban nation, but it will also be the last (Kenneth T. Jackson, *Crabgrass Frontier*, Oxford University Press, New York, 1985, pp. 297, 302, 304).

As of the early 1990s data suggest that the above prognostication is unlikely to occur. For example, in spite of the hopes of some of us, research done in the 1980s established that nationwide urban gentrification would be of limited scope and that, moreover, the much-discussed back-to-the-city movement was not actually occurring (J. John Palen and Bruce London, *Gentrification, Displacement, and Neighborhood Revitalization*, State University of New York Press, Albany, 1984). The myth of a substantial back-to-the-city movement, and that of incipient massive central-city gentrification, were largely creations of the popular media. Census or other data do not support the thesis that either cities or rural areas are making a strong comeback. Both continue to lose both population and economic strength to suburban areas. Central cities and rural places have become the edges which are losing to the suburban middle ground.

As someone who loves the vitality and variety of large cities, I have hoped for many years to see central cities make a strong comeback. However, research indicates that this is not what is occurring. Moreover, there are few reasons, except my wishing it to be so, to predict that such restructuring of current patterns will occur in the next decade or two. Whether we applaud it or lament it, suburbia has become the American Way of Life. It is already the life most of us live. And in spite of our laments for the central city, we don't want to give up the personal advantages of suburban living. The twentieth century, which began as the age of the city, is departing as the age of the suburb. As we approach the new century, North America increasingly is dominated by a *pax suburbia*.

Indexes

Name Index

229

Subject Index